THE
BASICS
of CRAFTSMANSHIP

THE BASICS
of CRAFTSMANSHIP

**Key advice
on every
aspect of
woodworking**

The Taunton Press

essentials of woodworking

Special thanks to the editors, art directors, copy editors,
and other staff members of *Fine Woodworking* who contributed to
the development of the articles in this book.

Front cover photo by Strother Purdy
Back cover photos by Vincent Laurence (top left and bottom),
Anatole Burkin (top right)

The Taunton Press
Inspiration for hands-on living™

Printed in the United States of America
10 9 8 7 6 5 4

The Taunton Press, Inc., 63 South Main Street, PO Box 5506,
Newtown, CT 06470-5506
e-mail: tp@taunton.com

Distributed by Publishers Group West

Library of Congress Cataloging-in-Publication Data
The basics of craftsmanship : key advice on every aspect of woodworking.
    p.   cm. — (Essentials of woodworking)
        Includes index.
        ISBN 1-56158-297-2
    1. Woodwork. 2. Woodworking tools.
            I. Series.
    TT180.B24   1999   98-47462
    684'.08—dc21   CIP

About Your Safety
Working with wood is inherently dangerous. Using hand or power tools improperly or ignoring
standard safety practices can lead to permanent injury or even death. Don't try to perform operations you
learn about here (or elsewhere) unless you're certain they are safe for you. If something about an
operation doesn't feel right, don't do it. Look for another way. We want you to enjoy the craft,
so please keep safety foremost in your mind whenever you're working with wood.

A journey of a thousand miles
starts with a first step.

CONTENTS

INTRODUCTION

When asked by a friend about why they work wood, most woodworkers can summon only vague and evasive answers. "Because the family needs furniture." "Because I've got to do something for a living." "Because it's, well, fun…?" Such answers rarely satisfy the questioner (especially if a child) and are generally followed with "But why, really?" Most people figure it's much easier to buy tables and chairs than to make them, so they can't see the motivation to build, except to make a living. But so few woodworkers do it for money, there must be another reason why—even if woodworkers themselves can't put a finger on it.

The attraction to woodworking is the tremendous satisfaction that comes from making beautiful, useful, and lasting things with your own two hands. A well-made table will be appreciated for many years, if not generations to come. To have the responsibility for that table's creation means that you can take the credit for the enjoyment and use it gives. And that's a thrill.

Moreover, the life of a finished piece of furniture is only a part of the gratification available to woodworkers. The construction and learning processes themselves are really the most enjoyable aspects. In the shop, woodworkers get to learn a new skill with almost every project, revel in the solutions they find to the endless little problems along the way, watch rough lumber become polished and beautiful, and even collect new tools that are interesting and beautiful in their own right. Only when sanding, perhaps, is woodworking a bore.

If you're not already a woodworker, these are excellent reasons to become one. This book will introduce you to what woodworkers do in their shops and will help you learn the basics. The chapters here, composed of articles from *Fine Woodworking* magazine, cover every major aspect of woodworking from buying tools and materials and setting up a shop to the basic techniques needed to make anything and everything. A few easy first projects and finishes will take you through the process step-by-step and won't leave you out on a limb. Still, remember that you don't need to know everything to be a woodworker. It's a title that doesn't depend on skill or the number of tools you have. It really only depends on one thing: getting into the shop and making something. Good luck and have fun.

ONE

Setting Up a Small Shop

When you're just starting on your own as a woodworker, it's hard to know what to do first. You might have a fairly good idea of the tools you'll need (or at least want) and a place for a shop planned out. But the devil's in the details: Knowing whether you'll use a set of bench chisels more than a bandsaw (and which you should buy first) can only be learned from experience. Buying everything and sorting it out from there is an option only a few have.

Most often, tool collections and the shops that house them are formed over the years through trial and error. In spite of this method's obvious problems, there probably isn't a better way. Every woodworker needs a collection of good tools to work, but no two will work successfully with the same ones. What is essential to one may be useless to another, depending on what kind of woodworking is intended. The tablesaw and the router appear to be central and versatile tools, useful in every shop. But some chairmakers don't use tablesaws, and some furnituremakers won't touch a router. Telling any woodworker which tools he must have is a fool's errand.

Nevertheless, there are ways to reduce the confusion while you find your own way. A first step is to get a sense of the types of tools available and some of the options. The articles in this chapter will go a long way to describe the vast range of woodworking tools available, what to look for when you buy, suggestions for what to get first, and some ideas for setting them up in your shop. Articles in later chapters will offer more in-depth descriptions of tools and techniques.

Also, when considering any one tool, think of what you want to make and how you want to work. Although tools are essential to woodworking, no one tool is crucial. You always have a choice of tools for any one job. Will you mostly make small gifts for friends and family? Or do you intend to fill your house with furniture and paneling? Do you enjoy relative silence while you work, or do you prefer the speed of power tools? What good is it if you suffer using a tool in your effort to enjoy a hobby? A handplane is slow and will make you work up a sweat. A router will fill your ears with noise and your nose with dust. If you can't stand some aspect of a tool, don't buy it. Thinking about these questions will make choosing the right tools a whole lot easier.

PROFESSIONAL ADVICE ON OUTFITTING A SHOP

It takes time, money and good sense to outfit a complete shop, but the principles involved are simple: Buy the best you can afford, cultivate hand-tool skills and acquire machines to perform those tasks for which they're best suited—the brute work of getting stock square, true and to size.

What tools do you need to set up a good basic shop to make functional furnishings you can be proud of? That's the question I posed to three accomplished woodworkers—and teachers of woodworking. Independently, each affirmed the importance of both accurate, reliable power tools and high-quality hand tools in the modern woodworking shop. Though sometimes contradictory, the advice they offer is surprisingly consistent. And where it varies it's often because of their different backgrounds and the kinds of work they do.

Peter Korn was a professional furniture-maker for 12 years and taught furniture

design at Drexel University for four of those years before becoming director of the woodworking program at Anderson Ranch Arts Center in 1986. He has written numerous magazine articles and newspaper columns on woodworking and two books, *Working with Wood: The Basics of Craftsmanship* (1993) and *The Woodworker's Guide to Hand Tools* (1998), both published by The Taunton Press. Korn left Anderson Ranch in 1992 to start his own woodworking school, the Center for Furniture Craftsmanship, which is in Rockport, Maine. The school offers two-week courses for basic and intermediate woodworkers.

Mario Rodriguez is a cabinetmaker and 18th-century woodworking consultant. He's been making 18th- and 19th-century reproductions for the past 17 years, specializing in Windsor chairs. He has been adjunct assistant professor of woodworking for the Fashion Institute of Technology's antique restoration program for the past 10 years and has lectured at the Brooklyn Museum, the Cooper-Hewitt Museum, Sotheby's, the Royal Oak Society and for other groups interested in Early American woodworking. He has taught workshops on planemaking and use, dovetailing and veneering. Mario's book, *Traditional Woodwork: Adding Authentic Period Details to Any Home*, was published by The Taunton Press in 1998.

Mark Duginske, a contributing editor to *Fine Woodworking*, is a fourth-generation woodworker. His books include *The Band Saw Handbook*, *Band Saw Basics*, *The Band Saw Pattern Book*, *Precision Machinery Techniques* and *Mastering Woodworking*

Machines, which was published by The Taunton Press in 1992. He has also done two videos, one accompanying his book *Mastering Woodworking Machines* and the other called *Mastering Your Bandsaw*. His restoration work on the Frank Lloyd Wright home and studio in Oak Park, Ill. has been featured on *This Old House* and PBS's *Frank Lloyd Wright* special.

Although workshops are as individual as their owners, there's a common thread of good sense in the suggestions these three teachers and woodworkers have to offer.

PETER KORN: Building a foundation for a lifetime of craftsmanship

Every year I teach classes in basic wood-working, and every year the students want to know which tools they should buy to set up their first workshop. The answer, of course, depends upon what they want to make and how. I teach the skills necessary for building fine furniture, emphasizing the use of machinery for milling rough lumber foursquare and hand tools for cutting joinery and smoothing surfaces. Machinery and hand tools are complementary aspects of a contemporary fine furniture workshop.

Whether you're setting up a home workshop or starting a small woodworking business, you should acquire the same basic equipment. In neither case should you stint on quality. Good tools may not ensure good work, but poorly made, undersized or underpowered tools will adversely affect both your results and the pleasure you take in the work. Unlike most consumer items, in which obsolescence is engineered, good woodworking hand tools and machinery will last a lifetime and beyond; if you buy the best from the start, you'll only have to buy once. In general, I consider Delta and Porter-Cable to be the minimum acceptable standard against which the quality of other power tools should be measured.

Power tools

If I could have only one piece of machinery in my workshop, it would be a bandsaw. This versatile tool can do anything from the brute work of resawing a 6-in. hardwood beam into planks to the delicate work of cutting the curves for a cabriole leg. With a bandsaw, handplanes and a little sweat,

rough lumber can be milled perfectly four-square. A 14-in. bandsaw is the standard size for most home and small professional shops. You should expect to pay around $700.

The truth is, though, I wouldn't consider getting started without a tablesaw, jointer and thickness planer if I could possibly afford them. Straight, flat, square stock is vital to well-crafted furniture, and these three tools work together to make the milling process easy.

The tablesaw is useful for many other tasks as well, such as making dadoes, tongues, tenons and miters. I recommend buying a good 10-in. tablesaw with a 3-hp motor, such as the Delta Unisaw, which will cost you around $1,500. If you try to save money by purchasing a smaller saw or a weaker motor, you will be itching to upgrade in no time at all.

I started my own shop with a 6-in. jointer, but if I had to do it over again, I would purchase an 8-in. jointer or an even wider one. Those extra inches of cutterhead width significantly reduce the number of boards you will have to flatten with handplanes or saw apart, joint and re-glue because they are too wide for the jointer. A good 8-in. jointer will run you approximately $1,500.

My first planer was a 12-in. Parks, sold by Sears in 1952. I found it abandoned and in pieces in the corner of someone's shop in 1977. While it's not a huge machine, it's been fine for me as a one-off furniture-maker. If I were buying a planer today, I'd stay away from the myriad of lightweight, portable offerings and get something built to last. I've heard good things about the Makita, Hitachi and Delta DC-33 stationary planers. Expect to pay upward of $1,300 for a solid 13-in. planer.

I've also heard good reports from students about some of the better jointer/planer combinations, such as the Robland and the Minimax, but I haven't tried them. Combination jointer/planers may be a good idea for woodworkers with little shop space and/or limited budgets, but separate machines provide an element of convenience I would hate to forego. I am constantly moving back and forth from jointer to planer, so pausing to change one into the other would slow me down considerably. Though I've only used separate machines, I also suspect that they

"Machinery and hand tools are complementary aspects of a contemporary fine furniture workshop."

hold their settings more dependably than do the combination machines.

A drill press, for accurate, straight boring of holes, is the final piece of stationary power equipment essential to a woodworking shop. The size of the drill press isn't all that important, and variable speed isn't really necessary either. Any drill press will do as long as its run-out is minimal, it has an adjustable depth stop and the table is square to the quill. A satisfactory drill press can be had for $300.

Other stationary power tools that are useful but secondary in importance are a lathe, a radial-arm saw or chop saw, a compressor and a belt/disc sander. A vacuum system makes a shop more pleasant to work in, but a dust mask and a broom probably make more fiscal sense—especially when you're just getting started.

Other power tools

Among smaller and portable power tools, I would purchase a grinder, drill and router straight off. A circular saw, jigsaw and biscuit joiner can wait, as can palm, belt and random-orbital sanders.

A grinder is indispensable for keeping chisels and planes sharp. You can get a cheap one for about $50, but if you can afford to—and they're substantially more expensive—you should buy a grinder that spins at about 1,750 rpm, rather than the standard 3,200 rpm to 3,400 rpm. A slower grinder is less likely to overheat steel and destroy its temper.

A router is perhaps the most versatile tool in the shop. A small router with a ¼-in. collet is perfectly adequate for a small shop. My first choice would be Elu's 1-hp variable-speed plunge router, which features a soft start. It is a sweet little machine—just a pleasure to use, and at about $170, it is a very good buy.

My first portable power drill would be a ⅜-in. variable-speed, reversible model. One of its main functions would be to drive drywall screws when building jigs and fixtures in the shop. Milwaukee makes some of the most reliable drills, but they're also among the most expensive—about $120 for the model I recommend.

Hand tools

While you may not think of it as a hand tool, the workbench is where most of your handwork takes place. It may well be your single most important tool. A good workbench should have a flat top, be sturdy enough to take a pounding and not wobble. The bench should also have both tail vise and shoulder vise or the equivalent. If you can't afford to buy a good European workbench (about $1,200), building your own bench should be one of the first projects for your new shop. You can find the bench hardware for about $115.

I've found the following hand tools to be indispensable. I've explained briefly what each is used for as well as what you should expect to pay for a good tool, assuming you shop smart.

Folding rule and a tape measure My favorite measuring device is a 6-ft. Lufkin Red End carpenter's rule with extension slide. It's durable, handy and accurate. $18 (for the folding rule) and $14 (for the tape).

Square I use several squares regularly: a 4-in. engineer's square, a 6-in. try square and a 10-in. try square. If I had to settle for only one square, it would probably be either a 10-in. or 12-in. try square. $25 (for a 10-in. try square).

Sliding T-bevel Indispensable for marking out dovetails and angles. $14.

Mat knife For many purposes, including marking out joinery. $4.

Chisels I recommend buying a set of durable, plastic-handled bench chisels, such as Marples Blue Chip, in sizes ¼ in., ⁵⁄₁₆ in., ⅜ in., ½ in., ¾ in. and 1 in. $45.

Handplanes The first two I'd get are a block plane and a jack plane. The block plane is for planing joints flush, planing across end grain, fairing convex curves, and breaking edges. The jack plane is for flattening wide roughsawn lumber and for smoothing machined surfaces. $45 (block plane) and $73 (jack plane).

Marking and mortising gauges (or a combination gauge) For marking mortises, tenons and dovetail shoulders and for marking stock to be resawn. $34 (for a combination gauge).

Hand scraper For smoothing surfaces. Sandvik makes the best. $7.

Backsaw For cutting joinery. I use a small, inexpensive saw with a 10-in. by $1^5/_8$-in. blade. Its 21 tiny teeth per inch leave a very thin kerf. $13.

Coping saw For removing waste when cutting dovetails and for sawing interior curves. $14.

Awl For marking pilot holes. $7.

Wooden mallet For driving chisels. $14.

Hammer For a multitude of uses. $16.

Twist drill bits From $^1/_{16}$ in. to $^1/_2$ in., by 64ths. $48.

Brad-point bits From $^1/_4$ in. to $^1/_2$ in. by 16ths, plus $^5/_8$ in. and $^3/_4$ in. $40.

Half-round rasp and wood file For smoothing curves and shaping edges. $16 and $14.

Mill bastard file, 8 in. For scraper preparation and for odd bits of metal filing. $6.

Waterstones, 1,000-grit and 6,000-grit For sharpening chisels and plane blades. $47 for the pair.

Clamps I recommend buying six $2^1/_2$-in. C-clamps, six 12-in. quick-action clamps, six 24-in. quick-action clamps, and six 4-ft. bar clamps. About $275.

Although $6,500 or so (a rough total) may seem like a lot of money now, it is almost a negligible sum when amortized over a lifetime of pleasure, productivity and value. Buying good tools to start with and making sure that they're the right tools for the job will get you off to a good beginning on your career as a craftsman.

—Peter Korn

MARIO RODRIGUEZ:
Quality hand tools and a few machines—a good start

When you decide to set up shop, you're immediately faced with decisions about space, equipment and tools. As your skills and experience grow, so will your collection of tools. But, to get you started, here's a good basic kit.

My suggestions are heavy on hand tools because I believe in a strong foundation of hand skills. But a combination of hand tools and machines enables a woodworker to achieve speed *and* practice a high level of craftsmanship.

Stationary power tools

Bandsaw If I could have only one or the other, I'd choose a bandsaw over a tablesaw. Bandsaws are cheaper, take up less floor space, can resaw and cut curves and are considerably quieter than the tablesaw. With a good, well-tuned machine, the quality of cut is excellent. And while it's true that a bandsaw's rip capacity is limited to its throat size, a resourceful woodworker can work around that. You can get a good bandsaw (the Delta 14 in., for example) for as little as $650.

Jointer Buy the best and largest jointer that you can afford. A jointer is useful for cleaning up edges cut on the bandsaw, straightening and squaring edges for gluing, and for flattening boards. The Delta 6 in. sells for about $1,100.

Sliding compound miter saw This saw is invaluable for clean and accurate crosscuts and miters. The sliding-arm feature lets you crosscut up to 12 in. wide (like a small radial-arm saw). Look for a model that takes

"A craftsman's training should be based on a strong foundation of hand skills."

a 10-in. blade instead of an 8½-in. blade. Not everyone carries 8½-in. replacement blades. I like Makita's version, which sells for around $450.

Portable power tools

Router You can do it all with this tool: dado, rabbet, mortise, joint or shape an edge, or follow a template. Porter-Cable's ⅞-hp router is a good value at $110.

Drill, ⅜ in. In addition to using it to drill holes, you can also use it for driving screws, light grinding and polishing. A basic unit can be had for $50.

Hand tools

Chisels Buy a good set of wooden-handled bench chisels (¼ in., ½ in., ¾ in., 1 in.) and a ¼-in. mortise chisel. Wooden handles are more comfortable and more visually appealing than plastic, and if ever they split or get chipped, you can replace them with little effort. I prefer traditional Western chisels (mine are made by Sorby) as opposed to Japanese chisels, which I think require too much work, especially if you're just getting started in woodworking. If you can afford to, buy a 2-in.-wide bench chisel in addition to the four smaller ones. Its extra-wide blade is ideal for paring tenons. A set of four

Sorby chisels costs about $80, the mortise chisel about $30 and the 2-in. paring chisel about $40.

Sharpening stones I prefer waterstones because they're cleaner than oilstones. I use 800-, 1200-, 4000- and 6000-grit stones.

Combination square, 12 in. This tool will mark out stock at 90° and 45° and can double as a ruler and a marking gauge. Buy the best you can afford: Starrett and Browne & Sharpe are both good brands. You can find the Starrett for about $50.

Engineer's square, 3 in. This is great for marking out and checking small parts and edges. It's smaller and handier than the combination square and generally more accurate. You can get a 3-in. engineer's square for around $5.

Sliding bevel This is an essential layout tool used for setting and copying angles. Shinwa makes a compact and inexpensive version (about $10).

Hammer A good 13-oz. claw hammer is ideal for general cabinet work and is useful for installation work as well. I use a one-piece, leather-handled Estwing, which costs about $18.

Carver's mallet This is useful for driving joints home and for chopping out mortises. I like a medium-sized turned lignum vitae mallet. Expect to pay about $15.

Marking gauge I use a compact version made by Reed, which, unfortunately, is no longer in production. It's simple, keeps its setting and has a removable (and replaceable) blade for easy sharpening. Starrett makes a very similar gauge (their #29A) for around $30.

Marking knife I use a pointed chip-carving knife for marking joints. Its slim, pointed tip lets me scribe a good line even in very tight spots, and the shape of the blade allows me to apply pressure for a deeper cut when needed. Less than $10.

Folding rule, 6 ft. I prefer a ruler over tape. I find it more accurate for cabinetwork, particularly when measuring inside cabinets and checking diagonals. Lufkin's Red End is the best and costs about $18.

Dovetail and tenon saws For cutting small pieces, I use an 8-in. dovetail saw with a turned handle and 18 teeth per inch (t.p.i.). I use a 10-in. brass-backed dovetail saw with 14 t.p.i. for cutting dovetails and

A basic kit of hand tools doesn't have to cost a fortune or take up a lot of space. Here, with some changes and additions, is Mario Rodriguez's basic kit. The chisel handles (and the brass-backed dovetail saw's handle) are all replacements made by Rodriguez.

tenons. Japanese saws will also do a great job, but they can require delicate handling, and replacement blades are often expensive. Expect to pay about $10 for the dovetail saw with the turned handle and about $40 for the brass-backed model.

Block plane I recommend the Lie-Nielsen block plane, either the low-angle or the regular. Solid, compact and well made, it's the best block plane on the market. A block plane is useful for planing small parts, flushing surfaces and planing end grain. It sells for $75.

Smoothing plane, #3 A smoothing plane is used for final planing of surfaces as well as for shooting edges on short pieces and for fairing joints. I don't care for any of the smoothing planes on the market for under $100; they're just not made as well as they used to be. I think a reconditioned Stanley, pre-1940, is your best value. I got mine from Tom Witte, an antique tool dealer (P.O. Box 399, Mattawan, Mich. 49071; 616-668-4161). Expect to pay from $60 to $85 for a good used #3.

Rabbet plane There are several planes that fit the bill, but the Stanley #93 is the most versatile because its front half can be removed to convert it to a chisel plane. This plane is used to trim rabbets, plane into corners and trim joints flush. It costs about $80.

Cabinet scraper I use Sandvik scrapers. They're inexpensive, work well and last forever (I still use one I bought over 14 years ago). Scrapers are good for smoothing hardwood and veneered surfaces, either before or in lieu of sanding. You can get a Sandvik scraper for about $6.

These tools are just a beginning. I've tried to keep the list short both to keep your initial outlay of cash from getting out of hand and because it's a good idea to become comfortable and familiar with the basics before adding to your collection. Just remember: Buy the best tools you can afford, take care of them and keep your blades sharp.

—Mario Rodriguez

MARK DUGINSKE: Buy the basics, and know when not to compromise

Setting up shop takes money, but it also takes time, thought and energy: a room full of tools doesn't make a shop. It's important

to reach a point of critical mass, though, having all the tools you need to do a job adequately. And while you don't want junk, you're better off with a shop full of inexpensive tools that allow you to get the job done than only one high-quality tool that leaves you stuck. At the same time, I believe, you're better off buying a good tool and buying it once. The trick is to know when a tool is good enough.

Tablesaw

The tablesaw is at the center of more shops, both figuratively and literally, than probably any other machine. This is partially because of the now ubiquitous use of sheet goods, which the tablesaw alone among stationary woodworking equipment is able to cut down to size. But it's also because the tablesaw can rip stock far more cleanly than the bandsaw and more safely than the radial-arm saw.

Your choices for under $1,000 are the Taiwanese contractor's saws (sold under more names than I can keep up with) and the Delta contractor's saw. The Delta is well made, easily adjustable and it holds its adjustments well. The problem with the Taiwanese saws is their inconsistency. Some are fine out of the box, but I've also seen one on which it was impossible to align the blade with the miter-gauge slot without disassembling the saw and filing out the trunnion holes. On other Taiwanese tablesaws, I've seen the finish on the inside of the miter-gauge slot as rough as a file. If you take the time to expand your miter bar to fit the slot tightly (either with a prick punch or by peening the bar), the adjustment will wear away very rapidly by the rough side wall. If you're going to buy a Taiwanese saw, buy it from a local dealer, and check it out before any cash changes hands.

Two of the best used tablesaws are the Inca 259 and Delta's old 9-in. contractor's saw. Both are excellent machines; if you see one for a reasonable sum, jump on it. Another excellent used saw is the Delta tilting arbor saw, which had cast-iron wings like the Unisaw but an open base like the contractor's saw.

Bandsaw

If you can afford only one really good tool, make it the bandsaw, especially if you'd like

"Setting up shop takes money, but it also takes time, thought and energy: A room full of tools doesn't make a shop."

to do restoration work or any kind of work that requires curve cutting. There are only two choices for an affordable first-rate bandsaw: the Inca 340 and the 14-in. Delta. Both are fine pieces of equipment and each has its strengths. The Inca weighs only 60 lb., which makes it quite portable. Also, with its optional micro-adjuster, it's well suited for joinery, such as cutting tenons and dovetails. The Delta's strength is its resaw capacity, which, with the optional riser block, is 12 in.

As for used tools, I'd look for a 14-in. Delta or an old Sears with a tilting table.

Saws for crosscutting

If you're doing more carpentry-type construction or you're just doing a lot of crosscutting, particularly of long pieces, then you should consider buying a radial-arm or a sliding compound miter saw, which has replaced the radial arm for most contractors and for many—if not most—woodworkers. The sliding compound miter saw has no rip capability, but it can crosscut up to 12 in. on most models and can cut accurate 45° and other miters as well as compound angles. These saws are portable, and their simple design keeps them surprisingly accurate.

Jointers and planers

The Ryobi and some of the other small planers have transformed the small shop by bringing the price of a planer into the range of most woodworkers' budgets. Along with a 6-in. jointer and a contractor's saw, anyone can afford to dimension his own stock now. Bring a reliable straightedge with you to check the beds when shopping for a jointer. A jointer is a precision-oriented tool, and its beds must be flat and parallel.

A combination jointer/planer is another affordable way to set yourself up to prepare stock. Hitachi, Inca and Robland make very good jointer/planers.

Gadgets and gimmicks: beware

Hand-tool skills and basic power-tool savvy are a woodworker's best foundation. A disturbing trend I've noticed in the past few years, primarily at woodworking shows, is the number of beginning woodworkers buying gadgets and gimmicks rather than investing in solid, basic tools. Granted, the basic power tools represent a more significant investment, but these jigs, fixtures and whatnot that promise to deliver flawless joinery with no effort are only distractions that insulate novice woodworkers from acquiring basic hand skills and mechanical knowledge.

The combination of hand-tool skills, a router and some medium-sized, well-tuned decent equipment will allow you to do just about anything. You may not get it done as quickly as if you had each one of Delta's industrial tools, but you will be able to do a variety of quality work without spending a ton of cash on equipment.

Buying tools is only part of becoming a woodworker. The other ingredient is skill, which is purchased with time and determination. Each tool—whether power or hand—has its own learning curve. The current trend—to learn machine woodworking before developing hand-tool skills—is backward. Compounding this problem, or perhaps causing it, is that we as a culture are so goal-oriented that we have to make things right away rather than playing with a tool and getting to know it. It's possible to develop the same kind of intimacy with power tools as you develop with hand tools, but it doesn't happen when you're in a mad rush to finish a project. Traditionally, knowledge was gained by continuous repetition during an apprenticeship period. Today, experimentation and practice are the best ways to learn. But there are no shortcuts—no matter how much you're willing to pay.

—Mark Duginske

HOW TO BUY USED HAND TOOLS

by Robert Hubert Jr.

I was excited. I had finally saved up a little extra cash to put toward new hand tools for my shop. I gathered up all my dog-eared woodworking catalogs to pick out planes, chisels and other tools. The shock came when I hit "total" on my calculator; my modest savings would buy only a fraction of the tools I wanted. But thanks to a neighbor who told me about an old plane he had seen at a local flea market, my tool-buying strategy changed.

The next Sunday I bought that plane, a usable Stanley #5, for just $15. Three years later, my collection of vintage hand tools has cost me less than half the price of new tools. And here's the best part: By carefully purchasing and reselling a few extra tools for a profit, my tool buying has begun to pay for the rest of my shop.

Preparing for a tool hunt

Whether you call them antique tools, vintage tools or just plain old tools, hunting for used tools requires preparation. The better equipped you are, the better your chances of acquiring high-quality tools at reasonable prices. Here's the systematic approach I use.

Make a tool "want list" for the woodworking you do. Use catalogs to jog your memory of your shop needs. Be specific. Don't just list "bench plane," put down "Stanley #3," and list whether you want a wood plane or an all-metal one. Being specific will keep you focused and help you avoid buying tools you don't need.

Behold the language of auctioneer Richard Crane. Most auctioneers initially start the bidding low; later, they'll open items high.

Study the tools you'll be buying. Start by becoming familiar with tool classes and makers. Certain tools, like drawknives, have changed little over the years. Others, like planes, have changed dramatically. One place to learn about hand tools is in original or reprinted owner's manuals and catalogs. Product literature can help you identify a tool as well. In addition, there are books and associations (see the sources of supply on p. 12) that offer a tour of secondhand tools and sellers, as well as supply information about repairing and using old tools. As a beginner, you can go a long way by studying up on Stanley tools alone.

Learn about fair prices and value of used tools. Although you shouldn't completely rely on price guides, current guides can give you ball-park figures for tools. If you're buying for speculation, the guides can tell you how valuable a tool is. Collectors typically look for limited-production tools or tools from unusual makers. Stay away from these

SOURCES OF SUPPLY

For a more complete list of tool groups, dealers, auctions and publications, send $1 to Bob Vogel, New England Tool Collectors Assoc., 164 Chestnut St., N. Easton, MA 02356-2611.

ASSOCIATIONS, AUCTION HOUSES AND WORKSHOPS:

Early American Industries Association, PO Box 2128, ESP Albany, NY 12220-0128

Society of Workers in Early Arts and Trades, 606 Lake Lena Blvd., Auburndale, FL 33823

Tool Group of Canada, 112 Holmcrest Trail, Scarborough, Ont., Canada NT M1C 1V5

The Tool and Trades Historical Society, 60 Swanley Lane, Swanley, Kent, U.K. BR8 7JG

Your Country Auctioneer Inc., 63 Poor Farm Road, Hillsboro, NH 03244

National Antique Tool Auction, 4729 Kutztown Road, Temple, PA 19560

David Stanley Auctions, Stordon Grange, Osgathorpe, Leicester, LE12 9SR, U.K.

Warwick Country Workshops (plane clinics), 1 E. Ridge Road, Warwick, NY 10990

ANTIQUE AND USED-TOOL DEALERS:

Tom Witte's Antiques, PO Box 399, Mattawan, MI 49071

Bob Kaune Antique and Used Tools, 511 W. 11th St., Port Angeles, WA 98362 www.olympus.net/bktools

Two Chislers, 1864 Glen Moor Drive, Lakewood, CO 80215

Iron Horse Antiques, PO Box 4001, Pittsford, VT 05763

Roger K. Smith, PO Box 177, Athol, MA 01331

Martin Donnelly Antique Tools, 31 Rumsey St., PO Box 281, Bath, NY 14810

BOOKS AND PUBLISHERS:

Dictionary of Woodworking Tools, R.A. Salaman, revised by Phillip Walker, 1990, The Taunton Press Inc., PO Box 5506, Newtown, CT 06470 www.taunton.com

The Antique Tool Collector's Guide to Value, Ronald S. Barlow, 1985, Windmill Publishing Co., 2147 Windmill View Road, El Cajon, CA 92020

Restoring, Tuning and Using Classic Woodworking Tools, Michael Dunbar, 1989, Sterling Publishing Co., 387 Park Ave. S., New York, NY 10016

Astragal Press, PO Box 338, Mendham, NJ 07945 www.astragalpress.com

OLD TOOL WEBSITES:

The Electronic Neanderthal, www.cs.cmu.edu/~alf/en/en.html

The Fine Tool Journal, www.wowpages.com/ftj/

---

tools if you want a bargain tool for woodworking. Always jot down a fair price range for each of the tools on your want list. An entry in my notebook looks something like this: "Jack Plane—prefer Stanley #5 w/corrugated sole—$15-$25."

Four basic rules for buying vintage tools

As I head into an uncharted used-tool market with my want list in hand and my head full of knowledge, I follow four basic rules.

Rule #1: Thoroughly inspect the tools you're buying. If a tool has many parts, take it apart and examine the pieces. I carry a simple tool-disassembly kit that consists of two screwdrivers, an Allen wrench set and a pair of pliers. A hidden crack (see the photo on p. 15) can make an old tool useless. Therefore, after you take a tool apart,

wipe away grime with a rag. Then, check the tool's stress points. On a plane, the blade area and mouth are susceptible to stress and so is the rear tote (for more on this, see the story on pp. 14-15). On chisels, check for mallet-caused damage and for splits where the tang meets the handle.

Check for missing or substitute parts. Here again, a manual makes it easy to compare a parts list against the actual tool. At the least, a catalog will show a drawing or photo of what the tool should look like. In addition, the tools themselves can reveal where parts are absent. A threaded hole with nothing attached may indicate a missing fence, for example.

Rule #2: Look at what tool collectors don't. One of my best bargains came about because a collector shunned a tool. The owner of a panel-raising plane had restored

Wise tool prospectors, armed with want lists and notes, scope out a table of handplanes and box lots of tool parts during the auction preview. A few of the bidders will snatch up bargains at the end of the auction just by outlasting their competitors.

his tool by refinishing it. The tool looked beautiful to me, but not to a collector. Without its original finish, the plane sold for one-tenth of its value.

Rule #3: Buy parts and pieces. Occasionally, it's a good idea to buy a box lot or two of tool parts because you'll often find a tool with something missing. The tool may be offered cheaply and be in good shape otherwise. To complete the tool, you can simply connect the right part from your stock. My best hand tools have come this way (see the photo at right).

Rule #4: Take it easy. There will always be another tool like the one you want. Don't feel forced into buying a marginal tool or one that costs more than it's worth. It took me nearly three years to put together my assortment of hand tools, and I'm still refining it.

Where to acquire old hand tools

Vintage tool hunters basically have three avenues where they can buy tools: flea markets, auctions and dealers. Depending on where you live, the used-tool scene can be quite disorganized and the prices arbitrary. Always remember, it's "buyer beware."

Flea markets offer the best bargains, but they'll cost you energy and time (pleasant work for me). At many flea markets, you may only find one tool. But, it's likely you'll be able to buy it cheap. My favorite buy was a mint-condition Millers Falls bit brace—just $3. You can cover a flea market quickly

Put together for less than one-fourth the price of a complete plane, this Stanley combination plane is the author's pride and joy. Assembled from parts acquired from flea markets, auctions and tool dealers, this non-original plane makes a perfectly good woodworking tool, even though it's unacceptable to a collector.

once you learn to spot tool tables from a distance. When you find a tool, don't be afraid to barter. Rarely have I had to pay the marked or asking price.

Auctions provide the best selection of tools, but be wary of auction fever. There'll be lots of tools for sale, so wait for a good tool at the right price. To minimize overbidding, first get the auction preview list, even if you

Stalking a secondhand plane

by Maurice Fraser

Buying a new handplane costs you time or bucks: Mass-produced ones, ill-machined, take hours to tune, while well-made deluxe models are pricey. Another option? Hunt for a usable old classic. So you won't have to hunt in the dark, I'll describe what to watch for when pursuing good used planes, and I'll examine their inner workings.

Basic plane anatomy

A plane is, essentially, a chisel locked to a guiding body. Standard bench planes are of three types—each for a special job. The jack plane, Stanley's Nos. 5 and 5½ (14 in. and 15 in. long), zaps wood to dimension; the jointer plane, Nos. 6 to 8 (18 in. to 24 in.), straightens the curves; and the smooth plane, nos. 1 to 4½ (6 in. to 10 in.), polishes surfaces. Except for size, the three types are built alike.

British and American traditions

Metal planes are of either the wooden-core British type, exemplified by the classic Norris, or of the familiar open-shell cast-iron type, perfected by Stanley of New England.

Norris and Stanley-type metal planes boast parallel-thicknessed blades, which ensure consistent mouth-to-blade fit, unlike old wood planes. Both Norris and Stanley blades have a cap iron (chip breaker) bolted to them called, collectively, the "double iron." Both brands secure the double iron with a pivoting lever cap.

Norris-type lever caps pivot on an axle and lock the blade by tightening a bolt. Stanley-type lever caps are captured under a bolt head and snap tight with a clever cam action: This gives identical blade-to-seat pressure each time. However, the ideal, an integral seat, isn't feasible in a cast body, so Stanley-types require a screw-on cutter seat or "frog," which allows adjustment. But, often more a liability than an asset, the frog permits chatter on heavy cuts, and its blade-positioning range is quite narrow. Furthermore, most frogs wander when adjusted, and realignment is by trial and error. (Lie-Nielsen, like old Bed Rock, remedies this.) But the Norris cutter seat is integral: cut true into the solid wood interior, it needs no adjustment.

Adjusters: Stanley vs. Norris

Both Stanley and later Norris metal planes rely on mechanisms to control both depth of cut and side-to-side evenness. Stanley planes separate the two modes of adjustment. For depth, a brass wheel's rotation pushes a forked lever downward, carrying the blade with it. Sideways movement is via a pivoting upright lever, whose end is captive in the blade slot. Norris planes combine the two motions in a single ingenious, but awkward, mechanism.

Stanley's two-part adjustment system is reliable and responsive. Old over-used Stanleys can adjust with finesse. But even pristine Norrises are awk-ward to adjust, and it's all too easy to over-tighten the lever cap.

What to look for

Since Norrises are rare and ultra expensive, start by looking for the upper-end Stanley models: Bailey, Bed Rock and Gage. Liberty Bell and Defiance are Stanley's cheap models and may not adjust easily. Most generic "Stanleys" (unsigned) are bad tools. Sargent, Union, and Millers Falls are often mediocre. Leave exotic brands to the collectors and, as a rule, avoid (or haggle for) planes with mixed parts.

If you're patient and observant, you can avoid buying a plane that will need major work. The photo on the facing page shows a few features that should make or break a deal.

Body: Normal rust and pitting won't affect a plane's function, but cracks (common around the mouth) are risky and can worsen. Check the sole's length against a straightedge or a sole of known flatness. If any light shows through, the sole will need flattening or the plane won't function at all.

Handles: Avoid planes without totes. Making them is hard work, and broken or badly mended totes are like ill-fitting running shoes—no bargain is worth the misery. Note that the totes of long and short planes are not interchangeable. Broken or missing front knobs are replaceable. Remedy a loose knob or tote by screwing in the retaining bolt, shortening it, if needed.

Blades: Original blades are best; *good* replacements are acceptable. A blade ground down to ¾ in. or less from its long slot has little life left (and may have only unhardened steel left in it). Rust pitting on a blade's bevel face is acceptable, but *not* on the cutting face. The blade's back should be flat and smooth—otherwise, proper cap-iron fit will be impossible. Reject bent blades.

Cap iron and lever cap: When screwed tight, no light should show at the cap iron's junction with the blade's edge (chips will clog here). If the cap iron is a substitute, its adjuster slot may not align with the depth lever and will limit blade motion—so check out the blade-depth range. A chipped lever cap corner won't affect planing, but the leading contact edge should lie flush.

Adjuster and threaded parts: If the brass wheel is rust-frozen, applying WD-40 or oil may or may not free the motion. The yoke should be astride the wheel and freely move with it without rattling. Reject a broken yoke. The lateral adjustment lever can be bent and still function perfectly.

Screws should all turn and have reasonably crisp slots and rust-free threads. The lever-cap capture bolt *must* turn to allow tension adjustment, but rusted frog bolts may never require further use if the frog is set right. It's a hard call and one of the risks of the hunt.

Disassembly reveals problems and virtues: The parts on the left of the photo show what to be wary of when buying an old plane. The assembled plane (below right) is fully restored. The Norris-type adjuster (inset) is taken from a Record plane (carried by Garrett Wade).

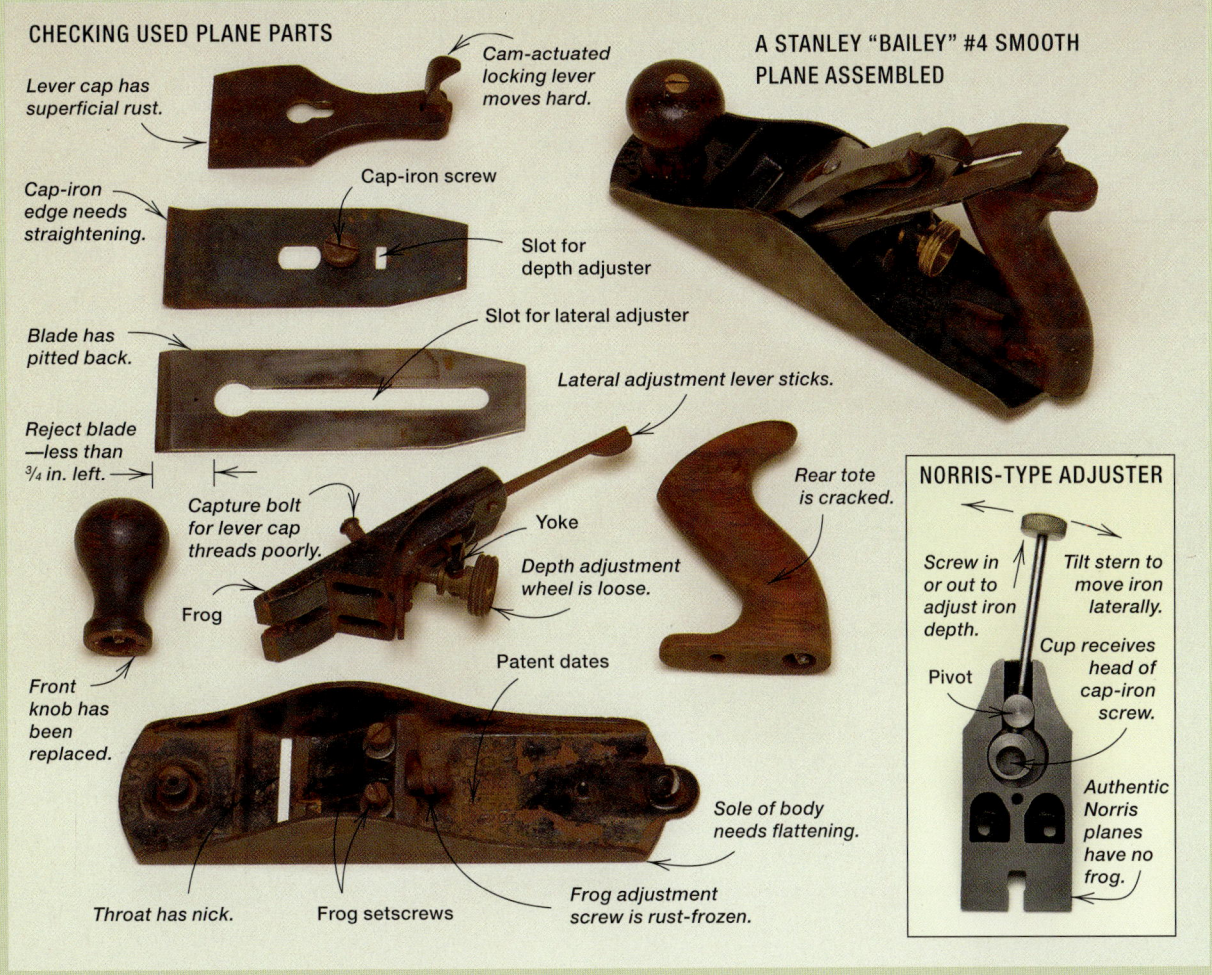

CHECKING USED PLANE PARTS

Lever cap has superficial rust.

Cam-actuated locking lever moves hard.

Cap-iron edge needs straightening.

Cap-iron screw

Slot for depth adjuster

Slot for lateral adjuster

Blade has pitted back.

Reject blade —less than ¾ in. left.

Lateral adjustment lever sticks.

Capture bolt for lever cap threads poorly.

Yoke

Rear tote is cracked.

Frog

Depth adjustment wheel is loose.

Front knob has been replaced.

Patent dates

Sole of body needs flattening.

Throat has nick.   Frog setscrews

Frog adjustment screw is rust-frozen.

A STANLEY "BAILEY" #4 SMOOTH PLANE ASSEMBLED

NORRIS-TYPE ADJUSTER

Screw in or out to adjust iron depth.

Tilt stern to move iron laterally.

Pivot

Cup receives head of cap-iron screw.

Authentic Norris planes have no frog.

There are other places to look for secondhand tools besides auctions and flea markets. Here, Hubert asks about a pair of calipers being offered by a tailgate dealer, who temporarily has set up shop in the parking lot outside the Cabin Fever Auction. This old-tool auction is held every February in Nashua, N.H.

have to buy it, and then use preview time wisely (see the top photo on p. 13). Some auctions have previewing the day before; and some require an admittance fee. After I check off items from my want list, I allow five minutes for inspecting each tool. This gives me enough time, even when there's a crowd. If there's no preview list, try to arrive when previewing begins. Do a once over to spot-check all the tools. Then go back and fully inspect items that interest you.

Second, mark down the maximum price you're willing to pay for a tool. I often write the figure on the back of my bidding card along with the lot number (this prevents me from bidding on a tool that looks identical to the one I want). Once you've arrived at a figure, don't exceed that limit. You'll be strongly tempted to bid another five dollars in hopes of winning a tool, but this rarely works. One exception is when you're bidding against a dealer—they're usually conservative, disciplined bidders. Once they reach their cutoff, you can often buy an item at just a slightly higher bid. On the other end of the spectrum are the collectors. Avoid getting in a bidding war with a

collector—they often bid quite aggressively when pursuing a tool for their collection.

Third, to save yourself grief, don't bid on something you haven't inspected. I've wound up with lemon tools because I didn't inspect them first. If you can't attend an auction, you may still be able to place a sight-unseen absentee bid, but it is risky. If you're determined to take a risk at an auction, buy a cheap box lot.

Fourth, check out the tailgate tool market, where dealers peddle their wares in event parking lots (see the photo above).

Dealers have hard-to-find tools, but their prices are frequently higher than those at flea markets and auctions. Many tool dealers sell via mail order and issue some kind of catalog. The catalogs usually list prices and describe tools and their condition. Before you order from a dealer, verify that he has a flexible return policy. Most dealers also have a listing service in which they'll locate something from your want list. Finally, keep an eye open for antique dealers who double as tool dealers.

GREAT SHOP IN A TWO-CAR GARAGE

by Curtis Erpelding

A workshop ought to be perfectly practical—just a place to work wood and to keep tools and materials dry and warm—but it never is. That's because it is also very personal. The problems you solve as you outfit your shop may be practical ones, but they arise for personal reasons: You make jigsaw puzzles as well as highboys; your shop is unheated in the winter and floods in the spring; you like to stand while drawing and sit down while cutting dovetails; you store your kayak for half the year suspended from the ceiling above your milling machines.

I've had six shops over the last 20 years, and I've found that improving a shop is a matter of learning about myself and the way I work, both in general and in each specific space.

In my first shop, which was the cleared-out end of a book-storage warehouse, I hung the few tools I had accumulated on the wall a good 10 paces away from my work table. It soon became apparent that constant trips between the wall and the work table were doing nothing for my productivity. I learned a specific lesson and applied it in my succeeding shops: Store drill bits by the drill press, sawblades by the saw, hand tools by the workbench, jigs and fixtures by the machines they were built for.

I also learned a more general rule of shop design: You'll rarely get it right the first time. It takes time and experience to create a well-functioning, efficient shop. All of the aspects of shop order—from tool and machine layout to work flow procedures and storage solutions—evolve over time.

My grinding setup is an example of Darwinism as it applies in the workshop. In that first shop, my grinding device was a hand-operated wheel clamped to the edge of the table. It had all the disadvantages: It was slow, it took muscle, its minimal tool rest made it difficult to obtain a consistent edge and, being clamped to the work table, it was in the way. It didn't take too long to realize that if I was serious about making a living while using hand tools, I would have to find a better system.

The first improvement was to motorize. I salvaged an old washing-machine motor that ran at a convenient 1,725 rpm and fitted it with a white vitrified wheel. Then I went about finding a better approach to the tool-rest problem. One drawback of most tool rests is that they don't fully support the blade being sharpened. Another problem is that they force you to hold the tool or blade at an unnatural angle. I built a tool rest in the shape of an open-sided box around the grinding wheel. The wheel emerges through a slot in the top of the box the way a table-saw blade emerges through the throat plate. This enables me to grind tools while they are lying flat and fully supported on the top of the box (see the photo at left on p. 23). Even spokeshave irons and small marking knives can be precisely ground without the need for positioning fixtures. With the motor mounted on a hinged board, I can adjust the grinding angle by raising or lowering the motor. That was my second sharpening setup, permanently mounted at the end of a wall bench. My current arrangement has the same grinder, but the box is now mounted on the wall at a comfortable height for grinding. The whole mechanism is on drawer slides and is pulled out of the box for use. This saves space but also keeps dust, debris and stray tools from ending up on the grinder.

Because everything evolves, being flexible is another inflexible rule of organization. Try not to make any feature of the shop permanent. The arrival of new tools, new types of work or simply better ideas will demand a new arrangement.

Having machines that are movable is particularly advantageous in a small shop. In my own shop spaces, I've kept my machinery small. One of the advantages of having

Overhead view of the shop

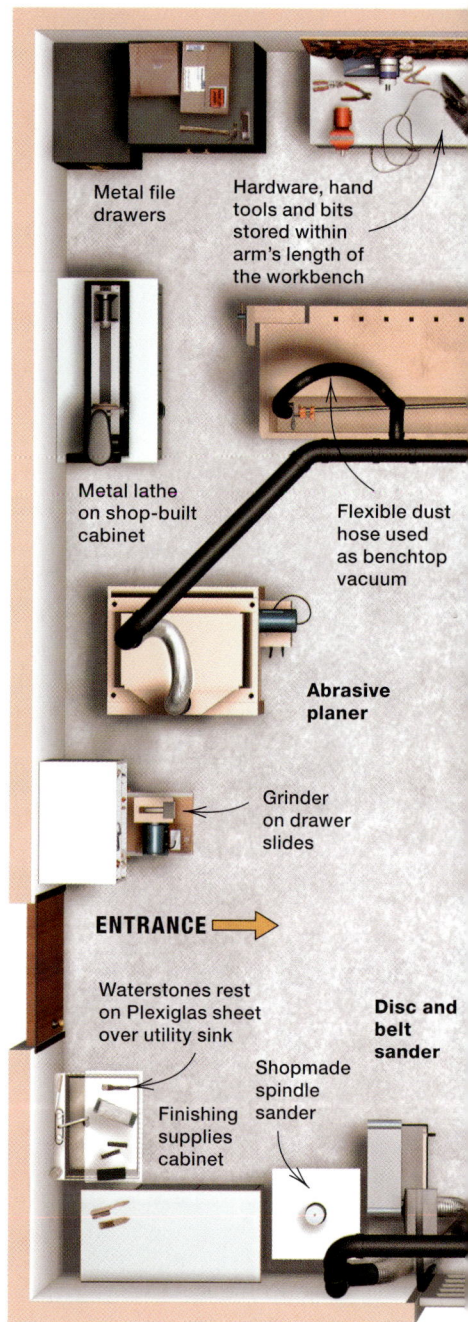

Metal file drawers

Hardware, hand tools and bits stored within arm's length of the workbench

Metal lathe on shop-built cabinet

Flexible dust hose used as benchtop vacuum

Abrasive planer

Grinder on drawer slides

ENTRANCE

Waterstones rest on Plexiglas sheet over utility sink

Disc and belt sander

Shopmade spindle sander

Finishing supplies cabinet

small, lightweight machines is that you can easily move them, even by yourself. With my 14-in. bandsaw, for example, I don't have room for the optimal 8 ft. or 10 ft. of clear-

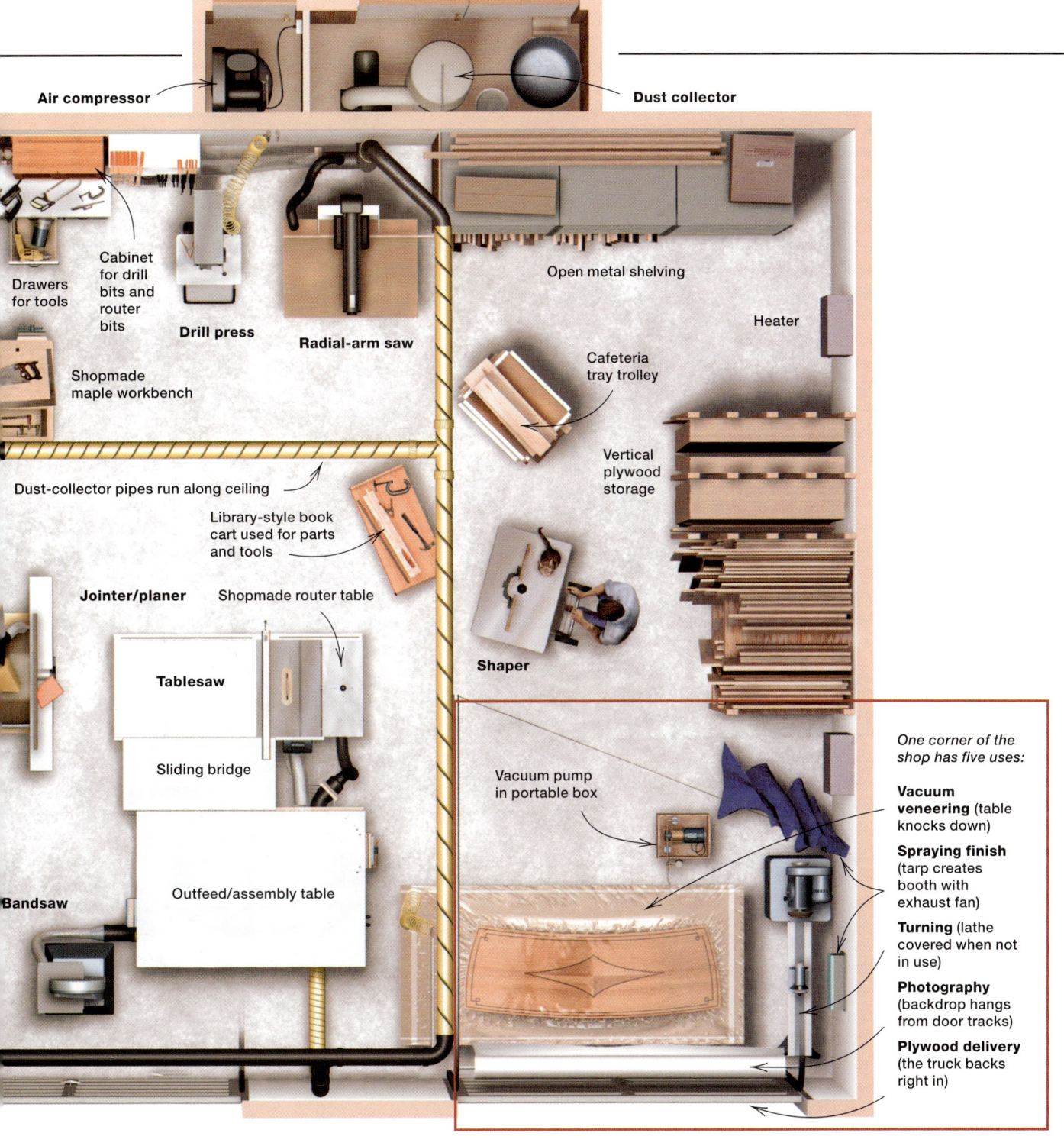

Air compressor

Dust collector

Drawers for tools

Cabinet for drill bits and router bits

Drill press

Radial-arm saw

Shopmade maple workbench

Open metal shelving

Heater

Cafeteria tray trolley

Vertical plywood storage

Dust-collector pipes run along ceiling

Library-style book cart used for parts and tools

Jointer/planer   **Shopmade router table**

Tablesaw

Sliding bridge

Shaper

Vacuum pump in portable box

One corner of the shop has five uses:

Vacuum veneering (table knocks down)

Spraying finish (tarp creates booth with exhaust fan)

Turning (lathe covered when not in use)

Photography (backdrop hangs from door tracks)

Plywood delivery (the truck backs right in)

Outfeed/assembly table

Bandsaw

ance on the outfeed side. In good weather, I increase outfeed clearance by opening the garage door. In poor weather, I simply pivot the machine. With heavier machines, I

improvise. I mounted two non-swivel casters and two adjustable glides inside the base of my shaper. They raise the machine ⅛ in. or so, without compromising its stability. I can

Tablesaw and assembly table linked at the heart of the shop

With all the room a tablesaw requires for infeed, outfeed and support on either side of the blade, its placement is the logical starting point for laying out a shop. The author decided to make his outfeed table do double duty as a fixed-in-place assembly table. A sliding bridge connects the saw with the assembly table.

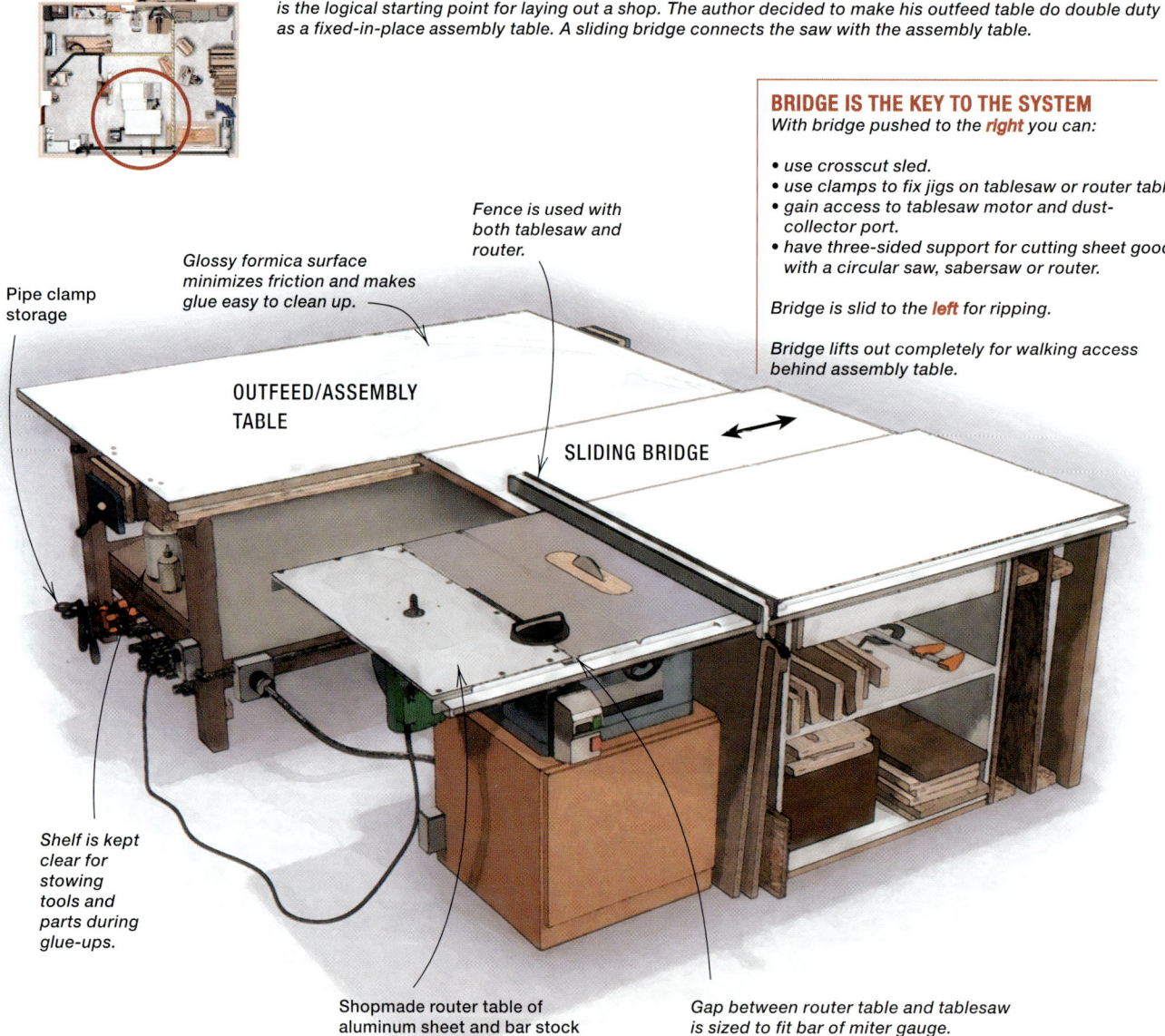

BRIDGE IS THE KEY TO THE SYSTEM
*With bridge pushed to the **right** you can:*

- *use crosscut sled.*
- *use clamps to fix jigs on tablesaw or router table.*
- *gain access to tablesaw motor and dust-collector port.*
- *have three-sided support for cutting sheet goods with a circular saw, sabersaw or router.*

*Bridge is slid to the **left** for ripping.*

Bridge lifts out completely for walking access behind assembly table.

Fence is used with both tablesaw and router.

Glossy formica surface minimizes friction and makes glue easy to clean up.

Pipe clamp storage

OUTFEED/ASSEMBLY TABLE

SLIDING BRIDGE

Shelf is kept clear for stowing tools and parts during glue-ups.

Shopmade router table of aluminum sheet and bar stock

Gap between router table and tablesaw is sized to fit bar of miter gauge.

move it short distances by lifting the side with the glides and pushing or pulling. For longer trips, I use a hand truck to lift and push the side with the glides. I could have bought a mobile base for the shaper, but I didn't want to raise the shaper significantly because I use it as a side support when I crosscut long pieces on the tablesaw.

Because each shop presents unique problems, it makes sense to make your own shop fittings and furniture. But that doesn't mean you can't find ready-made solutions. I have an old large metal cabinet full of drawers. It was originally used for storing Addressograph printing plates, and it was free for the hauling. I spent a couple of hours modifying the drawer interiors, and it is now brimming with neatly segregated screws, sandpaper,

In a small shop, most things should be movable

Tilt and roll

Lift and roll

Let it slide

Stationary disc and belt sander has wheels just off the floor, so you can tip it back and move it like a wheelbarrow. Offset, non-swivel casters are key.

A pair of non-swivel, heavy-duty casters make the shaper movable, and a pair of adjustable glides keep it level and stable. For a long move, a hand truck helps. The cat provides good ballast.

The jointer/planer often needs to be angled to increase feed clearance. A simple plywood box with nail-in glides at the corners makes a stable, slidable base.

hardware and glue. All sorts of card file cabinets are obsolete as a result of the computer revolution. The cabinets range from the fine wooden ones with dovetailed drawers that libraries used for their card catalogs to standing metal cabinets and two- or four-drawer desktop cases.

Used office-furniture stores are a good place to haunt. Metal file-drawer cabinets in legal or letter size make fine storage for

mid-sized items, and used ones can be had quite cheaply. And at a bankruptcy sale, I bought a metal storage rack for $20 that would have cost me at least a day of labor and $100 in materials to duplicate in wood.

Being a frugal sort, I like the idea of adaptive reuse. Two of my roll-around carts are sturdy aluminum trolleys that used to carry cafeteria trays. I bought them for $50 apiece

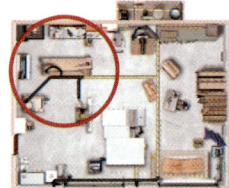

The author worked for years with his bench against a wall. Moving the bench away from the wall and building a cabinet with drawers behind it made him far more productive.

1 Pulled away from the wall, the bench can be used from both sides, and workpieces can extend from it in all directions.

2 With counter space and tool storage within arm's length, the workbench stays uncluttered.

3 Cabinet is used for router bits and drill bits.

4 Countertop with laminate surface and integral splash is available in various lengths at home centers. This 8-ft. section cost about $50.

5 Deep drawers run on heavy-duty, full-extension slides and hold routers, drills, sanders and air tools.

at a scrap-metal yard. I scrubbed them down and cut pieces of ½-in. particleboard to use as shelves where the trays once went. These 6-ft.-high carts, with their footprint of 1½ ft. by 2½ ft., can hold an enormous number of furniture parts that would otherwise be scattered over tables or benchtops or spilling onto the floor.

Like all shops, mine is a stage for the eternal battle between order and chaos. And true to thermodynamic law, chaos has the edge. As years go by, I collect more jigs and fixtures that somehow can't be thrown out, extra material from each job begins to add up and, of course, I can't resist that extra piece of equipment. The more I try to

FROM THE LUNCHROOM TO THE WORKSHOP
For $50, the author bought an aluminum trolley for cafeteria trays. A good scrubbing and some ½-in. flakeboard shelves turned it into a parts cart.

PUMP HOUSE
A quick plywood box, with cutout handles and a slide-in lid, makes a snug mobile home for the author's vacuum-veneering pump. When not in use, it is stored on a shelf.

GLIDING GRINDER
This grinder slides out of a box for use. For rigidity, two pairs of drawer slides are used: one pair side-mounting, the other bottom-mounting. The open box around the grinding wheel is the tool rest, which enables the author to grind blades while holding them flat. The blades ride on a steel wear plate. The motor mount is hinged, and changing its height adjusts the grinding angle.

REVIVE-A-VAC
The bottom half of a dead shop vacuum makes a rolling rag bin, trash can or a barrel for cutoffs. A scrap of flakeboard placed on top turns it into a utility table for mixing finishes.

squeeze in, the more chaos threatens to take over. At some point, after all the space-saving devices have been deployed, the issue becomes paring back (perish the thought) or expanding the space. This spring, after working in a two-car garage for six years, I am remodeling the shop, nearly doubling the working area. I have a pretty good idea how I'll use this added space—a dedicated

finishing room, a fold-up table for vacuum veneering, a place where the lathe is more accessible. Whether these ideas will work out as planned I don't know. But I am certain that over time my needs will change, my accessories will increase, the new space will evolve to accommodate them and chaos will slowly regain its lost ground.

TWO

Materials

If you've ever built furniture with clear pine, you know its many advantages. It's a pleasure to work, cuts easily, and has a nice warm color when finished bright. Pine is also cheap and widely available. However, you also know that it's soft and dents easily. A writing desk with a pine top can't even stand up to a ballpoint pen. The first letter you write will be etched into the top forevermore. While pine works well for a number of applications, tabletops are best made with a harder wood such as oak, maple or even a plywood with hardwood veneer.

No one wood is perfectly suited to every application. But there are enough varieties to suit every reasonable use. The difficulty is not just in knowing your options but in knowing how to find them. Special woods such as white oak, black walnut and mahogany aren't generally available at local lumberyards or home centers. The same is true of other shop materials, including hardwood-veneered plywood and some adhesives and abrasives. Home centers bias their inventory toward home construction rather than cabinetry. To find the right materials for cabinetmaking, you have to look a bit harder. Specialty lumberyards, sawmills, woodworking stores and mail-order catalogs are better places to look.

This chapter offers articles on all the major shop materials. The articles discuss the many options, what to look for, and where to find them. The right materials are always worth the extra effort for the difference they will make in your work. A dresser made from pine just isn't the same as one made from walnut. The beauty of walnut will make it a treasure and not just another dresser fated to end up in a tag sale. Even something as simple as the glue you choose can have a huge effect on the way you work and the quality of what you make. Quick-setting yellow glue is great for small work, but it's a nightmare for large projects. It can set before you've clamped the joints tight. In these situations, a slow-set epoxy or a polyurethane glue will eliminate the rush and stress. Material choices are just as important as tool choices. Skimp on them, and you'll regret the results.

BUYING LUMBER

by Vincent Laurence

I remember cruising the aisles of a home center, while still in college, looking for wood to make a stereo rack. I was making the move from pine 1x12s on cinder blocks, and I wanted to do it right. But something *wasn't* right with the hardwood lumber at the home center. It was stacked upright, all surfaced and plastic-wrapped. In its packaged uniformity, the lumber had all the appeal of shrink-wrapped chickens lined up in a supermarket cooler.

Today, there are few things I enjoy more than pawing through stacks of walnut, cherry or bird's-eye maple. Even roughsawn boards are enough to set me building projects in my head. For me, the wood itself is a big part of the reason for woodworking.

But you have to find the wood first. Then you need to know what you're looking for—and what to avoid. There are a lot of different places to find wood, each with its advantages and disadvantages. And wood is avail-

A LUMBER-BUYER'S GLOSSARY

BOARD FOOT (BD. FT.): A unit of measurement equivalent to 1 in. by 12 in. by 12 in.

BOW: A curve along the face of a board from end to end, like a ski.

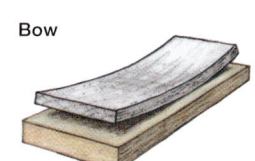
Bow

CASEHARDENING: A defect caused by improper drying, which results in a board with latent stresses and possible honeycombing. A casehardened board cannot be resawn without problems.

CHECKING: Cracks resulting from uneven drying. They may be at the ends of a board or throughout the board as a result of casehardening.

Crook

CROOK: A curve along the edge of a board from end to end.

CUP: A concave face on a board.

Cup

EQUILIBRIUM MOISTURE CONTENT (EMC): A board is at equilibrium moisture content when it neither takes up nor gives off moisture in the surrounding environment.

FLATSAWN: Sawn parallel to a tangent of the tree's growth rings. Flatsawn lumber shows face grain, with oval, U- and V-shaped patterns.

FLITCH: A slice of the tree from bark to bark.

FOUR-QUARTER (4/4): Lumberyard/sawmill jargon for 1-in. stock. And 6/4 (pronounced *six-quarter*) is 1½ in., 8/4 is 2 in., and so on.

GRAIN: The predominant orientation of cells in wood. Grain direction can be seen in the growth rings of a board.

HONEYCOMB: Large checks all the way through a board and evident on its surface, which indicate casehardening. The checks are a result of improper drying.

KILN DRIED (KD): Wood that has been dried in a kiln, usually to a moisture level of 6-8%.

PITH, PITH TRACKS: The pith is the very center of the tree. A pith track is the hollow or papery cross section of the pith that's exposed when a tree is cut into boards at its center.

QUARTERSAWN: Quartersawn lumber is made by sawing a tree into quarters and then

sawing boards so the growth rings run perpendicular to the face of the board. It's dimensionally more stable than flatsawn boards and often reveals beautiful fleck in species such as oak (red and white), cherry and sycamore.

ROUGH LUMBER: Unplaned lumber.

SAPWOOD: The outer rings of a tree, through which the sap flows. Sapwood always is light colored in contrast with the heartwood.

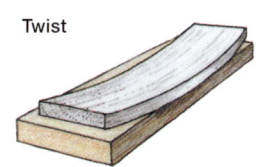
Twist

TWIST: Wood that looks like it's spiraling.

WANE, WANY: Wane is where the natural edge of the tree tapers so that it shows up on the edge of a board.

—V.L.

able in many forms: air dried and kiln dried, quartersawn and flatsawn, roughsawn and planed. Quartersawn and flatsawn are defined in the glossary on p. 27 and are discussed later in this article.

Given the opportunity, I always buy roughsawn. Lumber that's already been planed, especially 1-in. stock, may be too thin if I have to resurface it after I get it back to my shop. If you don't have a jointer and planer, you can often find a local professional woodworker who will surface your lumber for a fee. I've also known woodworkers who've taken woodworking courses at a local high school just to gain access to its woodworking equipment.

Wood is seldom defect-free. Lumber producers have developed grading systems to classify lumber quality (see the sidebar below for an explanation of lumber grading). That

Lumber grading: what you really need to know

Hardwoods and softwoods are graded differently and by a number of organizations. Even the names assigned to various grades differ from organization to organization. But let's concentrate on the most widely recognized rules for grading hardwood lumber, which come from the National Hardwood Lumber Association (P.O. Box 34518, Memphis, TN 38184-0518; 901-377-1818). The following NHLA publications explain all you could want to know about grading: *An Introduction to Grading Hardwood Lumber* ($2), *An Illustrated Guide to Hardwood Lumber Grades* ($5) and *Rules for the Measurement and Inspection of Hardwood and Cypress* ($7).

The fundamental premise in grading hardwood lumber is that any given board is going to be cut into defect-free furniture components. With this in mind, lumber graders calculate how many potential clear components (or cutting units) are in a given board. Three things count in determining grade: the minimum size allowed for the clear sections, how few of these sections there are, and what percent-

age of the board's total area consists of these sections. The basic principle is that the larger the clear sections and the fewer of them, the higher the grade.

The best way to get the lumber you need is to see what a mill or lumberyard is selling as No. 1 common or selects. Get what you can use from these lower grades, and spring for higher-grade lumber only when you absolutely need long, wide, clear boards.

The grades: The best lumber grade is FAS (firsts and seconds). Firsts and seconds are really two grades, but they're only sold together. Firsts must yield at least 91⅔% clear cuttings on the worst face. Seconds must yield 81⅔% clear cuttings on the worst face. FAS boards must be at least 6 in. wide and 8 ft. long, and the minimum size of clear cuttings that count toward the specified yield is 3 in. by 7 ft. or 4 in. by 5 ft.

The two next-best grades, FAS1F (FAS one face) and select, are graded using both faces. For both, the best face must meet FAS requirements, and the other face must be No. 1 common. FAS1F boards, like FAS boards, must be at least 6 in. wide and 8 ft. long. Selects can be just 4 in. wide by 6 ft. long.

No. 1 common lumber must be between 66⅔% and 83⅓% clear. The smallest No. 1 board can be 3 in. wide by 4 ft. long. Minimum clear-cutting size is 3 in. by 3 ft. or 4 in. by 2 ft.

No. 2A and No. 2B lumber usually is grouped together. Boards must be at least 3 in. wide and 4 ft. long. Minimum clear-cutting size is 3 in. by 2 ft.

No. 3A, No. 3B and "below grade" lumber generally is not considered furniture grade. *—V.L.*

information is helpful in a general way, but the small-shop woodworker is better off knowing about particular defects—which are acceptable, which are not—and what to do about them.

Where to find it

Wood for building furniture is available from a lot of different places. I've disassembled pallets. I've picked up burls left by the side of the road when a tree's been taken down. I've even taken logs out of the firewood pile. But mostly, I buy wood from lumberyards and sawmills.

Lumberyards

Lumberyards—not building-supply dealers —are the obvious place to start looking. These places deal primarily in hardwood lumber, though most also sell sheet goods like plywood or medium-density fiberboard (MDF). Hardwood lumberyards generally carry kiln-dried rather than air-dried stock, sometimes roughsawn and sometimes planed. Planed lumber costs more because more labor has gone into it. If you want your lumber planed, most lumberyards will do it for you for a price.

To find a local lumberyard, look under "lumber" in the yellow pages. The places that specialize in hardwood lumber usually will say so in their advertisements. Ask other woodworkers or your local woodworking store about good yards, too. Lumberyards generally have a wide selection of both local, nonlocal and exotic species (see the photo above). Many will order something for you if it's not in the yard. Some yards require minimum orders, but even if they don't, buying 100 bd. ft. usually entitles you to a price break. The next price break may be at 300, 500 or 1,000 bd. ft.

Check out several yards, and weigh selection, attitude and price. I've been treated wonderfully on many occasions by the staff at a big yard near where I live, but I've also had to deal with surly, unhelpful staff. If you're not buying what they consider a significant amount, the staff may not consider your business worthwhile.

Choosing lumber is part of the pleasure of woodworking. Hardwood lumberyards generally have a broader selection than local sawmills.

Lumberyards buy from a number of different suppliers. The beautiful cherry you see today may not be available next week, so buy plenty while you have the opportunity. One final item: Some yards sell primarily to furniture manufacturers or large-volume shops and don't want you to pick through their stacks. Explain that you need certain boards for the project you're about to begin, and tell them that you'll restack everything neatly when you're done (be sure to deliver on that promise). If they still won't let you pick your own lumber, go elsewhere.

Sawmills

Generally, sawmills are more friendly than big lumberyards. You can get to know the guy who's sawing your wood, ask him to be on the lookout for something special or have him saw something just for you. Prices at a mill tend to be lower than at lumberyards, too—sometimes dramatically so. Besides, you're supporting a small business and buying a local product. To find them, look in the yellow pages under "sawmills," or just ask around.

About the only downside to buying from a mill is that the wood selection is limited to what's available locally. In addition, the wood may not have been kiln-dried, so you may have to acclimate the wood for a while before using it. Ask the mill owner if the wood is kiln-dried or air-dried.

Some mills, like lumberyards, aren't interested in your business. They're perfectly happy making baseball-bat blanks, pallet stock or whatever is their bread and butter. Still, it's worth checking out. A Vermont woodworker I know got all his figured maple for pennies on the dollar from a mill that sold all its plain maple to furniture manufacturers. The furniture manufacturers just didn't have any use for that irregular stuff, and the mill was happy to get rid of it.

Woodworking stores

I haven't bought lumber from a woodworking store, primarily because I haven't been able to get over the sticker shock. These businesses, which sell tools and books as well as lumber, generally look like boutiques and have prices to match. Usually, their lumber is already surfaced to make it more appealing. It is attractive, but if it starts warping while on display (which often happens), the ¾-in. board you take home likely will have to be taken down to ⅝ in. or even ½ in. before it's flat again. High prices and surfaced wood also have kept me from buying wood from building-supply companies or home centers.

Other sources

Check the classifieds. I once bought more than 100 bd. ft. of walnut at $1.25/bd. ft. from a guy who was being transferred by his company. There are lots of ways to find wood. Many woodworking tool stores have bulletin boards listing tools and wood for sale. Industrial arts teachers may have recommendations. Even your local chamber of commerce may know who's selling lumber nearby.

What to look for, what to avoid

Wood is an organic material. It's not uniform. That's its curse and its beauty. Some of wood's "defects" are spectacular, like burls and bird's-eyes. Others, like loose knots or knotholes, checks, pith and bark pockets, are less desirable and must be worked around. Count on buying at least 30% more than you think you need.

Defects and what to do about them

Some defects are fatal. Others aren't. Sapwood, for instance, while not considered a defect by grading organizations, is avoided by many woodworkers because its lighter color doesn't match the heartwood. You can work around it by putting it on the inside of a case piece or on the underside of a table. Or you can just live with it. Some woodworkers make sapwood part of a design.

Boards with pith tracks (see the glossary on p. 27 for unfamiliar terms) aren't a problem as long as they're thick enough to allow the pith to be planed off. I've filled pith tracks on the edge of a board with five-minute epoxy darkened with artist's oil colors. The pith ended up looking just like a sound pin knot.

A sound knot is not a problem if you're looking for a rustic feel, if you can incorporate it into your design, or if it's at the end of a board. Even a knot that's in the middle of a board is not a problem if you can take components from both sides of it.

End checking is normal, but you'll lose the checked portion of the board plus at least an inch or so. Extensive face checking most likely means the wood's casehardened, which is a serious defect. You won't want the board.

Cup or crook in a board isn't a problem. Because the deformation is in one plane, a jointer should take care of it quite easily. If you buy a cupped or crooked board, be sure that it's sufficiently thick or wide, so it will be useable once it's flattened or straightened. Cutting boards into smaller pieces before milling and using the jointer will take care of mildly bowed boards. Twisted boards are best avoided.

Grain, figure and color
Quartersawn lumber will move less than flatsawn lumber, so it works better in situations where tolerances are critical. A door frame is a good example. Quartersawn lumber is more work for the sawyer, however, so it's more expensive. For the same reason, it's also sold separately from flatsawn stock of the same species.

Figured woods are beautiful but generally difficult to work. Bird's-eyes in particular want to pull right out of the board when being planed. Curly woods also will tear out if you're not careful. Still, I buy figured

woods and love them. You can identify most kinds of figure in the rough by looking for irregularly fuzzy patches on the faces of the boards.

Try to get boards from the same tree when you can. How can you tell? Color, grain density and figure are clues. Also, look for knots in the same location and similar profiles if the boards are flitchsawn. For straight-edged boards, dimensions are a good clue. If you run across three or four that look alike and are all 97¼ in. long, ranging from 6 in. to 8 in. in width, that's a pretty good indication they're from the same tree. Often, you can figure out the order in which the boards were cut.

What to bring to the lumberyard or mill
When I buy lumber, there are a few items I always bring (see the photo below). They include leather work gloves, a tape measure and a rough cut list, broken down by thickness and the sort of grain I'm looking for in each component. I bring a calculator for figuring ballpark board footage and a pad to

Tools for buying lumber include leather gloves, a tape measure, and a notepad. A block plane and alcohol help reveal grain and color.

Buy your wood where you can pick your own. But whatever you don't take should be restacked the way you found it.

keep track of boards, board footage and how much I'm spending. A pad is also helpful for sketching, so I can figure out whether I can get the components I need from particular boards.

I try to remember to bring a block plane (if I forget, I use my knife), so I can expose a bit of smooth wood on rough planks, as shown in the photo on p. 30. This is especially important if the lumber's been stored outside for a while; walnut will turn a gray that's almost white, and maple turns a dark gray. I like to know what sort of color I can expect after the wood's been planed. (Before cutting or planing, it's a good idea to ask someone at the yard or mill if it's okay to cut or plane the wood.)

I sometimes bring a rag and a small can of denatured alcohol. The alcohol gives an instant preview of what the wood will look like finished. And I usually bring a handsaw for cutting long boards down to size.

At the yard, I try to be as independent as I can. Once a worker at the yard takes down a stack or two of wood with a forklift, I restack the pile as I'm going through it, and I stay out of the way. The less of a pain you are to the yard staff the more welcome you'll be.

After I've loaded my lumber and paid up, I tie an old red T-shirt to the end of the longest board and head off into the sunset. And if I've spent more than I'd planned, which is usually the case, I just remember James Krenov's maxim in *The Fine Art of Cabinetmaking*, "A good rule is to buy as much as you can sensibly afford of any wood that excites you and then, quickly, buy a little bit more."

Ordering wood sight unseen

by Ken Textor

Ordering lumber from faraway dealers is a good way to buy wood that isn't available locally. The prices are comparable, even with shipping, and there are many woods you just can't get any other way. I've ordered dozens of species from all over North America for more than 15 years, and I've learned that there are three steps in getting what you want: specify, specify, specify.

You want what? The first time I ordered poplar I was asked, "That yellow poplar or white poplar you want?" Later, I found out that yellow poplar is also known as tulipwood, tulip poplar and canary wood. Learn all you can about the species you want, including its many names, before you call a dealer.

The next thing you must specify is the grade. This can be a real quagmire. If the dealer uses the National Hardware Lumber Association's grading standards, you're all set. But if his system's unconventional (many are) or if you haven't done business with this dealer before, you're better off just asking for clear planks. That's not an official lumber designation, and it will cost more, but it's generally understood to mean no knots, bark pockets, splits, gouges or the like.

Also, even though some dealers may be insulted, tell them you can't use seriously warped, cupped or twisted stock.

Once you've agreed on the specifications, find out what the total price is and what you're paying per board foot. Write it down along with the description of the lumber that you and the dealer have settled on, and send the dealer a confirming fax or letter with all that information on it. As for payment, most dealers these days prefer one of the major credit cards.

The wood's in the mail: I've had lumber arrive looking as if it was dragged behind the truck, not shipped in it. It's a good idea to ask the dealer how he'll package your wood. Make suggestions if you're not satisfied with his reply.

These days, lumber shipments are usually sent by UPS or a similar courier service. If the load exceeds size or weight requirements, the dealer probably will choose a common carrier. Some common carriers will only deliver to the shipping terminal nearest you, so ask if this is the case. Once, I assumed that the freight carrier would deliver to my door. Late one Friday afternoon, I received a surprising phone call. "You've got 500 bd. ft. of hickory here," the terminal dispatcher told me. "You've got 48 hours to pick it up." I managed to get my wood before the terminal closed for the weekend, but not without difficulty.

SHEET GOODS FOR THE WOODSHOP

by William Duckworth

I became a woodworker almost by accident. Living alone, just out of college and far from home, I started to build furniture for myself because I couldn't afford to buy it. The living room of my three-room tenement apartment, a fifth-floor walkup in New York City, was my shop. The most basic hand tools were all I had to work with. When the downstairs neighbors had heard enough noise, they'd start banging on their ceiling with a broomstick, so even my working hours were limited. Materials? I made everything out of pine—it's all I could buy at the local lumberyard.

I fell in love with the process so much that I started building furniture for friends at no charge. It took a few years before I realized I might be able to do this for a living. So I quit my job, rented a small space in a nearby basement and paid $350 for a Sears Best 10-in. tablesaw.

One of my first commissions was a wall of bookcases. I'll never forget my astonishment when a friend of mine suggested I consider making them with birch plywood. My local lumberyard didn't stock it. I didn't even know what it was. That soon changed, and I started using birch plywood all the time. It wasn't long before I graduated to oak, ash, walnut and mahogany panels.

Hardwood plywood has transformed the furniture and cabinet trades. I don't share the belief that woodworking projects are necessarily inferior if not entirely constructed of solid lumber. Lumber and veneered sheet goods can work well together in a fine finished product. Purists who eschew the use of manufactured veneer panels are blind to the realities of the marketplace. These products are the backbone of the business of modern cabinetmaking. They save time and, in some applications, actually improve the quality of the end result. For those who believe otherwise, I would argue that, given access to the technology, Thomas Chippendale or Duncan Phyfe would have jumped at the chance to use a plain-sliced, book-matched Honduras mahogany panel with a medium-density fiberboard (MDF) core. Whether they were making tabletops, desks or the carcases of small chests of drawers, these two were businessmen as well as artists. Can anyone doubt that the same would be true for the Shakers?

Core follows function

I surveyed the following owners of custom woodworking shops to get an idea of which panels they used for what purposes: Lars Mikkelson of Santa Margarita, Calif.; Sven Hanson of Albuquerque, N.M.; Ron Barzyk of Madison, Tenn.; and partners Marcus Santora and Janis Melone of New Haven, Conn. Each shop has its own particular niche, from residential furniture to commercial case goods, so preferences varied widely. In all cases, though, I asked about panel products meant for interior applications only and those most commonly available to the small shop (see the photos on p. 36).

This press is hot. Workers at a manufacturing plant in Oregon unload a plywood press that can glue 24 sheets at 240°, 150psi.

Core construction and material performance _____

Plywood characteristics are based on research by the Hardwood Plywood Veneer Association and the Architectural Woodwork Institute. Values are averages only. The face species in these samples are (from left to right, top to bottom) plain-sliced Honduras mahogany, rotary-cut birch, rotary-cut bird's-eye maple and plain-sliced ash.

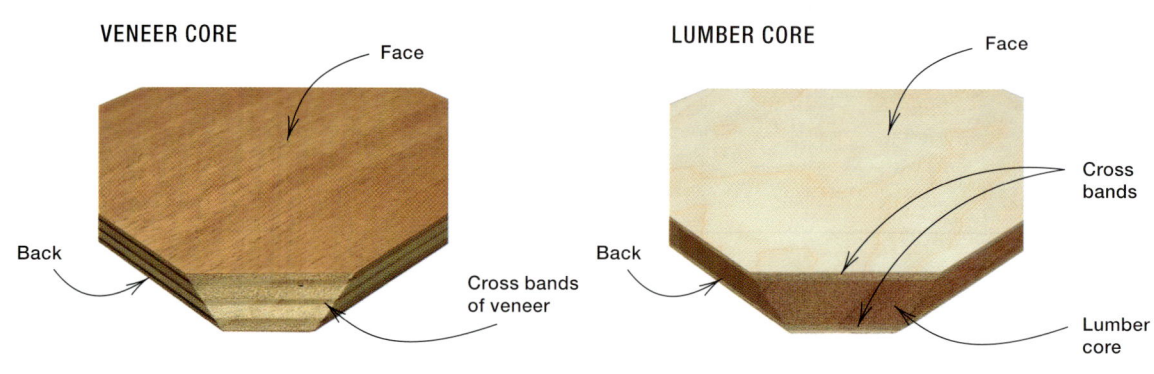

VENEER CORE

Face

Back

Cross bands
of veneer

Flatness: *Fair*
Visual edge quality: *Good*
Surface uniformity: *Good*
Dimensional stability: *Excellent*
Screw holding: *Excellent*
Bending strength: *Excellent*
Availability: *Good*

LUMBER CORE

Face

Cross
bands

Back

Lumber
core

Flatness: *Good*
Visual edge quality: *Good*
Surface uniformity: *Good*
Dimensional stability: *Good*
Screw holding: *Excellent*
Bending strength: *Excellent*
Availability: *Limited*

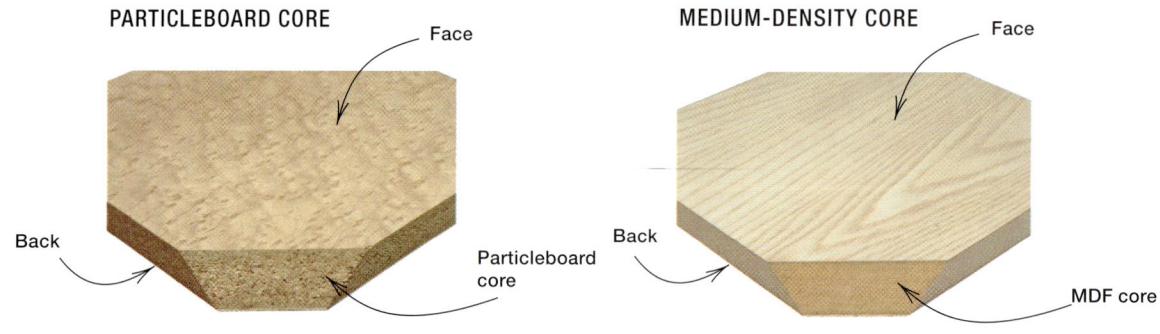

PARTICLEBOARD CORE

Face

Back

Particleboard
core

Flatness: *Excellent*
Visual edge quality: *Good*
Surface uniformity: *Excellent*
Dimensional stability: *Fair*
Screw holding: *Fair*
Bending strength: *Good*
Availability: *Good*

MEDIUM-DENSITY CORE

Face

Back

MDF core

Flatness: *Excellent*
Visual edge quality: *Excellent*
Surface uniformity: *Excellent*
Dimensional stability: *Fair*
Screw holding: *Good*
Bending strength: *Good*
Availability: *Good*

Veneer core is lightweight and strong
Veneer core is what most people mean when they refer to plywood. (The Architectural Woodwork Institute defines plywood as any panel product made from three or more layers of wood or wood products.) Like Lars Mikkelson and Sven Hanson, who both use it for case work and shelving, I prefer veneer core for wall-hung uppers or floor-to-ceiling cabinets, where weight might be a problem. I also use it for applications like torsion boxes, where strength is important.

Ron Barzyk says quality standards have declined in the veneer core he's bought in the last two years: more voids and a poor second face, or back. My own gripe about veneer-core panels is that I never met one that was flat and stayed that way. Once exposed to a change in temperature and humidity in the shop, veneer-core plywood often warps.

Ideally, each panel should be manufactured with an absolutely symmetrical construction from the center of the panel. That means the panel should be made from the same materials on either side of its centerline. Materials should contract and expand at the same rate. Somehow, in the real world, it never seems to work that way.

Poplar and aspen make the best cores. Less desirable are those made from meranti and virola, which are less stable. Virola is a species harvested in Panama and Guatemala. The logs are often stored in ponds to prevent them from rotting, and they sometimes absorb a fungus from the mud. When the logs are dry, the fungus prevents the absorption of glues in the manufacturing process. This problem results in cores that can come apart. The fungus also happens to smell bad: Virola is nicknamed stink oak.

Lumber core costs more

Lumber core is the most expensive and the least available. The core stock can be either hardwood or softwood, depending on the manufacturer. Basswood is the best.

According to industry standards, which are published by the Hardwood Plywood and Veneer Association (HPVA) and based on procedures set forth by the American National Standards Institute (ANSI), lumber-core grades are regular, sound and clear (the best). Regular grade allows butt joints within the core; sound requires full-length or finger-jointed pieces and allows discolorations, repair patches and sound knots; clear is the same as sound except that no knots are allowed.

Sven Hanson uses lumber core for drawer cases. He bevels the top edges of drawer sides to make the core appear more like solid lumber. He cautions anyone who lives in a dry climate to check lumber-core panels with a moisture meter. Industry standards allow plywood leaving the manufacturing plant to have a moisture content of 12%. That's

Veneer faces laid up five ways ____

The way veneer is cut from a log makes a big difference in the way it looks when it's applied to a panel and how much it costs.

Whole piece rotary cut: *A single sheet of veneer is cut from the tree like paper towels off a roll. This method produces the least waste.*

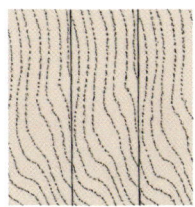

Slip match: *Sheets of veneer pulled from a flitch are joined side by side with the same face side up.*

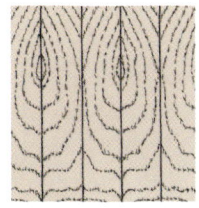

Book-match: *Every other sheet of veneer is flipped as it's pulled from the flitch. This pattern results in the best-looking panels. Book-matched panels also are the most expensive.*

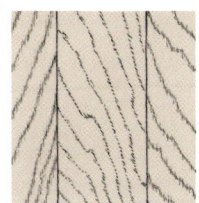

Pleasing match: *The veneers in this category match in color more than in grain characteristics.*

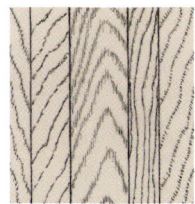

Random or mismatch: *Veneers don't match either in color or grain pattern.*

twice the figure recommended for interior woodwork in Sven's neck of the woods.

Ron Barzyk found a source for some panels with a pine lumber core that he likes to use for toe kicks under cabinetry in kitchens and baths. It holds up well to wet floor conditions. Other uses for lumber core include flat-panel doors and shelving that will not need edge treatment.

Lumber core stays flatter than veneer core, but it's hard to justify using it when it can cost twice as much as a panel with the same face veneer on another core. A ¾-in., 4-ft. by 8-ft. birch panel with a clear basswood core sells for more than $80 and walnut for $125. You could get the same veneers on particleboard for about $35 for birch and $75 for walnut.

Particleboard core is heavy in the hand

Sometimes referred to as flakeboard or chipboard, particleboard core is composed of small particles of wood and wood fibers bonded together with synthetic resin adhesives under heat and pressure. It is manufactured in low, medium and high densities. None of the four shops uses it as a plywood panel (with a hardwood face and back). Ron Barzyk likes the core material only when he's making countertops with plastic laminate. Sven Hanson commented that it's good for garage shelving, but I don't think he meant that to be taken literally.

Particleboard is the least expensive, and it has an excellent rating for flatness and surface uniformity. So why don't they like it? One problem is weight. A ¾-in., 49-in. by 97-in. panel weighs about 93 lb. Unless you

have a separate scoring blade on your tablesaw, particleboard will sometimes chip out in small pieces on the edge. It will warp easily under even moderate loads, like a bookshelf full of paperbacks. It does work well as a core material for solid-core door manufacturers. It would be a good choice for a well-supported tabletop. And it does make good use of natural resources: What was once waste material has become core stock.

MDF core is the answer to many needs

Ah, MDF, now that's another beast altogether. Like particleboard, MDF is made from small wood fibers bound by synthetic resins under heat and pressure. It's also less expensive than veneer-core and lumber-core panels, but it costs more than particleboard and weighs about the same. However, if you try to break the same size scrap of each over your knee, you'll discover the tensile strength of MDF is much greater than that of particleboard. It will deflect under load more readily than veneer core.

MDF holds a screw well, properly piloted, and it machines beautifully. Crisp and clean edges result when it meets up with a sawblade, a router bit or a shaper cutter (carbide is a must). When you order a ¾-in.-thick panel, that's exactly what you get—not the $^{23}/_{32}$-in. or even $^{11}/_{16}$-in. sheets that sometimes show up in a delivery of veneer core or lumber core.

Lars Mikkelson appreciates the way the smooth, flat and uniform substrate provides a fine surface for the veneer. The smooth surface won't telegraph the cross-grain patterns you sometimes get with veneer core and lumber core. Sven Hanson says thermal-set glue on edge tape holds well on the dense edges. Ron Barzyk uses MDF-core plywood for all his cabinetry, whether stained or painted, including shelves and door panels. Marcus Santora and Janis Melone use it only occasionally. They don't like the really fine dust kicked up when machining it.

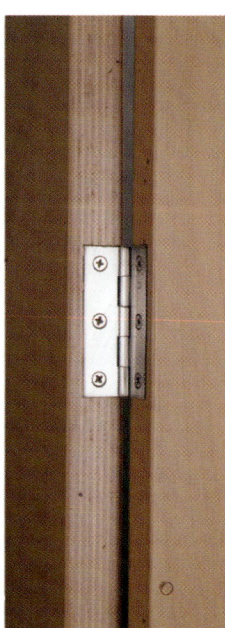

ApplePly doesn't have to be banded. Thin, uniform plies become part of the design in case work by Janis Melone and Marcus Santora, partners in a New Haven, Conn., shop.

MDF takes a crisp edge when machined. Lars Mikkelson of Santa Margarita, Calif., uses MDF with no face veneer for work that will be painted, like this door panel.

MDF-core birch cases with alder faces. From left to right, Ron Barzyk, his son Brook and Floyd Parker of Madison, Tenn., dry-fit wall unit cases. Barzyk prefers MDF core over any other.

What's new or different?

Innovations abound in the sheet-goods industry. Boise-Cascade (208-384-6610) recently came out with a product called Electrically Conductive particleboard. Loaded with carbon, it's designed to discharge static electricity and meant to be used in computer rooms and medical and military facilities.

The Baltek Corporation (201-767-1400) offers a panel fabricated with a core of plantation-grown end-grain balsa. It's extra light and very strong. And the Norfield Corporation (203-792-5110) offers a product with similar characteristics made from a core of rigid honeycomb plastic. It's available from ¼ in. to 3 in. thick and can be sold in small quantities.

Tim Smith of F.W. Honerkamp Co., a large plywood and lumber distributor in New York, tells me that his company is selling a lot of pre-finished panels made by States Industries. Called Nova by the manufacturer, the finish is a formaldehyde-free, ultraviolet-cured topcoat over four coats of a sanding sealer. The manufacturer will apply it to any kind of core panel.

I saw two products at the Woodworking Machinery and Furniture Fair in Anaheim, Calif., a couple of years ago that looked very interesting. The first, made under a variety of trade names (Classic Core, Armorcore, Fiber-Ply), has been around since 1986. It has a combination core (veneer-core plies in the center with outer layers of ⅛-in.-thick particleboard or MDF) over which face and back veneers are glued. It's been very slow to catch on, and I can't figure out why. Lars Mikkelson is the only person I've spoken with who uses it, and he loves the stuff. You get strength, reasonable weight and a smooth substrate under the veneer.

The second new product I saw in Anaheim is manufactured by Weldwood of Canada. It's called

Fiber-Ply (left) and Multi-Core are strong and less expensive than standard veneer-core plywood.

Longlac Multi-Core (LMC), and it's different from any other panel product. The core of a ¾-in.-thick panel consists of 7⁄16 in. of aspen flakes, or wafers, highly compressed and glued together with waterproof phenolic resins. I would characterize it as a sort of disoriented strand-board core. On either side of the core are cross bands of aspen veneer and face and back veneers. LMC is light and strong like veneer core, but it stays flat like MDF and particleboard-core panels. It's rated far better than any other core for screw holding through the face and about the same as veneer core for edge screws.

Formaldehyde emissions are one-sixth those of MDF. The aspen used for the core is a species that regenerates quickly, which makes for more environmentally friendly forestry management. Bob McKenna, a salesman for Atlantic Plywood in Woburn, Mass. (a large wholesale plywood distributor), tells me that his company is selling a lot of this product. He says that the cabinet shops love its low cost and its good machinability. They use it mainly for case work but also for doors.

—W.D.

What size, how much and where to get it

Plywood mills can make more than the standard 4-ft. by 8-ft. panel, up to a maximum sheet size of 5 ft. by 12 ft. You pay a premium for those larger sizes, and most distributors stock them in only a few species. I once placed a special order for a large conference table: four sheets of plain-sliced walnut, 1¼-in.-thick MDF core, 10 ft. by 5 ft. (the grain ran with the width, not the length), flitch-matched. They were beautiful, but they cost around $300 a sheet. Any domestic hardwood, from ash to wormy chestnut, that's available in lumber also is available as the face veneer on plywood. The same is true for what makers and sellers call exotics, woods grouped by the location of their origin—Africa, Asia, Australia, Europe and South America.

Panel products designed for special jobs

Plywood manufacturers compete to come up with panel products that will serve their customers' needs. The items listed below are among some of the more successful results.

Melamine saves finishing time: Melamine is a panel whose surface is plastic-impregnated paper fused to a substrate by heat. It's a curse to many woodworkers. They hate its heavy core and sharp edges, but their customers love it because it's easy to clean and maintain. It's well suited for kitchen and bathroom cabinetry. Melamine is most commonly available with a particleboard core, although Sven Hanson has a source that supplies him with

Melamine for hospital built-ins— These cabinets were built by Jacob Cabinets in Nashville, Tenn.

an MDF core. It responds with less chipout and holds edge tape better. A ¾-in. standard sheet, 49 in. by 97 in., costs about $25.

ApplePly is not apple: This product was developed in Oregon by States Industries. It's designed to compete with the makers of Baltic- and Finnish-birch panels from Europe. The original versions came in odd sizes (roughly 5 ft. sq.) and were often way out of square and warped. ApplePly cores are made from ¹⁄₁₆-in.-thick western red alder veneers. Seven plies make a ⅜-in.-thick panel and 13 plies make a ¾-in. panel (face and back are sanded to ¹⁄₃₂ in.). The face is maple or birch. The decorative edge is considered an asset because of the uniformly thin and light-colored veneers. Of the shops surveyed, only Marcus Santora and Janis Melone use it, and they use it for almost everything. I have used it in a ⅝-in. thickness for drawers; the core has no voids, and ½-in. screws for slide hardware do not telegraph through the other side. A ½-in.-thick, 4-ft. by 8-ft. panel costs about $65.

Three-eighths-inch bending lauan for curves: Also called wacky wood and wiggle board, ⅜-in. bending lauan was developed for curved work (see the right photo below). It's made from two thick but pliable veneers with a sandwiched sheet of thread-thin cloth between them. It will bend easily to a radius of 3 in. Sales of this product have overcome those of ⅛-in. bending poplar ply, which was the only bendable plywood until this hit the market in 1986. A sheet will run about $30. —*W.D.*

Bending lauan for curves. Sven Hanson assembles the core of an apron for a demi-lune gate-leg table.

Lumber core is only available in ¾ in., 1 in., 1⅛ in. and 1¼ in. thicknesses. Veneer, particleboard and MDF cores are standard in the following sizes: ⅛ in., ¼ in., ½ in., ¾ in., 1 in., 1⅛ in. and 1¼ in. Other thicknesses exist, but they're not commonly stocked.

Prices run the gamut from particleboard core, MDF, veneer core to lumber core, in that order, no matter what the face species.

In general, prices will range from $35 for rotary-cut birch on a particleboard core to $125 for plain-sliced walnut on a lumber core. That's the least and most you should expect to pay for any commonly stocked ¾-in. panel.

Birch and walnut are respectively the most common and the most dear of domestic-species plywood panels. All other face veneers on different cores will fall somewhere between those figures. Quantity matters, too. If you're buying 10 sheets or more, you should be able to get a price break.

There was a time when many distributors would only sell their products on a "to the trade" basis. Some of them have changed that policy. If you can't find what you want at the local lumberyard and your fingers have walked through the yellow pages with no success, there's a source book you might find useful. It's called *Where to Buy Hardwood Plywood and Veneer*. It costs $5 and is published by the HPVA (P.O. Box 2789, Reston, VA 22090; 703-435-2900). About a third of its 120 pages is devoted to advertisements. The rest of the book includes background on the HPVA, information about available veneer species and names, addresses and phone numbers of manufacturers and distributors throughout North America. If you don't live close to a distributor, go to some professional cabinet shops nearby and ask them to buy plywood for you. Be nice; offer to pay a handling fee.

Grading veneers toward a standard

In the past, every manufacturer had its own system of grading panel products, which has led to a lot of confusion. Hardwood plywood makers and suppliers may be moving toward a revised and realistic agreement when it comes to grading sheet goods, which should benefit the end user (see the photo below). Now, except for a few holdouts, most manufacturers have begun to comply voluntarily with standards published

by the HPVA and ANSI. The latest version, approved in January 1995, can be purchased for $15 from the HPVA. It is a 24-page booklet that details face, back and inner ply grades.

Specifications on grading can be complex. Tolerances vary among the face species, so it takes some study to know what you're ordering. This booklet also spells out terms for allowable formaldehyde emissions, moisture content, sanding and grade marking on each panel shipped. It's the source for the Architectural Woodwork Institute's *Quality Standards*, the book professional shops use to communicate construction details to the design trades. If you buy plywood, it's worth the money to know how to specify what you want.

Thicknesses keep getting thinner

With the advent of improved veneer cutting and handling machinery and the desire (environmental and economical) to stretch expensive natural resources as far as possible, veneers really are getting thinner. When I first started working with wood, $1/28$ in. was the standard. It seems hard to believe, but furniture manufacturers buy and use more veneer than the plywood mills. So the equipment manufacturers use determines, to a large extent, the prevailing thickness standard. Nowadays, it's $1/36$ in. But in response to European competition, they're gearing up with machines that can safely handle veneers up to $1/42$ in. So that's likely to be where we're headed. Put away those belt sanders, the future is drawing near.

Final grading at the sanding station at a Columbia Forest Products plant in Klamath Falls, Ore. The birch panels on this machine, called a star grader, will soon be bundled and shipped.

ADHESIVES FOR WOODWORKING

by Chris Minick

Everyday, woodworkers across the country glue wooden parts together to make furniture, cabinets, toys, boats, turning blanks and musical instruments. Yet most of us don't pay much attention to this critical operation until, for some reason, our standard glue fails. Then the search for an alternative adhesive is on. Although about 1,500 adhesive products are manufactured in the United States, less than a dozen of them are suitable for most woodworkers' needs (see the top photo on the facing page). In this article, I'll explain the most common types of woodworking adhesives, how they work and what to expect when you use them. And in the sidebar beginning on p. 52, I will discuss the steps necessary for successfully gluing wood, from preparing the stock to clamping up.

How glue bonds wooden parts together

Before I discuss individual adhesives, it's helpful to understand a little about the chemical makeup of wood and how an adhesive interacts with these components during the bonding process. Wood is a complex mixture of organic chemicals and water. About 95 percent of a board consists of cellulose, lignin and hemicellulose, which form the structural matrix of wood and give it its strength, rigidity and elasticity. The remaining 5 percent contained in dry wood is composed of resins, tannins, essential oils, gums, coloring agents and sugars. This chemical mixture of extractives is responsible for wood's smell, color and decay resistance. Unfortunately, extractives in some resinous woods, such as teak and rosewood, can interfere with the gluing process (for an explanation of how to overcome this problem, see the sidebar on p. 52).

Once an adhesive is applied to adjacent wood surfaces and the pieces are clamped up, the structural elements of wood are linked together by the bonding process. First, the liquid adhesive is absorbed into the wood, and its polymer molecules intermingle with the structural fibers of the wood. Next, the adhesive's polymer molecules coalesce (come together), surround the structural fibers and harden, mechanically interlocking the fibers. *Thermosetting* glues, such as epoxy, urea formaldehyde and resorcinol, cure by a chemical reaction (usually after two components have been mixed) while *thermoplastic* adhesives, such as white and yellow glue, cure by evaporation. Once either type of glue is dry, the thin layer of cured adhesive between the two wood surfaces acts like a bridge holding the boards together.

Although all the glues in this article (except hot melts) will produce bonds that are actually stronger than wood itself, each adhesive has special properties that make it better suited to some gluing tasks than others. These factors are discussed in the chart (summarizing adhesive properties) on p. 46.

Less than a dozen popular woodworking adhesives perform 99 percent of the gluing tasks in the shop today. But different types of glue have different characteristics that make them better suited for some jobs than others. From left to right, the adhesives are cross-linking polyvinyl acetate (PVA), two-part epoxy, cyanoacrylate ("super glue"), solvent-based contact cement, yellow PVA (aliphatic) resin, urea formaldehyde, resorcinol and hot-melt glue sticks shown with the glue gun that heats them for application.

Polyvinyl acetates

White and yellow glue are probably the two most popular glues used in woodshops today. Both are polyvinyl acetate (PVA) adhesives that come in three main varieties: white or craft glue, yellow aliphatic resin glue and cross-linking PVA emulsions. All of these have a balanced set of properties, which make them ideal for gluing wood. They are easy to use, have quick grab, set rapidly, clean up with water, are non-toxic and work in most wood-gluing situations. Also, the liquid adhesives will spoil if frozen. However, PVA adhesives have poor creep resistance (under a sustained load the adhesive slowly stretches), and they should never be used in structural assemblies, like load-bearing beams, without some form of mechanical fastening.

White glue

While general-purpose white glues are considered by many woodworkers to be hobby glues, white glues have a unique flexibility and a high sheer strength that make them particularly well suited for use in flexible joints, such as bonding the canvas backing to wood slats for tambour doors. The flexible adhesive bonds allow the slats to move

Woodworking adhesive properties

Glue name/type	1 part, 2 part or water mix (W)	Gap-filling ability ▲	Moisture resistance ▲	Solvent resistance ▲	Creep resistance ▲	Open assembly time (minutes) ▶	Minimum drying time (hours) ▶	Minimum application temperature	Cleanup solvent	Safety equipment
White/PVA	1	P	P	P	P	3-5	1 ◆	40	Water	None
Yellow/PVA	1	F	F	F	P	5	1 ◆	40	Water	None
Cross linking/PVA	1	F	G	F	F	5	1 ◆	50	Water	None
Hide	W	P	P	G	G	2-5	2	70	Water	None
Epoxy	2	E	E	E	E	5-90	12-24	50 ●	Lacquer thinner	Gloves
Urea formaldehyde	W	F	G	E	E	10	12-24	65 ●	Water	Vapor mask Gloves
Resorcinol	2	G	E	E	E	10	12-24	65 ●	Water	Vapor mask Gloves
Contact cement	1	P	E	F	P	2-3 hrs.	None	40	■	Vapor mask ▶▶ Gloves
Cyanoacrylate	1	P-F	E	E	E	30 sec.	1-2 min.▲	40	Acetone	Gloves
Hot melt	1	E ✳	E	G	P	10-30	None Sec.	—	Scrape	None excess

Notes:

▲ E=excellent, G=good, F=fair, P=poor

■ See container label for proper solvent

✳ Very low strength

▲ Much faster when accelerator is used

● Higher temperatures decrease pot life

◆ Humidity slows down drying; more clamping time needed

▶ Higher temperatures speed up drying time, reduce open time

▶▶ Not needed for waterborne contact cement

Explanation of chart headings

Gap filling: Most glues are stronger than wood when applied thin; choose best gap-filling glues for bonding imperfect joints.
Moisture resistance: Excellent-rated glues are waterproof and suitable for outdoor use; good-to-fair rated glues are only moisture resistant.
Solvent resistance: Use best-rated glues for veneered work where solvent in finish could penetrate veneer and affect glue.
Creep resistance: Choose high-rated glues for lamination and structural bonds; a poor rating means that the dried adhesive has a rubbery glueline.
Open assembly: Maximum time between application and assembly/clamp-up. Long open time best for complicated assemblies.
Drying time: Minimum time joints must stay clamped and undisturbed.
Application temperature: Lowest allowable shop temperature for optimum bonds.
Safety equipment: Some glues produce irritating fumes and require special equipment for safe handling.

freely, and the high peel strength prevents the cloth from pulling loose. On the downside, dried white glue forms a rubbery glueline, which gets gummy from the heat generated during sanding and clogs the sandpaper. White glues have no water resistance whatsoever and should only be used for indoor projects that won't get wet.

Yellow glue

Aliphatic resin glues are probably the best all-purpose wood adhesives made today. Technically, both yellow aliphatic resin and white glues contain the same polymer: polyvinyl acetate; the yellow color is a dye added to distinguish the two glues. Aliphatic resins share many properties with their white cousins—high bond strength, easy cleanup and rapid set. But yellow glues have better moisture resistance, improved creep resistance, higher tack and better sandability. They do have a pretty short shelf life, though; after about a year, most brands are usually too viscous to be useful. Adding a small amount of water to revive a slightly thickened adhesive will do no harm, but resist the temptation to salvage one that is stringy out of the bottle, as shown in the top photo at right. It's better to buy a new bottle than risk having the joints fail on your project.

Cross-linking PVA glue

Once only available to large shops and commercial users, cross-linking PVA glues like Franklin's Titebond II are the most advanced members of the PVA family. Titebond II is a one-part self cross-linking glue that does not require the addition of a catalyst to activate the adhesive. Chemical bonds formed within the adhesive during drying improve the toughness of the glue bond and increase its water resistance. I've found that Titebond II handles like regular yellow glue but has a little higher tack and a shorter drying time. To test Titebond II's water resistance, I prepared identical maple test panels: one glued with Titebond II, the other with regular aliphatic resin glue. Both panels were submerged in a bucket of water and allowed to soak overnight. The next morning, the aliphatic resin sample came

When yellow glue exceeds its usable shelf life, it becomes thick and snotty. You can test this by dipping a small stick into the container. If it's stringy as shown, throw the unused portion away (it contains no solvents, so this is environmentally acceptable).

apart as I pulled it from the bucket. But after 48 hours underwater, the Titebond II sample was still holding firm, and I could not break the joint by hand. To test Titebond II's gap-filling ability, I glued up some maple boards with gap sizes ranging from a tight fit (zero gap) to $1/32$ in. After the samples had dried for a week, I tested them on a laboratory tensile tester to determine the bond strength of the joints. All the samples with gaps up to $1/64$ in. split apart at about 2,600 psi (pounds per square inch) before the glueline failed. At a gap size of $1/32$ in., huge by woodworking standards, the adhesive strength of Titebond II was close to 1,700 psi—sufficiently strong to keep the boards together for a typical woodworking project.

Resorcinol and urea formaldehyde

Urea formaldehyde and resorcinol formaldehyde adhesives are most frequently used for bonding wood when strong, creep- and water-resistant bonds are required. Urea formaldehyde (UF) adhesive, sometimes called plastic resin glue, comes as a one-part powder. The powder is a mixture of dry

resins and hardeners that if kept dry will remain storable indefinitely. Water is added by the user to dissolve the chemicals and activate the adhesive. The pot life after mixing is relatively long, but the viscosity of the activated glue slowly increases until, after about an hour, the adhesive is too thick to be usable. Once cured, UF adhesives produce structural bonds, and the tan glueline is hardly noticeable even on light-colored woods. Interior load-bearing beams and hardwood plywood paneling are often glued with UF adhesives. Not 100 percent waterproof, most UF glues slowly degrade in moist environments. While continuous immersion is not recommended, UF adhesives can be used outdoors, say, for patio furniture, where an occasional soaking from a passing rainstorm will not seriously affect the strength of the bond. UF has only fair gap-filling qualities; therefore, the mating surfaces must be cut accurately and clamped for 24 hours to produce a structurally strong bond. The long working life of UF glues (about 20 minutes) is a real advantage in veneering operations, allowing precise positioning and repositioning of the veneer without loss in ultimate bond strength.

Resorcinol formaldehyde, or RF, adhesives have high strength, exceptional solvent resistance and when properly cured, will withstand prolonged immersion in water, making them perfect for marine applications. RF glues come as two-part kits: one part contains the resorcinol resin dissolved in ethyl alcohol; the other contains powdered paraformaldehyde. The premeasured components are stirred together to activate the adhesive, but careful mixing is necessary to avoid lumps. I've found it best to sift the powder into the liquid resin while constantly stirring the resin (an operation that sometimes takes three hands). RF adhesives produce mahogany-colored gluelines, which show in blond woods, and are a bit harder and more brittle than those produced by UF glues. Their increased hardness makes cured RF glue squeeze-out more difficult to remove. Application procedures, clamping and cleanup with water, are the same as for urea formaldehyde glues.

Unfortunately, both RF and UF adhesive systems release formaldehyde gas when in the liquid state and present a very real health threat to some users. Although test results regarding the carcinogenic nature of formaldehyde gas are not conclusive, it is known that many people are highly sensitive to this chemical. Even low concentrations of formaldehyde in the air can cause irritation to the nose and eyes and cause pounding headaches. Working in a well-ventilated shop will decrease the risk, but I consider heavy rubber gloves and a face mask rated for organic vapors to be necessary to prevent dangerous exposure.

Epoxy

With their high strength (shear tests around 4,000 psi), great gap-filling capacity, uncanny ability to structurally join difficult-to-bond materials and waterproof nature, epoxies are surely the high-performance adhesives of the woodworking world. Epoxy adhesives are solvent-free, two-part systems consisting of an epoxy resin and an amine hardener. Typically, equal parts of resin and hardener are mixed to activate the adhesive and start the curing process, which works by chemical reaction rather than solvent evaporation. The exact mixing proportions are fairly critical; too much of either component will adversely affect bond strength. Epoxy's lack of solvent is responsible for its low shrinkage and exceptional gap-filling ability. In tests, I've found no loss of bond strength —even on glued samples with a $1/16$-in. gap. Common epoxies are designed for optimal

Japanese rice glue: the edible adhesive

by Sandor Nagyszalanczy

Contrary to the western attitude that the best glue is the strongest, Japanese craftsmen consider more than strength when choosing the ideal glue for a job. Traditionally trained craftsman Toshio Odate uses rice glue for his shoji screens because "It is a super assistant; rice glue not only secures the mortise and tenons that join the shoji screen parts but also acts as a lubricant to aid assembly." Rice glue is also tacky, so the many components of a frame don't fall apart during clamp-up. The glue dries transparent and doesn't discolor with age, so the glueline won't show on the blond woods usually used for screens. While rice-glued joints in softwoods are strong enough to sustain normal use, they can't stand shock, so a broken screen can be easily knocked apart for repair—even if it's 100 years old.

Toshio Odate prepares rice glue in his workshop. Cooked short-grain rice taken from a covered bowl is mashed on a wooden work surface with a special tapered and beveled stick until it becomes a smooth and creamy paste. Odate makes a fresh batch whenever needed.

On a recent visit to his house, Odate was kind enough to teach me how to make *sokui*, which is Japanese for rice glue. This adhesive is traditionally prepared fresh, right in the shop whenever needed. The secret? "First, learn how to cook good rice," Odate said. Start with regular rice (not converted, like Uncle Ben's). Odate told me that Japanese kokuho rice (he uses Rose brand), a short-grain rice, works best. Wash the rice with cold water, rinsing until the water runs clear. Drain the rice overnight in a colander (in Japan, these are bamboo), and cover with a cloth to keep moisture in. In the morning, take one part rice, one part water and put them into a heavy lidded pot, and bring them to a rapid boil until it nearly boils over. Turn the heat down to the lowest setting, allow the rice to simmer for about 20 minutes, shut off the heat and let it sit for another 10 minutes. Get the rice kernels well cooked but tight, not mushy.

Now in the shop, prepare a glue-mashing surface by selecting a smooth board or a small sheet of plywood clean on one side. You can make a small mashing tool, like the one Odate uses in the photo at left, from a piece of fir or pine. It should be beveled back about 30° and tapered to a sharp point. Take the rice to the shop in a small, covered bowl, put a small pat of rice on the work surface and bring the flat part of the mashing tool down on it. Work the tool back and forth, lifting the leading edge on each stroke. Continue mashing until the rice is smooth and pasty. Remove any bits of debris with the tool's point. Mix only as much as you can use right away; throw away any that has skinned over. Use the masher to apply the paste. If the paste is too thick to spread, add a little cool water to thin it down—but don't make it too thin.

Excess glue can be wiped away immediately with a damp rag, although any excess left on the surface won't show or splotch under stain and finish. Wait at least half a day for the glue to dry before unclamping; by then, it's easy to scrape or plane off squeeze-out. This glue won't chip your plane or chisel like dried yellow glue will. If you work up an appetite from the strenuous mashing and gluing up, Odate pointed out that you can always eat the rice remaining in the covered bowl.

curing at 65°F to 70°F, but curing and clamping time are temperature dependent: Below 50°F, the reaction rate slows dramatically; at 40°F, an epoxy can take several days to cure fully. Unmixed epoxies have very long shelf lives, but they will eventually go bad. If either part becomes granular, it's time to buy new glue.

Epoxies do have some drawbacks. At about $18 to $20 per pint, they are expensive. Undried epoxies are irritating to the skin and can cause contact dermatitis in sensitive people, so it's best to wear gloves when using them. Epoxies have very low tack and poor uncured strength, so joints have to be clamped until the adhesive is fully cured, usually overnight. Uncured epoxies are not soluble in common workshop solvents, making cleanup difficult (acetone or lacquer thinner can be used in a pinch). Cured epoxy sands and machines well, but the completely hardened squeeze-out is difficult to scrape or sand off. I've found it easier to let the squeeze-out harden until it is rubbery and scrape it off with a sharpened putty knife. Rapid-setting "five-minute" epoxies are a poor choice for woodworking because they are generally lower in strength, and once mixed, they gel very quickly.

Contact cement

Synthetic neoprene rubber forms the base of most modern contact cements. As you might expect, these adhesives have very low strength in the traditional woodworking sense and suffer from high creep. Contact cements are easy to use and produce instant clamp-free bonds, but they aren't suitable for structural uses. Their strong suit is their ability to bond a wide variety of porous or non-porous mate-

rials (such as metal or plastic to wood), which explains their popularity for gluing plastic laminates, such as Formica, to particleboard substrate for kitchen countertops.

Contact cements come in three main varieties based on solvent type: flammable solvent, non-flammable solvent and waterborne. The choice is more a matter of preference than performance; I've found all three types bond equally well. Safety is another matter. Because these products are usually spread over very large areas, a lot of solvent evaporates into the shop or job site. Flammable-solvent contact cements pose a very real fire and explosion hazard unless used in a well-ventilated area. Alternately, non-flammable contact cements aren't a fire hazard but release chlorinated solvents that are known to cause severe health problems in some individuals. A respirator specifically designed for chlorinated solvents must be worn while using this type of contact cement. From a safety standpoint, waterborne contact cements are best, though only for non-porous materials.

Regardless of type, the procedures for using contact cements are very simple. The bonding surface of each part is coated with adhesive and allowed to dry until tack free. One part is then positioned over the other with sticks or waxed paper between the coated surfaces. This allows alignment while preventing contact, necessary because once the adhesive-coated surfaces touch, they stick and cannot be repositioned. To prevent trapping air between the layers, remove the sticks, one at a time, and push the surfaces together as you go. On large panels, start in the middle and work toward the ends. Apply pressure to the face of the lamination with a veneering roller to complete the bond.

Cyanoacrylate

Although they're very expensive (about $170 per pound), cyanoacrylate (CA) adhesives are usually used a drop or two at a time, so they're fairly economical. These fast-setting glues are wonderful for repairing small cracks and tearouts in wood (see the left photo on the facing page) and have found popularity among woodcarvers and turners. Some use cyanoacrylate adhesives to firm up punky areas in spalted wood before turning or carving. CAs come in several forms

including a low-viscosity liquid and a gelled version that's best for more porous woods, like basswood and butternut. Both varieties cure by reacting with water vapor in the air to form colorless, water-resistant joints. But while such rapid setting is a great advantage for gluing up hard-to-clamp parts, the CA bond tends to be very brittle and can be easily broken by a sharp rap with a hammer.

Gluing acidic woods like oak and walnut with CA requires special treatment because the acid content of these woods inhibits the glue's ability to dry. Special accelerators can be sprayed on the joint to neutralize the acid (wiping the surfaces with ethyl alcohol also works). Curing also can be accelerated by breathing on the glue-coated parts before assembly; the humidity starts the adhesive's polymerization reaction.

Most CAs exude vapors that are extremely irritating to the eyes, but are relatively nontoxic, so no special protective equipment is needed when working in a well-ventilated area. The biggest drawback with cyanoacrylates is their propensity to glue things together that shouldn't be glued—like the cap to the bottle or your fingers to the workpiece. Further, cured cyanoacrylates are very solvent resistant and require special CA solvent for dissolving the bond (in a pinch, try using an acetone-base fingernail polish remover). Once opened, cyanoacrylates have a short shelf life: about six months. Storing the adhesive in your freezer will considerably extend its useful life (more than two years in my experience). However, allow the glue to warm to room temperature, and dry the container before opening the bottle.

Hide glue

While modern synthetic adhesives are the workhorses of the woodshop, old-fashioned hide glue has a few unique properties that still make it useful. Fresh, hot hide glue easily bonds to old, dried hide glue, making it great for restoring pre-1940 furniture, which was probably originally assembled with hide glue. Hide-glued joints can be disassembled by applying steam or hot water, a quality embraced by those who repair furniture and stringed-instruments. Because hide glue is a natural protein, it will absorb an oil-base stain just as the wood does. Thus, if any glue remains on the wood, the piece can be stained or dyed without light splotches appearing, a common problem with synthetic glues.

Chemically, hide glue is a protein-base adhesive derived primarily from the hides and hooves of cattle. It comes in several different grades (most woodworking supply catalogs sell it) with gram strengths between 164 and 251. Gram strength is *not* an indication of the glue's bond strength—all grades of hide glue are strong enough for woodworking. Rather, glues with a higher gram strength are more viscous and gel quicker.

Unlike synthetic liquid adhesives, traditional hide glue is prepared by soaking the glue granules in cool water for a few hours. Typically, a mix of $1^1/_2$-3 parts water to 1 part glue granules (by weight) yields the proper consistency. The exact amount of water needed is different for each glue grade (see the instructions that come with your glue), but don't exceed 3 parts water to

Three steps to good glue joints

The process of gluing boards together seems simple enough. Only three steps are involved: preparation of the joint or planing of the surfaces, application of the glue and clamping the assembly. It is so simple that we often take it for granted. Unfortunately, neglecting the basics during any one of these steps can lead to weak or failed bonds, regardless of the wood species or the gap-filling ability and strength of the adhesive you use.

Surface preparation

Edge-gluing boards into larger panels is probably the most frequent gluing activity in the woodworking shop. And, while matching boards for grain patterns and color is important to the final appearance of the panel, careful attention to the machining and preparation of edges before glue-up will reward you with the strongest and longest lasting joints possible. All edges should be planed straight, true and perfectly perpendicular to each face, a job for a sharp, well-tuned jointer or a long handplane equipped with a fence (as shown in the photo at right). Some woodworkers prefer to glue up boards with edges as they come right off the tablesaw. While this method probably will produce joints of adequate strength, I prefer to plane my edges for two reasons. First, sawblades damage bonding surfaces by tearing the wood fibers as they cut through the board. Subsequently, excessive clamping pressure often is required to flatten the uneven areas of the bond line. Second, a sharp jointer or handplane shears the fibers leaving an undamaged, flat gluing surface, which minimizes the clamping pressure necessary to achieve an almost invisible glueline.

Jointing square edges on a board before glue-up is essential for a strong bond. Clamping a 90° fence guide on the side of a handplane will help to keep your cuts square and true.

It is likely that more joints fail due to having been machined with dull jointer knives than from any other problem. Dull knife edges crush and glaze the wood fibers instead of cutting them cleanly. These abused wood fibers don't absorb the glue properly, which results in a weak bond. To test for this problem, simply place a drop of water on a jointed edge; if the water stays beaded up after about

1 part glue because the resulting mixture will be too weak for proper bonding. When the soaked granules resemble mushy oatmeal, liquefy the hide glue by warming it. Special glue pots are available for this, but a double boiler or any heating device that keeps the glue at around 140°F will work well. Use a candy thermometer to read the temperature, and don't let the glue boil, or you'll weaken its bonding strength. Incidentally, for small jobs, you can use unsweetened gelatin powder from a grocery store, which is really hide glue that's been purified. Mixed $2\frac{1}{2}$ parts water to 1 part powder, gelatin's high gram strength gives it an open time of about 60 seconds, too fast for veneering large panels but perfect for quick repairs.

Once the glue is hot and of even consistency, it is ready for use. Brush the hot glue on the joint, and assemble the pieces quickly. Regular hot hide glue has a short open

30 seconds, then the surface is probably glazed. Sharpen your knives or plane blade and resurface the edges before gluing.

Before glue-up, plan to dry-assemble each edge joint to make sure that it's tight and gap free when lightly pressed together by hand. Avoid using warped lumber, because distorted boards usually put unequal stresses on a dried glueline that may ultimately cause the joint to fail.

Highly resinous woods like teak or rosewood require special care during preparation to ensure adequate strength in the final glue joint. The extractives that resinous woods contain concentrate at the surface as the lumber dries and tend to make the wood water repellent, preventing most adhesives from being properly absorbed (check for this with the water-drop test previously described). A common practice among woodworkers is to wipe these joints with lacquer thinner or alcohol in an attempt to remove the excess resins. This practice sometimes works but often just worsens the problem as capillary action from the evaporating solvent pulls more resin to the surface, recontaminating the freshly cleaned surface. The best way to sidestep the problem is to joint the edge just before gluing: Milling temporarily removes most extractives at the surface. But don't let the wood sit around too long, the extractive will accumulate again if the lumber is stored. An alternative is to switch to a less oil-sensitive adhesive, like epoxy or resorcinol.

Endgrain gluing: The glued strength of most edge-to-edge joints, such as panels, depends on long-grain to long-grain contact. Gluing endgrain to side grain or endgrain to endgrain directly is okay for small parts but isn't recommended in most cases because endgrain is extremely porous (similar to a box of soda straws viewed from the top). Capillary action at the endgrain wicks the liquid adhesive away before it has a chance to set and bond the parts together. To achieve adequate strength in situations where endgrain must be glued (for example, a typical cabinet face frame), joints such as mortise and tenons are employed to increase the long-grain bonding area. Spline joints, biscuit joints and doweled joints also can be used for endgrain to side grain bonding with equal success. Scarf joints, popular with wooden boatbuilders, are good for joining boards end to end. A scarf joint is really a low-angle miter cut to expose as much long grain as possible. The USDA Forest Products Research Laboratory recommends a slope of about 1:8 (about a 7° angle) for best bonding strength.

Spreading the adhesive

Woodworkers often ask, "Should one or both sides of a joint be covered with glue before clamping?" I prefer spreading a thin layer of adhesive on both sides of the glueline because this ensures that the proper amount of adhesive will be absorbed into both parts. If only one side is coated, the adhesive may be squeezed from the joint by clamping before it has a chance to absorb into the mating surface.

For ultimate bond strength, it's imperative for the adhesive to be spread evenly over the entire bonding surface. Areas that haven't been coated with glue will not bond. I have two glue applicators that satisfy most of the gluing needs in my shop. A stiff parts-cleaning brush (I purchased mine at a local auto parts store) applies glue to tenons, dovetails

continued on p. 54

time—two to three minutes—and the joint must be assembled while the glue is still liquid. Warming the wood with a hair drier will extend open time, as does adding small amounts of water to the glue. Products called liquid hide glue come premixed with chemical gel depressants (to keep them liquid and extend their open time) and are an alternative to cooking your own. While some woodworkers claim that liquid hide glue is weaker than hot hide glue, I haven't found this to be true. All hide glues cure in about 24 hours, but the clamped joints can be unclamped after two hours provided the piece isn't handled too roughly. Excess glue is easily cleaned off with warm water or by peeling the squeeze-out off the surface with your fingernail before the glue has a chance to set.

Specialty adhesives

Among the hundreds of special adhesives available to woodworkers, hot-melt glues are

Applying glue with a rubber veneer roller is one way to ensure that the adhesive is spread evenly over the edges to be joined. The small parts brush setting on the water container (foreground) is handy for getting glue into joints, like the plate-joinery biscuit kerfs in the boards shown.

and other irregularly shaped joints. I use a hard rubber veneer roller for edge-gluing solid stock (not a hard plastic roller, I find these tend to skid over the top of the adhesive and not spread it properly). A rubber roller is fast and easy to use and automatically coats the entire surface with the proper amount of adhesive (see the photo above). To mix two-part thermoset adhesives, such as epoxy, I use disposable paint brushes or small sticks as disposable applicators because these adhesives are hard to clean up. Incidentally, fingers don't make good

applicators for any type of adhesive. It's hard to get an even coating of adhesive with your fingers, and besides, you're more likely to contaminate some other part of the project with adhesive residue and get your clothes gluey.

Clamping

The object of clamping is to hold the parts in position until the adhesive has set. Dry-assembling parts before glue-up will ensure that everything fits together as it should and also provides an indication of the number of clamps needed and where to place them. When the joints are tight and properly milled, surprisingly little clamping pressure is usually needed to achieve good bonds. Small gaps and cracks can not always be avoided, and they can usually be closed with slight pressure. If excessive clamping pressure is needed to close a joint during the dry-assembling stage, then the glued joint will be under high stress and may spring apart once the clamps are removed or sometime in the future. In such cases, it is best simply to recut or to resurface the joint.

How tight should you make the clamps? If the joint surfaces are well machined, just enough pressure to squeeze any excess glue from the joint is plenty; try to keep clamping pressure even by spacing clamps uniformly for long glue-ups and using clamp blocks to distribute clamping pressure. Blocks also keep the wood from getting dented by the clamps. While it's not advisable with structural components or

among the more useful. Sold in the form of solid sticks, hot melts are dispensed from an electrically heated glue gun (see the photo at left) at about 350°F and rapidly set as they cool—in about 15 to 20 seconds. Hot melt's poor penetration, thick glueline and low strength coupled with its poor sandability limit its uses in woodworking (it's also capable of burning you). I've found hot melts to be a convenient way of attaching glue blocks to furniture and for tacking drawer bottoms in place during assembly. Edgebanding veneers, precoated with hot-melt glue, are used extensively in production furniture shops to cover the edges of plywood and

particleboard. This kind of edgebanding can be applied with a household iron. Also, a few dabs of hot-melt glue serve as a good temporary fastener for jigs and fixtures. The adhesive can be released by heating (a paint-stripper gun works well), and the rubbery residue is easily scraped from the wood.

An interesting adhesive I've used, Scotch brand 934 Adhesive Transfer Tape, defies categorization: The product applies like tape, but sticks like glue. An applicator rolls it on to one side of the joint, releasing it from a paper backing as you roll it along. Pressing the parts together increases bonding strength. I've used this adhesive-tape

Even clamping pressure ensures uniform squeeze-out of excess glue and a maximum strength bond. To keep dripping glue off his workbench, Minick covers the surface with water-resistant kraft paper.

like birch or rock maple, can lead to starved joints.

I wanted to test this theory of excessive clamping in a fairly scientific fashion, so I prepared and pull tested three sets of hard-maple samples, one rubbed together, one standardly clamped and one overly clamped (to the point of crushing the mating surfaces). The results were somewhat ambiguous: I found that all three samples had glue joints of acceptable strength. Using moderate clamping pressure still yields the strongest joint and seems to make the most sense, if for no other reason than to avoid dents in clamped edges.

The drying time for a glue and glue-curing time are often confused. Drying time (as shown in the chart on p. 46) is the average amount of time, under normal conditions, that glued joints must remain clamped and undisturbed before the assembly can be handled. But curing time is the length of time necessary for the *maximum* bond strength of the adhesive to develop. Most adhesives take much longer to cure than to dry—typically two to three days. Other conditions, such as excessive or inadequate temperature or humidity, also can affect drying time. Extending the clamping time beyond the minimum specified by the glue manufacturer is necessary for joints whose mating surfaces are less than perfect. The extra time allows the glue to cure more fully and minimizes the chances of joint failure. —*C.M.*

large surfaces, you can even achieve decent adhesive bonding by rubbing two glued parts together, a common practice for adding glue blocks to reinforce a carcase. In theory, excessive clamping pressure will force the adhesive from the glueline, starving the joint and resulting in bonding failure. Further, as the density (weight per volume) of a wood species increases, its ability to absorb adhesive decreases. Thus, overclamping dense woods,

product for gluing metal and plastic to wood and as a veneering adhesive on small wooden puzzles with good success. This tape is handy for temporarily gluing templates to jigs (see the photo at right) and for stack cutting pieces on the bandsaw. After cutting, remove the tape by rolling it up with your fingers, like rubber cement. If pieces are left bonded overnight, the tape develops a tenacious bond, making it great for permanently applying small moldings. I purchase transfer tape at an office-supply store, but I've seen it in specialty mail-order catalogs, too.

Temporarily attaching a template to a part to be routed is quickly done with a special adhesive tape made by 3M, which dispenses from an applicator like tape but sticks like glue.

MAKING SENSE OF SANDPAPER

by Strother Purdy

What goes on between belt sander and board? Sandpaper is a kind of cutting tool, like a saw or a plane. Magnified at right, swarf from sanding with the grain looks like shavings from a ripsaw.

Years ago at a garage sale, I bought a pile of no-name sandpaper for just pennies a sheet. I got it home. I sanded with it, but nothing came off the wood. Sanding harder, the grit came off the paper. It didn't even burn very well in my wood stove.

Sanding is necessary drudge work, improved only by spending less time doing it. As I learned, you can't go right buying cheap stuff, but it's still easy to go wrong with the best sandpaper that's available. Not long ago, for example, I tried to take the finish off some maple flooring. Even though I was armed with premium-grade, 50-grit aluminum-oxide belts, the work took far too long. It wasn't that the belts were bad. I was simply using the wrong abrasive for the job. A 36-grit ceramic belt would have cut my sanding time substantially.

The key to choosing the right sandpaper is knowing how the many different kinds of sandpaper work. Each component, not just the grit, contributes to the sandpaper's performance, determining how quickly it works, how long it lasts and how smooth the results will be. If you know how the components work together, you'll be able to choose your sandpaper wisely, and use it efficiently. Then you won't waste time sanding or end up burning the stuff in your wood stove.

Sandpaper is a cutting tool

What sandpaper does to wood is really no different from what a saw, a plane or a chisel does. They all have sharp points or edges that cut wood fibers. Sandpaper's cutting is simply on a much smaller scale. The only

Sandpaper in cross section _____

Sandpaper is made of abrasive minerals, adhesive and a cloth, paper or polyester backing. The abrasive minerals are bonded to the backing by two coats of adhesive; first the make coat bonds them to the backing; then the size coat locks them in position.

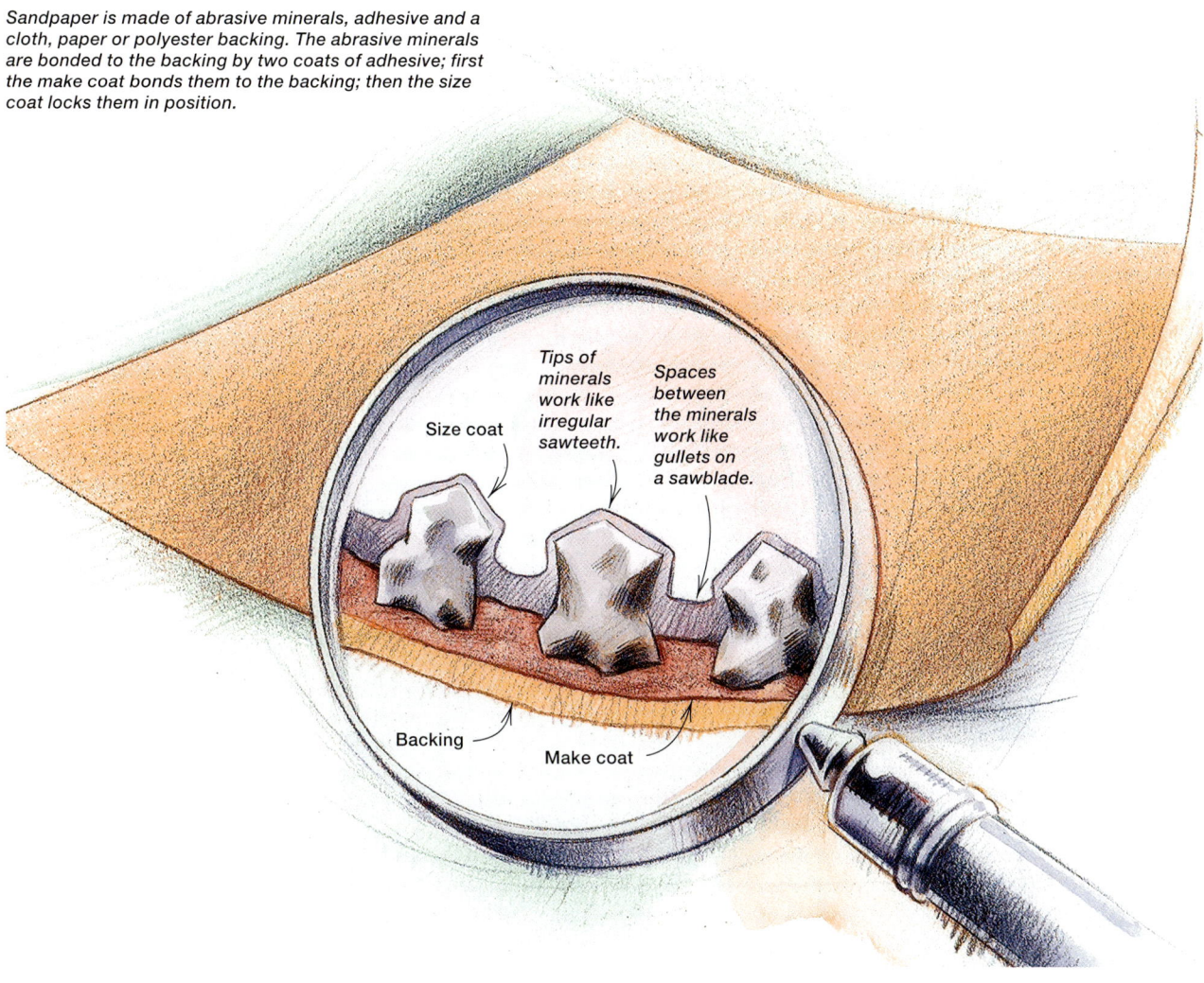

Size coat

Tips of minerals work like irregular sawteeth.

Spaces between the minerals work like gullets on a sawblade.

Backing

Make coat

substantial difference between sandpaper and other cutting tools is that sandpaper can't be sharpened.

Look at sandpaper up close, and you'll see that the sharp tips of the abrasive grains look like small, irregularly shaped sawteeth (see the drawing above). The grains are supported by a cloth or paper backing and two adhesive bonds, much the way that sawteeth are supported by the sawblade. As sandpaper is pushed across wood, the abrasive grains dig into the surface and cut out minute shavings, which are called swarf in industry jargon. To the naked eye, these shavings look like fine dust. Magnified, they look like the shavings produced by saws or

other cutting tools (see the bottom photo on the facing page).

Even the spaces between the abrasive grains serve an important role. They work the way gullets on sawblades do, giving the shavings a place to go. This is why sandpaper designed for wood has what's called an open coat, where only 40% to 70% of the backing is covered with abrasive. The spaces in an open coat are hard to see in fine grits but are very obvious in coarse grades.

Closed-coat sandpaper, where the backing is entirely covered with abrasive, is not appropriate for sanding wood because the

Aluminum oxide

TRADE NAMES

Adalox

Aloxite

Imperial

Metalite

Production

Three-M-ite

346U
PRODUCTION RN
Paper D wt.
Open Coat

Aluminum oxide is a sharp and blocky mineral. It is the most common, all-purpose woodworking abrasive, and for good reason. It is the only abrasive mineral that fragments under the heat and pressure generated by sanding wood. This characteristic is called friability and is highly desirable. As you sand, aluminum oxide renews its cutting edges constantly, staying sharp and cutting much longer than other minerals.

Aluminum oxide is also a relatively tough abrasive, which means that its edges won't dull much before they fragment. Its friability and toughness make aluminum oxide the longest lasting and the most economical mineral.

All aluminum oxides are not created equal. 3M alone manufactures 26 different kinds, ranging greatly in toughness and friability. The toughest grades are nearly white in their raw form and are used on premium-grade sandpapers. The softest grades are dark brown and more appropriate for sandblasting than sanding. Some cheap sandpapers have blast-grade aluminum oxide on them. No manufacturer is going to tell you which kind is on which sandpaper, however, and it's impossible to judge by the color of the sandpaper because a size coat covers and colors the mineral. If one brand's aluminum-oxide paper doesn't work well, don't judge all aluminum oxides by it. Simply try another.

Silicon carbide

TRADE NAMES

Durite

Tri-M-ite

Fastcut

Powerkut

Wet-or-dry

435N
TRI-M-ITE
FRE-CUT
Paper C wt.
Open Coat

Silicon carbide is black and iridescent, and the grains are shard-shaped (see the photo below). Unlike aluminum oxide, there is only one kind of silicon carbide. It is harder and sharper than most aluminum oxides, making it the better choice for cutting hard materials, such as finishes, paint, plastic and metal. Consequently, you'll probably find the widest range of silicon carbide sandpapers in a good auto-body supply store.

Silicon carbide sandpapers for woodworking are almost always on waterproof paper and intended for sanding finishes. Though silicon carbide is a friable mineral, it is so hard that sanding wood will not cause it to fragment and renew its cutting edges. Though it will sand faster at first, it will dull more quickly than aluminum oxide. It is also generally more expensive than aluminum oxide.

Abrasive grains are little saw-teeth. This is 24-grit silicon carbide sandpaper before a size coat has been applied. It is easy to see how sharp the particles are.

Ceramics

Garnet

TRADE NAMES

Norzon

Dynakut

Regalite

REGALITE
RESIN BOND
Paper E wt.
Open Coat

TRADE NAMES

None

110N
GARNET
Paper A wt.
Open Coat

Ceramics come in a wide variety of shapes, from blocks and heavy wedges to flake-like shards. They're all more costly and less common than other abrasive minerals. All of them are very tough and very aggressive.

Like silicon carbide, ceramics are not friable, and do not renew their cutting edges when sanding wood. But they don't dull as quickly because of their extreme toughness. This makes them the best choice for hogging off stock, roughing out shapes, removing finish and leveling uneven boards. For this reason, they are generally available only in coarse-grit cloth belts for stationary and portable sanders.

Ceramic mineral names and the trade names they're sold under are not easy to sort out. Though Cubitron sounds like a trade name, it's a ceramic mineral. One of its trade names is Cubicut. When mixed with aluminum oxide, it's sold as Regalite. Alumina zirconia is the name of a ceramic mineral. Sometimes it's marketed as aluminum zirconia, as if it were another type of mineral. It's also sold under the trade names Norzon and AZ as a ceramic mineral.

Abrasive manufacturers make these names intentionally confusing to avoid losing their copyrights. If a trade name becomes synonymous with the product in the public's mind (think of a thermos), then any company can use it.

Garnet is the only natural abrasive mineral still widely used for woodworking. Like aluminum oxide, it is blocky in shape. Unlike aluminum oxide, it is non-friable, not very tough and dulls very quickly. This is not necessarily a defect. The softer cut of a garnet paper, though slow, will produce the smoothest finish of all the abrasives within a given grit size. Because it is so soft,

garnet will not leave pigtail-like scratches the way an aluminum oxide will when used on a random-orbit sander. This makes it well suited for final sanding of wood surfaces.

Garnet is an excellent choice for final sanding end grain and blotch-prone wood. Garnet's peculiar tendency to burnish wood—close off pores—makes a stain penetrate far more evenly though less deeply (see the photo at left).

Pigmented stain prefers a garnet-sanded surface. Both sides of this test board were sanded to a 150-grit, the left with an aluminum-oxide paper and the right with a garnet paper.

swarf has no place to go and quickly clogs the paper. Closed-coat sandpaper is more appropriate on other materials such as steel and glass because the particles of swarf are much smaller.

Some sandpaper is advertised as non-loading, or stearated. These papers are covered with a substance called zinc stearate—soap, really—which helps keep the sandpaper from clogging with swarf. Stearated papers are only useful for sanding finishes and resinous woods. Wood resin and most finishes will become molten from the heat generated by sanding, even hand-sanding. In this state, these substances are very sticky, and given the chance, they will firmly glue themselves to the sandpaper. Stearates work by attaching to the molten swarf, making it slippery, not sticky, and preventing it from bonding to the sandpaper.

Methods for sanding efficiently

Sanding a rough surface smooth in preparation for a finish seems a pretty straightforward proposition. For a board fresh out of the planer, woodworkers know to start with a coarse paper, perhaps 80-grit or 100-grit, and progress incrementally without skipping a grade up to the finer grits. At each step, you simply erase the scratches you made previously with finer and smaller scratches until, at 180-grit or 220-grit, the scratches are too small to see or feel. But there are a fair number of opinions on how to do this most efficiently.

Don't skip grits, usually

Skipping a grit to save time and sandpaper is a common temptation, but not a good idea when working with hardwoods. You can remove the scratches left by 120-grit sandpaper with 180-grit, but it will take you far more work than if you use 150-grit first. You will also wear out more 180-grit sandpaper, so you don't really save any materials.

When sanding maple, for instance, skipping two grits between 80 and 180 will probably double the total sanding time. This, however, is not as true with woods such as pine. Soft woods take much less work overall to sand smooth. Skipping a grit will increase the work negligibly and may save you some materials.

Sand bare wood to 180- or 220-grit

For sanding bare wood, 180-grit will generally give you a surface that looks and feels perfectly smooth and is ready for a finish of some kind. Sanding the surface with a finer grit is only necessary if you're going to use a water-based finish. These finishes will pick up and telegraph the smallest scratches. Sanding the wood to 220-grit or finer will prepare the surface better. However, it's not always wise to sand to a finer grit. You will waste your time if you can't tell the difference, and you may create problems in finishing. Maple sanded to 400-grit will not take a pigmented stain, for example. Pigments work by lodging themselves into nooks and crannies on the surface; without them, they will have no place to stick.

Sand faster across the grain

How many times have you been told never to sand across the grain? True enough: The scratches are much more obvious, look terrible and are hard to remove with the next finer grit. But what holds true for planing wood is also true for sanding. You will plane and sand faster and more easily when the direction of your cuts is between 45° and 60° to the grain, because the wood-fiber bundles offer the least resistance to the cutting edges. Cross-grain scratches are harder to remove simply because they are deeper.

Use a combination of cross-grain and with-grain sanding to get the smoothest surface in the fastest manner. First make passes at 45° to 60° to both the left and the right, making an X-pattern on the workpiece. Then, with the same grit, sand with the grain to remove the cross-grain scratches. Do this with each grit when belt-sanding and hand-sanding. The non-linear sanding action of random-orbit and orbital sanders can't take advantage of the wood's grain properties. When I use my orbital, I just sand with the grain.

Choosing from the four abrasive minerals

Four common abrasive minerals are aluminum oxide, silicon carbide, ceramics and garnet. Except for garnet, they are all manufactured, designed if you will, for different cutting properties. Harder and sharper minerals cut deeper scratches and, consequently, sand the wood faster. But these deep scratches leave a coarse finish, whether you sand with or across the grain.

Softer minerals within the same grit size will cut far more slowly but leave a smoother finish. For example, if you sand a board on one side with a 120-grit ceramic, the hardest abrasive mineral, and the other side with 120-grit garnet, the softest, you will be able to feel a distinct difference between the surfaces. It will seem as if you sanded the two sides with different grit sizes.

It's easy to rate each mineral's hardness and sharpness, but it's not as simple to prescribe specific uses beyond generalizations. There are many other factors that influence the appropriateness of a sandpaper for a job (see pp. 58-59).

Some fine points about grading scales

If you don't mind that we have two measurement systems, the U.S. Customary (foot, gallon) and the International (meter, liter), then you won't mind that we have three major abrasive grit-grading systems. In North America, the Coated Abrasives Manufacturers Institute (CAMI) regulates the U.S. Standard Scale. CAMI-graded

Abrasive grading systems

The most common grading systems used in North America are CAMI, FEPA and micron grading. CAMI and FEPA are similar in grades up to about 220. Beyond that, they diverge greatly.

	CAMI (U.S. Std.)	FEPA (P-scale)	Micron (μ)
			5
Finishing	1,200		
			9
	1,000		
	800		
			15
		1,200	
	600		
		1,000	
	500		
			20
		800	
	400		
		600	
	360		
			30
		500	
		400	
	320		
			40
		360	
	280		
			45
		320	
			50
		280	
	240	240	
			60
		220	
	220		
	180	180	
Smoothing			80
	150		
		150	
			100
	120		
		120	
	100		
			150
		100	
			180
	80		
		80	
		60	
	60		
		50	
	50		
		40	
	40		
		36	
	36		
Shaping		30	
	30		
	24		
		24	
	20		
		20	
	16		

The three systems grade particle size to different tolerances but by the same methods. From the coarsest grits up to about 220, particles are graded through a series of wire mesh screens. Smaller grit sizes are graded through an air- or water-flotation process.

CAMI-graded abrasives tolerate the widest range of particle sizes but are perfectly good for sanding wood.

P-graded abrasives are to tighter tolerances than the CAMI grades.

Micron-graded abrasives are most uniform in size and best for sanding finishes.

sandpapers simply have numbers, such as 320, printed on them. The Europeans have the P-scale, regulated by the Federation of European Producers Association (FEPA). These abrasives are identifiable by the letter P in front of the grit size, such as P320. Finally, to make sure everyone is really confused, there is a totally different micron grading system. This system is identified by the Greek letter mu, as in 30μ.

The chart on p. 61 is helpful in comparing grits of the three grading systems, but it doesn't tell the whole story. Abrasives on the P-scale are graded to tighter tolerances than CAMI-graded abrasives. This means that the CAMI-scale tolerates a wider range of grain sizes within the definition of 180-grit than the P-scale. Tolerances are even tighter for micron grading. P-graded and micron-graded abrasives give more consistent cuts with fewer stray scratches from outsized minerals.

Micron-graded abrasives on polyester films are about three times as expensive as paper products and probably not worth it for sanding wood. I have a hard time telling the difference between wood sanded with a 100μ finishing film abrasive and standard 120-grit sandpaper. But for polishing a high-gloss finish, I find micron-graded abrasives make a substantial difference.

The supporting role of backings and bonds

The backing's stiffness and flatness influence the quality and speed of the sandpaper's cut. For the most part, manufacturers choose adhesives and backings to augment the characteristics of a particular abrasive grit. You will have a hard time finding an aggressive abrasive mineral, for example, on a backing suited to a smooth cut.

The stiffer the paper, the less the abrasive minerals will deflect while cutting. They will cut deeper and, consequently, faster. Soft backings and bonds will allow the abrasives to deflect more, giving light scratches and a

Soft pads let the sandpaper deflect. Soft backings on sanding tools won't support the sandpaper and make it cut more slowly.

Discs don't flex, they break. The adhesive and backing on a random-orbit sanding pad can crack if the disc is folded like ordinary sandpaper.

smooth finish. You must even consider what's behind the backing. Wrapping the sandpaper around a block of wood will allow a faster cut than sanding with the paper against the palm of your hand. For instance, an easy way to speed up your orbital sander is by exchanging the soft pad for a stiff one (see the photo on the facing page). The other consideration is the flatness of the backing, which has nothing to do with its stiffness. Flat backings position the minerals on a more even level so they cut at a more consistent depth, resulting in fewer stray scratches and a smoother surface.

Cloth is the stiffest but least-flat backing. It will produce the coarsest and fastest cut. Cloth comes in two grades, a heavy X and a light J. Paper is not as stiff as cloth but it's flatter. It comes in grades A, C, D, E and F (lightest to heaviest). A-weight paper that has been waterproofed is approximately equivalent to a B-weight paper, if one existed. Polyester films, including Mylar, look and feel like plastic. They are extremely flat

and pretty stiff. They will give the most consistently even cut and at a faster rate than paper.

The backings for hand sheets and belts are designed to flex around curves without breaking. This is not true for sanding discs for random-orbit sanders. They are designed to remain perfectly flat, and if used like a hand sheet, the adhesive will crack off in large sections (see the photo above). This is called knife-edging because the mineral and adhesive, separated from the backing, form knife-like edges that dig into and mark the work.

Adhesive bonds on modern sandpaper are almost exclusively urea- or phenolic-formaldehyde resins. Both are heat-resistant, waterproof and stiff. Hide glue is sometimes used in conjunction with a resin on paper sheets. It is not waterproof or heat-resistant, but hide glue is cheap and very flexible.

THREE

Tools

Tools and techniques are so intimately related that dividing them into separate sections is a little artificial. You really can't have one without the other. To know a tool well is to know several techniques and vice versa. However, you have to start somewhere. This chapter will focus on tools and what they're capable of doing. The next will focus on the particular tool techniques that produce furniture.

Every woodworking tool requires a distinct skill to master. Some, such as clamps, take maybe five minutes, while a router takes a lifetime to exploit fully. Taking a woodworking course is probably the best way to learn about basic tools and their potential. There are few good substitutes for seeing a tool in action and being able to try it with the guidance of an experienced woodworker. But when a course isn't available, the next best thing is a book like this and a lot of practice in your shop.

Here you'll find the basics of some fundamental hand tools and power tools. The articles focus on individual tools, showing how they work, how to make them operate properly and what types of work they do best. You'll get an overall sense of the place each tool can have in the shop. You'll also get some guidance on picking them up for the first time and making a cut.

There's a good reason why so many basic woodworking books begin with a chapter on handplanes. (The bench comes first in this section because it's just slightly more fundamental than a handplane.) Planes and other hand tools are much safer to put in the hands of a beginner than power tools. Using a handplane also teaches you things about wood and woodworking beyond the plane's immediate application. The features and importance of wood grain are obvious from the start when planing wood by hand. Power tools tend to mask these collateral lessons. Grain direction poses a much smaller problem when routing. Often, you can ignore it completely.

On the other hand, starting out like a monk on a strict diet of hand tools isn't the answer. The tremendous usefulness of power tools shouldn't be ignored by the beginner, unless you aim to reenact an 18th-century apprenticeship. Power tools are often the first choice of the beginner because they accomplish so much so quickly. But a word of caution. A chisel and a handplane can give nasty cuts when misused, but no more. A tablesaw and a jointer can take fingers off before you realize what happened. Always put caution and safety before every other consideration. You'll be thankful you did.

POWER-TOOL WORKBENCH

by Lars Mikkelsen

Space is at a premium in my small shop, so the more functions any one thing can serve the better. I had two things that needed improvement—my hand power tools were cramped in a small cabinet, their cords always entwined, and my bench needed a good base. So I decided to kill two birds with one stone and build a base cabinet for the bench with cubbies for my tools.

These cubbies have worked out very well for me. Each tool has its place, where I also keep the miscellaneous wrenches and screwdrivers needed for that particular tool. The small size of the cubbies makes the tools much easier to find than if they were stored on long shelves. The cords never get tangled, and it's so easy to get and put away a tool that I avoid the usual clutter on the benchtop. The power strip that I attached to the bench makes it possible for a tool to be in its cubby while still plugged in ready to go.

Quick-access tool cubbies

I made the base cabinet from ³/₄-in. birch plywood edged with ¹/₄-in. strips of solid birch and biscuited together, as shown in the main drawing on the facing page. The biscuits could be replaced with tongue-and-groove joints or dadoes and rabbets, but biscuits are the simplest. I measured my biggest tool to determine the maximum width and depth of the sections. The desired final height of the benchtop sets the base height, and the shelves are adjustable. The dimensions can all be adapted to your own situation, but it is helpful to keep the combined width of the benchtop (mine is 29 in.) and depth of the base cabinet (mine is 18 in.)

below the standard 48-in. width of a sheet of plywood, so you can use the cutoffs from ripping the top to make parts for the base. And while I used all the space for cubbies, one of the sections could easily be set up to hold simple sliding shelves for bit storage. The shelves could slide in dadoes cut across the width of facing vertical dividers before assembly.

I used ¹/₄-in. plywood for the back of the base and anchored my bench to the wall with 3-in. screws driven through a ledger strip on the underside of the top. For a freestanding bench, I would recommend, at minimum, a ³/₄-in. back and a hefty face frame to add stiffness against racking. For maximum strength in a freestanding bench, cubbies could be made to fit beneath a traditional mortise-and-tenon trestle base.

A plywood work surface

The top of my bench is made from two layers of ³/₄-in. shop-birch plywood and one layer of ¹/₂-in. Baltic-birch plywood. Unlike shop-birch plywood, which has a core of thick softwood veneers between thin outer layers of birch, Baltic birch is all birch with a core of thin, high-quality veneers, free of voids. (Baltic birch sheets are often sized metrically and will run approximately twice the cost of shop birch.) This sandwich of shop birch and Baltic birch makes the benchtop amply stiff, and the Baltic birch has a surface hard enough and thick enough to withstand some abuse. I laminated the three sheets of plywood with Liquid Nails construction adhesive. I did not have any way of clamping something this big, so I used lots of screws coming up from the bottom. I removed the screws once the

Tool storage within an arm's length of the job

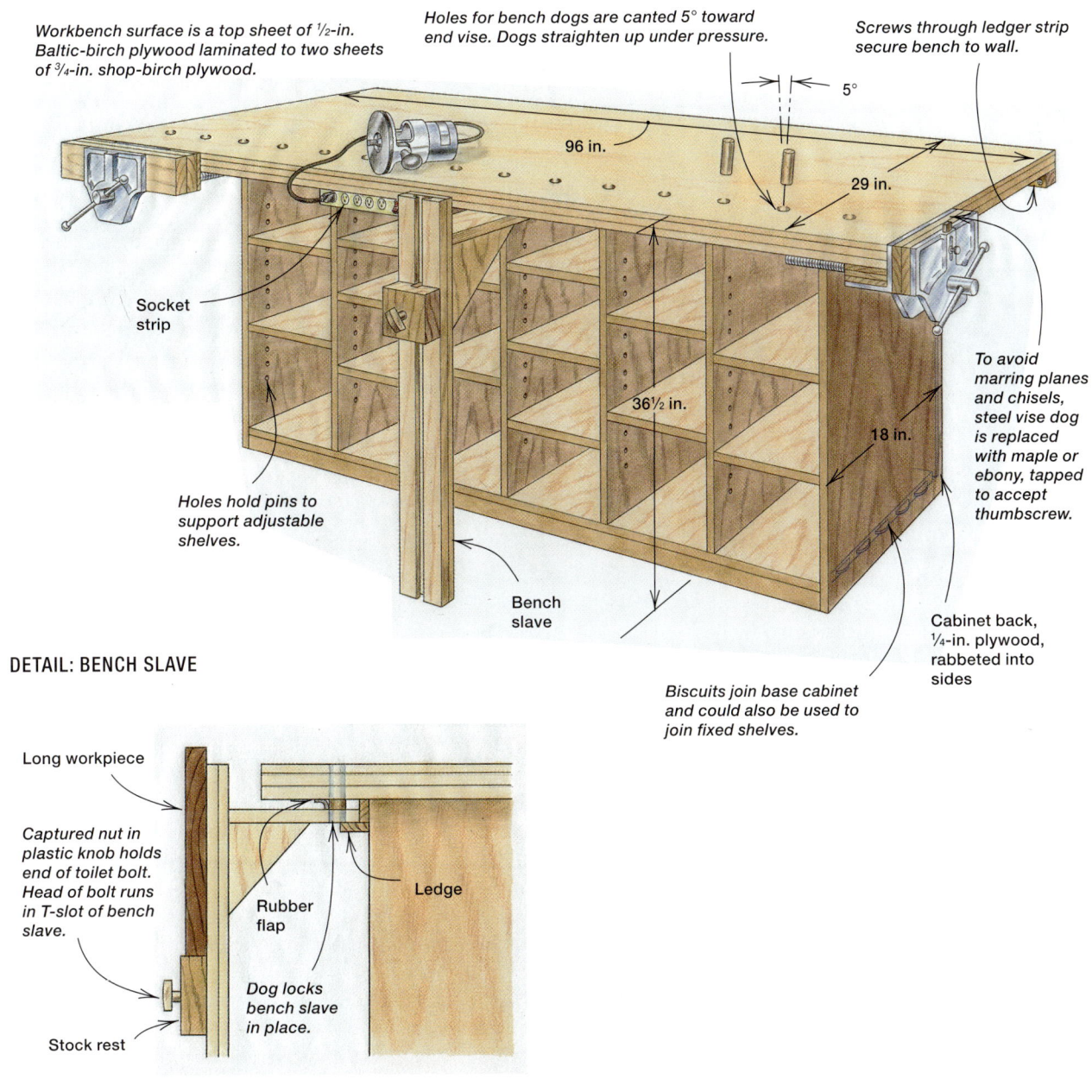

Workbench surface is a top sheet of ½-in. Baltic-birch plywood laminated to two sheets of ¾-in. shop-birch plywood.

Holes for bench dogs are canted 5° toward end vise. Dogs straighten up under pressure.

Screws through ledger strip secure bench to wall.

5°

96 in.

29 in.

Socket strip

36½ in.

18 in.

To avoid marring planes and chisels, steel vise dog is replaced with maple or ebony, tapped to accept thumbscrew.

Holes hold pins to support adjustable shelves.

Bench slave

DETAIL: BENCH SLAVE

Biscuits join base cabinet and could also be used to join fixed shelves.

Cabinet back, ¼-in. plywood, rabbeted into sides

Long workpiece

Captured nut in plastic knob holds end of toilet bolt. Head of bolt runs in T-slot of bench slave.

Ledge

Rubber flap

Dog locks bench slave in place.

Stock rest

adhesive had set, so I wouldn't run into them later when drilling for the bench dogs or other fixtures.

A new twist on old dogs

I mounted two Record #52$\frac{1}{2}$ ED vises to the top, one as an end vise, the other as a front vise. Both have wooden jaw faces. I tapped the metal jaws, so I could change the wooden faces easily without removing the vises from the bench. The front vise has oversized jaws to get a better grip on large pieces. To make bench dogs, I cut up a 1-in.-dia. dowel. I drilled a series of 1-in. holes for the dogs in line with the end vise dog. The holes angle toward the vise at 5° so the bench dogs straighten up under pressure. To keep the dogs from sliding down when in use, I tacked small strips of rubber to the underside of the bench, partially overlapping the dog holes. But I was afraid vigorous pounding on the bench might make the dogs fall out, so I screwed and glued a ledge to the base that supports the inside half of the dogs. I can easily reach under the bench to push the dogs up, and when not in use, they are firm against the ledge.

Long stock support

For the times when I have a long piece of stock clamped in the front vise, I made a bench slave to support the free end (see the photo above). The outer face of the slave leg is in the same plane as the inner jaw of the shoulder vise. I use the bench dogs and the ledge beneath them as a way of locking the slave to the table. Instead of making it freestanding, with feet that might get in my way, I built a kind of peg leg with a brace near the top that slides under the benchtop and rests on the ledge beneath the bench dogs. I drilled a slightly oversized hole through the brace, so it can easily be locked in place under any of the bench dogs.

Bench slave holds long stock—The author made a bench slave with a brace at the top that locks into the 1-in. dowel bench dogs he uses. Round dogs are easier to make and install than traditional square dogs.

The stock rest, a block of solid wood, is attached to the leg with a toilet bolt that slides in a T-slot (as shown in the drawing detail on p. 67) and can be locked at any height on the slave. To make the leg, I cut a shallow groove in a piece of ¾-in. solid wood and glued it, grooved side in, to a piece of ½-in. plywood; then I cut a narrower groove in the outside face, forming a T-slot for the head of the toilet bolt. A spline glued into the back of the stock rest rides in the stem of the slot.

My bench was relatively inexpensive to build and serves my purpose well. I like the big top, and the vises can hold everything I work on, from big doors to the occasional miniature. Doors on a base like this might look good, but the ease of access would be lost, and in a shop, efficiency comes before aesthetics.

FOUR PLANES THAT EARN THEIR KEEP

by Sven Hanson

After 20 years of mechanizing and jigifying my woodshop, I have to admit that the four planes shown in the photo below are still my most cost-effective tools. Not all by themselves, mind you. But they work as part of a complementary system that capitalizes on the efficiency of machinery and power tools to do the bulk work quickly and on the versatility of hand tools, especially planes, to do fine detail work. The four planes that I use regularly—smooth plane, jack plane, low-angle block plane and bullnose plane—also happen to be my favorite tools to use, period.

The Stanley Co. refined the designs of their cast-iron planes back in the late 1800s. Stanley-style planes, which are now made by a number of manufacturers, still deliver the goods in 1995. Sure, they take some time to master, but so do power tools. You have to set up planes properly and maintain them (see the sidebar on pp. 72-73), but investing

Handplanes complement power tools. Clockwise from left: a No. 4 for smoothing and flattening, a No. 5 for truing edges, a bullnose chisel plane for cleaning up rabbets and joinery, and a low-angle block plane for chamfering and trimming.

Buy a thick blade to stop chatter

More than one authority on handplanes has said that the route to clean planing is paved by a thicker blade. After trying several of them, I have to agree. Even if a thick iron is poorly seated to the frog, the iron's greater thickness reduces vibration and, hence, the stuttering that you often get with a thin blade as it skips across the wood.

Thick blades used to be the norm. Some of the earliest ones were tapered in thickness over their length. Luckily, you can still get thick antique blades, which offer the advantage of laminated construction. Old blade forgers put a layer of very hard but brittle steel on the top of the blade over cheaper, softer and more flexible steel. This yields a heavy blade that holds its edge for a long time.

Hock Handmade Knives offers new, thick replacement blades in a variety of sizes (available from Garrett Wade, 161 Avenue of the Americas, New York, N.Y. 10013; 800-221-2942 or Frog Tool Co., 700 W. Jackson Blvd., Chicago, Ill. 60661; 800-648-1270). You can find thick antique blades at auctions, tool swaps and flea markets.

But antique blades usually need work, such as removing rust pits, flattening the backs and sharpening. Also, you may have to narrow the iron to fit a new plane body or extend the cap-iron screw slot. But boy, can these irons cut and last.

—S.H.

a little time here will raise your work to a higher level. Even better, planes are quiet and don't make any dust. The joy of using finely crafted handplanes, woodworkers' mainstays since Roman times, just puts the frosting on the cake.

Integrating planes into everyday shop work

For serious stock preparation, I use a tablesaw, a bandsaw, a planer, a jointer and several routers. Then I turn to my arsenal of planes. I'm not talking about antique, wooden planes here. These are modern, metal planes, carefully tuned to have flat soles with sharp, well-bedded blades set at the right depth of cut.

The Stanley Co. assigned numbers to their various planes. Bench planes started with a No. 1 (the smallest and least common) and ended with a No. 8 jointer plane, which is the largest. Numbers higher than eight just identify the type of plane and do not indicate size. In everyday shop work, I use a No. 4 smooth plane to level and smooth surfaces, a No. 5 jack plane to joint edges for glue-up and a No. 90 bullnose plane to clean up rabbets and bevel inside corners.

I also use a low-angle block plane (Stanley No. 60½) as a utility player. It's great for one-handed jobs, like planing end grain,

chamfering and truing. And it's great for getting into tight places. I like it for smoothing certain difficult woods, too. Here's the way I use each of the four planes in my normal work:

Use two smooth planes: one for flattening, one for smoothing

I once tried to save six cents per board foot by buying unsurfaced boards and planing them to the right thickness with a scrub plane. After my arms turned to rubber and I was soaked in sweat, I decided to skip the scrub plane. It's much easier to buy surfaced lumber that's already fairly flat and smooth and consistent in dimension, color and grain pattern.

I still use a plane to do a little hogging, though. Once in a while, I use my No. 4 Bailey (a high grade of Stanley) smooth plane fitted with a thick, spare blade that has its edge rounded, like the tip of an adze. (See the sidebar above to learn more about thicker irons.) I grind and hone this plane iron at the usual 25° to 30° bevel, and by moving the frog and the iron, I adjust the throat (the opening formed by the edge of the blade in the mouth of the sole) so that it's fairly wide.

For general planing, however, I use two planes: a "roughing" smooth plane, which has the throat ⅛ in. open and the cap iron set back $\frac{1}{16}$ in. from the edge of the blade, and a "finishing" smooth plane, which has a $\frac{1}{16}$ in. or smaller throat and the cap iron set $\frac{1}{64}$ in. or less back from the blade edge.

When making heavy cuts, like flattening a board, I skew the roughing plane to the grain to make a slicing cut. Because I slightly crown the edge of the blade in this plane, there's less contact with the wood. This, combined with the skew, makes for relatively easy work and minimal tearout.

I find smooth planes especially handy in two common situations. The first is where two pieces of wood intersect—as they do in a door frame. I plane the adjoining surfaces one at a time until they are flush. The other is when I'm taking down high spots to get an even surface. For both of these jobs, I use the finishing smooth plane, fitted with a blade set for a light cut. Because the frog is adjusted for a small throat, it supports the blade edge. Taking the time to make these adjustments makes the plane easy to push and produces a smooth finish. The drawing on p. 72 shows what happens when the plane is adjusted correctly.

With the finishing smooth plane, I leave the cutting edge straight, but I round just the corners of the iron so they don't dig in. I skew the plane slightly and use shallow strokes in overlapping passes, which reduces tearout when I have to plane across or against the grain. I use slight pressure at the front of the sole during the start of a cut and shift pressure to the back as I finish. I do this to prevent rounding over the ends of the work. I'm actually lifting the heel and then the toe. To picture this, visualize the board from the side, and work as if you were planing a hollow in the middle by easing up on each end of the cut.

Regardless of which type of smooth plane I'm using, I hold the plane firmly without strangling it by the handles. Your hands can't feel what's happening if you use a death grip. Use a lighter grip, and let your fingers help guide the plane. To plane the edge of a board, wrap your fingers part way around the plane, and touch the sides of the wood. Use your fingers as a fence (see the photo above). To plane wide surfaces, rest your thumb on one side of the

Two versatile workhorses. The author uses a No. 4 smooth plane to flatten and smooth boards. With its sole waxed and skewed to the work, the plane easily removes millmarks from a piece of padauk. To joint edges, he uses the No. 5 jack plane in the background.

plane and fingers on the other. You can point your forefinger in the direction you're planing. If you aren't getting a good shaving, then expose less blade or sharpen it.

A jack plane with a crowned blade is great for edge-jointing

The jack plane, slightly longer than a smooth plane, probably got its name from either jack-of-all-trades or a mule. From either origin, you get the idea that this tool is a hard worker. Most furnituremakers take a No. 7 or No. 8 plane to joint edges because they are long (over 20 in.) and heavy. I prefer a No. 5, 14-in.-long jack plane for this task. It takes more trial fitting of the boards, but the jack is easier to handle. You could even substitute a smooth plane for jointing, but it is a bit short. In any case, you'll need a blade profile suited to jointing, not smoothing.

The blade for jointing should be crowned so that the middle of the edge is about 0.01 in. higher than the corners. I've tried other shapes and found that an iron without a crown wanders like a car without a steering wheel.

There's another reason to crown the blade. To correct the edge of a board that's out of square with a straightedge blade, you have to choose between angling the blade to the sole or tilting the plane to cut down the high side of the edge.

It's hard to tilt the tool freehand such a small amount. Likewise, it's not easy to angle the blade in the plane accurately (I angle it the wrong way half the time). But if you use a crowned blade, you can correct a beveled edge by planing with one side of

Five steps to tune your plane

A tune-up will improve any plane's performance. Sadly, many new planes need this more than old ones. Manufacturers often machine the sole before the casting is fully cured, which can leave the sole twisted or cupped. Most new planes don't have sharp blades either. Before using a plane, I correct these problems by following an easy, five-step tune-up procedure.

Bench-plane adjustments ___

A cutaway view of a Bailey-style smoothing plane shows what the cap iron does (detail A) and what happens to a shaving when the throat is small (detail B).

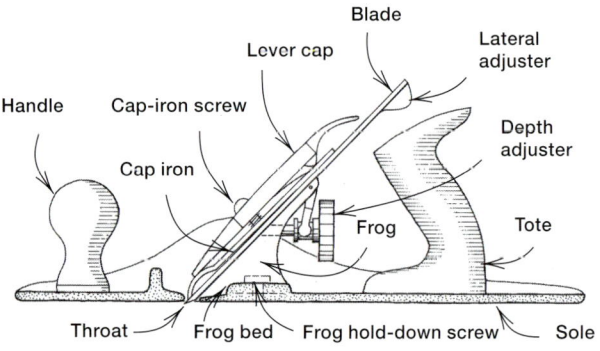

DETAIL A: CAP-IRON FUNCTION

With the cap iron set close to the tip of the blade, you can take a fine cut without tearout. The chipbreaker forces the shaving to curl, not tear out.

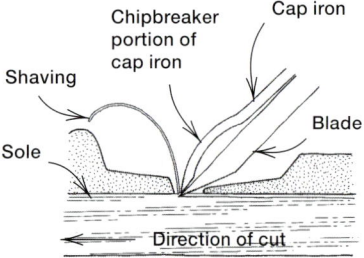

DETAIL B: PLANING WITH A SMALL THROAT

Down pressure of throat's leading edge keeps wood from lifting and splitting out.

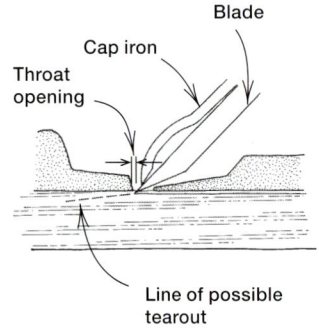

1) Flatten the sole: To check the sole for flatness, I install the blade 1/64 in. short of the sole and tension the lever cap as if I'm about to plane. Then, with a strong light shining from behind, I drag a straight-edge along the sole diagonally while looking along the bottom. Where light is peeking through, I draw lines across the sole with a permanent marker. Then I hold the sole to the platen of my 6x48 stationary belt sander. I use a worn 120- or 150-grit belt. If you don't have a stationary sander, you can make a fixture for a portable belt sander (see the top photo at left on the facing page).

After less than a minute of steady pressure, I check my progress. The disappearing lines tell me how I'm doing. I make sure that, at the least, the area just in front of the throat is flat. By installing an ultra-fine belt, you can polish the sole.

2) Sharpen the blade: To sharpen my irons, I mount an old 150- or 180-grit aluminum oxide belt to my sander. Using a protractor, I check the blade's existing bevel for its proximity to 25°, so I know whether to adjust the angle when sanding. Don't worry about being exact. Sharpness is far more important than a bevel at exactly 25°. I darken the bevel with a marker and draw cross lines using a square on the blade's back, behind the edge. Now I can see where I'm working and which way to tilt the blade. While I'm set up, I bring out all my plane irons and sharpen them too.

After flattening the back of the iron and dressing the bevel, I grind both surfaces on a soft Arkansas stone that's lubricated with Neatsfoot or glove oil, which I get at a local Kmart or sporting-goods store. I can go directly to this step if I haven't let the blade get too dull.

To find the proper angle (see the top right photo on the facing page), I touch the thick part of the bevel and then tilt the blade forward until oil squishes out from under the tip. I usually tilt up a bit more (about 5°) to create a microbevel. You'll hear a slightly higher pitch as you reach the tip. Following the

Belt sander dresses plane parts. A simple fixture allows Hanson to clamp his belt sander on its side with the trigger on. He trues up the leading edge of a cap iron, so it mates tightly to the blade, preventing shavings from clogging the tool.

To touch up blade edges quickly, Hanson uses oil-stones lubricated with Neatsfoot oil. Without losing much planing time, he can dress an edge before it gets dull. He uses a soft Arkansas stone and then a black oilstone for a surgical edge.

Power drill makes a portable honer—By clamping his electric drill to a worktable and chucking in a polishing wheel, Hanson creates a makeshift honing station. Used like a buffing wheel, the setup works well in the shop or at a job site.

4) Dress the cap iron: A cap iron has a sinuous-looking chipbreaker that acts like a speed bump to prevent shavings from shooting up the ramp as the blade is shearing off wood. The leading edge of the cap iron should contact the flat side of the blade tightly to prevent shavings from getting clogged between the two. To dress the cap-iron edge (I undercut it a bit), I use a file and my belt sander (see the top photo at left). I polish the chipbreaker, so the shavings will glide over it. And I ease the front of the lever cap with a file, so there's not an abrupt junction between it and the top of the cap iron.

Arkansas stone, I use a black oilstone. Alternating between the back and the bevel on the last strokes eliminates any wire edge.

An optional last step is honing. I rig up a fixture to hold my electric drill (see the photo above). Holding the bevel of the blade to a polishing wheel, I make sure I'm at the correct angle. While honing, I apply buffing compound to the wheel occasionally and cool the blade with water from a spray bottle.

3) Seat the blade: Plane chatter usually is caused by poorly machined areas in the frog bed or gunk between the bed and the blade. On better planes, I unscrew and lift out the adjustable frog. If cleaning the bed doesn't seat the blade, then I grind the bed flat, like the sole. Other styles of planes are trickier. I have to reach inside with a bastard file and flatten the whole bed without rounding it at the back of the throat.

With the first three tune-up steps done, a plane can cut smoothly with the grain. But because I'm planing against the grain half the time, I usually take the tune-up two steps further to reduce tearout.

5) Adjust the throat: On a bench plane, the front of the throat holds the shaving down and forces it around a sharp bend. The smaller the throat opening, the tighter the turn and the better the resistance to tearout. With a small throat, about the worst you will get is shallow, misdemeanor damage instead of felony tearout.

On a block plane with an adjustable throat plate, I decrease the throat to the smallest opening that won't choke on chips. For bench planes, I experiment with moving the frog and setting the blade depth. The blade isn't supported as well when you move it away from the back of the throat. Because of this, thin blades often chatter. I fix that by using a thick blade. I can usually guess the right combination of adjustments to get a small throat. However, because I've reduced the depth of cut, I've incurred a multi-stroke penalty, meaning that the job will take longer to finish. That's why I set up a second smoothing plane with a larger throat for rougher work.

To reduce plane-to-wood friction, I wax the sole with a candle. When you're prepping wood for glue-up or finishing, though, clean off the wax with mineral spirits before you make the last few passes.

—S.H.

the iron on the high side of the board. With practice, you can straighten a twisted edge in a pass or two. Once you learn the right body English, you'll be getting joints that close as tightly as the doors to Scrooge's vault.

Other than having a crowned blade for jointing and a relatively open throat, I set the rest of my jack plane just like a finishing smooth plane. That is, the blade has a razor edge, the sole is flat and the frog is seated firmly in the sole. It's also important that the leading edge of the cap iron mate tightly to the flat side of the blade (see the sidebar on pp. 72-73).

To joint a pair of boards for glue-up, I first run the mating edges over the power jointer. This usually leaves a bit of snipe on the end. Next I clamp one board into the bench vise and balance the second on top to see how the two butt. I look for areas of no contact and mark high spots on the sides. Lifting the top board off, I draw pencil lines across the edge of the bottom board every inch or so. The idea isn't to plane off the pencil lines, but to use them as indicators. I plane the high areas and leave the low ones. The disappearing marks let me know where and how deeply I'm cutting and whether the blade is sitting level.

A block plane is a great multipurpose tool

Block planes are little gems. If I were stranded on a desert island and could only own one plane, I'd have a block plane. They've been around a long time but were dormant in many tool chests for years—until British Arts-and-Crafts woodworkers reintroduced exposed joinery in furniture at the turn of the 20th century. Block planes are ideal for trimming the end grain of through-tenons and dovetails. A block plane's absence of a cap iron and its easy-to-remove lever cap make it the fastest plane to sharpen and put back into service. That makes it a good choice any time you think you might nick the blade on an embedded nail or gum up the blade with old paint.

A block plane's blade sits upside down in the plane—at a 20° slope in a standard block plane or a $12\frac{1}{2}°$ angle in a low-angle block plane. With the blade inverted, there's no place to fit a cap iron. To control tearout, you need to adjust the cutter depth and throat opening carefully and recheck it often. The better models have adjustable throats. Changing the direction of your strokes and the amount that you skew the tool also improves the cut.

Block planes work well as one-handed tools. When a workpiece needs a quick

A block plane is a handy trimming tool. Conveniently held in one hand, a block plane can pare the end grain of a stile in a frame and true up hard-to-get-at places.

Chamfer adds a finished look to pieces. With a block plane, you can relieve edges and corners to make them easier on the hands and on the eyes. Here, the author chamfers a cypress door frame.

swipe and I can steady it with one hand and plane with the other, I use a block plane (see the bottom left photo on the facing page). I like the low-angle variety best because it cuts plywood, fiberboard, plastics and laminates cleaner than other planes. Freshly sharpened, a block plane can trim projecting plugs and tenons without fracturing the wood fibers below the surface. Block planes also can chamfer crisply (see the bottom right photo on the facing page).

A bullnose plane refines joinery and gets into corners

Once you're hooked on the first three planes, you'll soon add a bullnose plane, which is actually a shoulder plane with a short, stout nose. Because the body of this plane is square, it does a great job on tenon shoulders and cheeks, and in dadoes and rabbets (see the photo at right).

I prefer Stanley and Record models because they are a combination shoulder and chisel plane. You can buy other bullnose planes for around $20, but they lack a removable front piece to make it easier to work in tight quarters, and they don't have a screw for adjusting blade depth for making ultra-fine cuts.

Like a block plane, a bullnose plane has its blade bevel-side up. But unlike a block plane, a bullnose plane is very demanding to set right. More than any other plane I own, the bullnose has to be adjusted carefully to coax out its peak performance. I hone the straight bevel of the blade razor sharp with perfectly square corners. The cutting edge and the sides of the blade must align with (or be just a hair over) the bottom and sides of the plane. Otherwise, you'll get stepped cuts that will slowly drive you out of a corner and out of square. I grind about a 10° bevel on each side of the blade.

Bullnose planes are great for several things: truing up the rabbets in a carcase to receive the back of the cabinet, beveling an edge near an adjacent surface, trimming corners in mitered frames or shaving down fat tenons. Further, you can widen a rabbet or dado by extending the blade past the side of the body to scrape the sidewall lightly. Last, but not least, with the front shoe removed, you can plane right up to a corner or joint.

It's like using a chisel in a steadying jig. This is helpful for things like cleaning up the rabbet for the glass in a mirror frame.

Other handplanes worth honorable mention

Besides the four planes mentioned, I have another standby plane in my trusty collection: a Stanley Multiplane. Though I use it less often, it's handy for shaping moldings that router bits can't duplicate and getting into places that bits can't reach. Because a Multiplane (a No. 45 or the less-common No. 55) has a fence and rides on rails instead of a continuous sole, it is more involved to use than other planes.

It's also worth mentioning rabbet and dado planes, which do what their names suggest. Rabbet planes can have one or both sides of the blade flush to its sides, and, like a Multiplane, a rabbet plane comes with a fence and a depth gauge. By making their own paths, dado planes can work below a surface to plow a groove or dado. Good rabbet and dado planes are expensive. But because they do their jobs so well, it's worth hunting around for them at flea markets.

A bullnose chisel plane cuts into a corner. After routing rabbets in a padauk mirror frame, the author uses a Record bullnose plane to clean up the rabbets inside the mitered corners. With the nose removed, it works just like a chisel.

FURTHER READING

The Handplane Book, Garrett Hack, The Taunton Press, 63 S. Main Street, Newtown, CT 06470

The Antique Tool Collector's Guide to Value, Ronald S. Barlow, Windmill Publishing, El Cajon, CA 92020

Plane Basics, Sam Allen, Sterling Publishing Co., 387 Park Avenue S., New York, NY 10016-8810

Fine Woodworking #14, #65 and #99 (tuning bench planes)

Fine Woodworking #35, #98 and #99 (choosing and using bench planes)

Fine Woodworking #39, #54 and #105 (block planes)

Fine Woodworking #67 and #76 (shoulder and rabbet planes)

Fine Woodworking #29, #61 and #81 (sharpening blades)

THREE EVERYDAY CHISELS

by Sven Hanson

Basic bench chisels—Bevel-edge chisel (left), firmer chisel and mortise chisel all have different tasks in the workshop.

The number one cleanup device in my shop isn't a broom or a vacuum, as any visitor can tell you. It's a chisel. Every ragged rabbet, gloppy glueline or oversized tenon can be improved by the touch of a sharp chisel. When fine joinery is required, it's a sure thing chisels will be part of creating the perfect fit. You need chisels to chop out hand-cut dovetails, to square the corners of router-cut rabbets and to trim countersunk plugs.

The bench chisel family tree has three main branches: bevel-edge chisels for a variety of trimming and paring work, mortise chisels for serious chopping, and the catchall category of firmer chisels for light-duty mortising or heavy-duty paring (see the photo above).

There are other, more specialized types of chisels. But your workshop will be well equipped if you carefully choose a few chisels from each of the three main groups.

The main thing to consider when shopping for chisels is your needs. If you plan to do a lot of heavy chopping in hardwoods, the money invested in tools with reinforced handles and properly tempered steel will be well worth it. But if you use chisels infrequently or if you use them for light-duty work, you could get by with moderately priced tools. And if you need chisels to do some rough work, like chopping away at interior trim where there's the likelihood of hitting nails, buy inexpensive chisels.

Chisels demand proper striking tools. Handles with metal striking caps or ferrules at both ends can be whacked with a hammer; unreinforced handles require a mallet. Wooden mallets, which come in a variety of weights and shapes, give you the most control and are friendly to a chisel's handle.

Choose the chisels for your shop

I have collected a pretty full set of each style of chisel, but they're not all necessary. Bevel-edge chisels, so called because they have three bevels on their faces, fit easily inside dadoes and dovetails. I use my $^1/_2$-in. and $^3/_4$-in. chisels all the time and chop out dovetails with $^3/_8$-in., $^1/_2$-in. or $^5/_8$-in. chisels.

When picking out mortising chisels, select ones based on the size mortises you plan to chop. These are costly; there's no value in owning a whole set if you routinely chop out only $^1/_4$-in. mortises. I find $^1/_8$-in., $^1/_4$-in., $^3/_8$-in. and $^1/_2$-in. mortise chisels serve most of my needs.

My firmer chisels play the utility infielder position, doing the work that might damage a thin-blade bevel-edge chisel or chopping small mortises on more delicate projects. You might need a few, ranging in size from $^1/_4$ in. to $^3/_4$ in.

Bevel-edge chisels are used in tight quarters

Along one leg of my Bermuda work triangle formed by bench, tablesaw and jointer, I've mounted a kitchen-style magnetic knife holder. It holds a handful of bevel-edge chisels, which I use more frequently than either my firmer or mortise chisels.

Bevel-edge chisels are sometimes called paring chisels, and there are two sub-categories. Short, sturdy paring chisels are

BEVEL-EDGE CHISEL
Beveled sides allow a dovetail chisel to squeeze into tight quarters.

called butt or carpenter's chisels, and long-blade ones are known as dovetail chisels.

Butt chisels get into tight quarters

You'll find some version of the short, sturdy chisel in every carpenter's tool belt. You don't need a long, delicate chisel for chopping out a $^1/_8$-in.-deep door hinge mortise. And if you're working inside a cabinet, the short butt chisel allows you room enough to swing a hammer without striking the other side of the case. This chisel is easy to hold and maneuver across a glued-up panel when scraping squeeze-out.

Dovetail chisels have long blades

A dovetail chisel's long blade makes it easier to see your work and gauge whether you're holding the tool perpendicular to the workpiece. Dovetail chisels have blades that are sharply beveled on the sides to allow you to work right into the triangular bottom of a dovetail joint (see the photo above).

I rely on countersunk and plugged screws to hold a lot of things together. Dovetail chisels are great for paring off the screw plug flush to the frame, because I can approach the cut with the long blade nearly flat on the wood. I take a careful trial cut across the top of the plug to find the paring direction that goes with the grain. I take

FIRMER CHISEL
Instead of heading back to the tablesaw to narrow a tight tenon, use a razor-sharp firmer chisel. Its square edge rides along a tenon's shoulder and makes paper-thin shavings.

class tools. As a result, they're usually the sharpest of the bunch. These chisels come in handy when you have to pare down a tight tenon (see the photo at left). For good control when taking off a thin shaving, you can use their square sides to ride along the tenon's shoulder.

If you want to do some serious chopping, the double-hooped handle with leather shock ring at the blade's shoulder can take a hard shot with a 22-oz. framing hammer. The only maintenance besides sharpening is grinding off the mushroom edge that forms on the hoop that protects the butt end from splitting. I round it back by rolling the edge against the belt sander.

Mortise chisels need to be strong

Mortise chisels are the big brutes of the chisel world. They have rectangular blades that can be thicker than they are wide. You need this heft when prying out a chip that's wedged deep inside a mortise.

Quality mortise chisels have a very hefty tang, a steel extension of the blade that fits up into the handle. The sturdiest have re-inforcing ferrules, also called hoops, at the tang and at the butt of the handle to prevent splitting when the chisel is struck with a hammer or mallet. If a mortising chisel does not have a ferrule at the striking end of the handle, it's meant to be used with a non-metal mallet.

To reduce the chance of splitting a work-piece when chopping mortises, I clamp a hand screw to the sides of the stock where the waste will be removed (see the photo on the facing page). A second clamp holds the whole piece firmly to the workbench. Besides preventing splitting, this clamp system lets you cut faster and with more control while keeping chips from creeping under the workpiece and dinging it.

roughly $1/16$-in. slices off the plug to pare it flush to the surrounding surface. It's not as fast as beltsanding but if done carefully, you get better results with less noise and less risk to the surrounding surface.

Firmer chisels look like skinny mortise chisels

The firmer chisel is a compromise tool that is often too light for heavy-duty mortising but too thick to work inside the confines of furniture joints. This chisel is also called a sash mortise chisel, named by American makers of window sashes, or a registered mortise chisel. Firmer chisels have only one bevel on the face, like mortise chisels, and the blades are thinner than they are wide.

I own a set of ash-handled Greenlee firmers. They reside in their own drawer away from the squalor of everyday working-

MORTISE CHISEL
Mortise chisels are as thick as they are wide and are built to withstand the heavy forces inherent in chopping and prying out waste.

Anatomy of chisels

There are two main components to chisels: the steel and the handle. Determining what kind of steel and how well a tool has been tempered can't be done by eye. You can get an idea about the strength of the handle by looking for reinforcing ferrules or striking caps and examining how it's fastened to the steel, whether by a socket (strongest) or a skinny tang (weakest).

I'm not obsessed with finding just the right hardness rating for my chisels. If you order tools from big mail-order outlets, you can usually find out about the type of tool steel and hardness of the chisels they carry. But if you pick up a set at the local hardware store, that information may not be available to you.

Michael Burke, technical advisor at Garrett Wade, a mail-order tool supplier, told me that "most chisels range around Rc58 to Rc61 (Rockwell C hardness scale) with Japanese chisels running about three points higher. The precise hardness doesn't really matter because a difference of a point or two is like the difference between 600-grit and 700-grit sandpaper."

I have noticed that the most inexpensive chisels on the market are often on the soft side, although I have seen a few that were quite hard and brittle. Hardness is both a function of the metal's carbon content (and other additives) and how the tool was hardened and tempered.

Good tool steel has enough additives to allow hardening, which is accomplished by heating the metal to cherry red and then quickly cooling the tool. It is then reheated to a lower temperature, which reduces or tempers the hardness, making it less brittle and easier to sharpen. A chisel with a very hard tip is prone to chipping.

Conversely, poor steel that has not been hardened properly or steel that has been tempered too soft will bend at the thin cutting edge when pounded into hardwood. It will, however, be easy to grind and sharpen. Toolmakers aim for a balance between these two qualities.

Good steel, quality control in hardening and tempering, and strong handles add to the price of a chisel. Medium- and high-quality chisels will cost about $10 to $30, sometimes more, apiece.

Sockets are found on the best chisels
Top-of-the-line older chisels were hand-forged with sockets. The blacksmith would pound one end of the metal around an anvil and create a conical section for the handle to fit inside. Modern socket chisels have their sockets machine-forged or welded on.

Angling for precision cuts

Not all bevels are created equal. If you cut hardwoods, a steeper bevel on your chisel will stay sharp longer. If you cut softwoods, you will need a shallow bevel angle to shear the wood fibers, not crush them. I use secondary, or microbevels, on all my chisels. The bevel-edge and firmer chisels get a very short microbevel at the cutting edge, which is created when I'm doing my final honing on a superfine stone. I lift the chisel up just slightly to create that microbevel. That way, when I resharpen, I only have to hone a very narrow edge, not the entire bevel.

For softwoods, a microbevel of 27° or so allows easier entry into the wood (see the near drawing at right). For hardwoods, a microbevel of 30° to 35° cuts cleanly enough and stays sharp longer than a more acute bevel. If you plan to do a lot of hand-paring, you'll want microbevels in the 27° to 30° range. But if you plan to use a heavy mallet, microbevels of 30° or more will hold an edge longer.

For fine work on delicate projects no matter what the wood, I use a 27° to 30° microbevel, especially when using the chisel without a mallet. This angle decreases the force necessary to cut. I pay for it with more frequent sharpening.

I modify the bevels on my mortise chisels by grinding the long bevel about 28° and honing a

secondary bevel of about 35° to 40° at the tip (see the drawing at right below). The long bevel permits easy passage of the chisel body into the nether regions of a cut. The blunt tip leaves more metal where it counts. —S.H.

SHARPENING ANGLES FOR BEVEL-EDGE AND FIRMER CHISELS

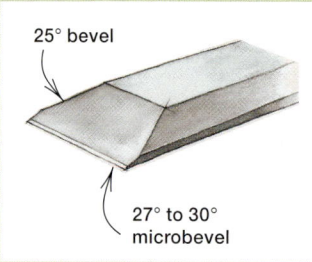

25° bevel

27° to 30° microbevel

For chiseling softwoods or hand-paring, grind a shallow microbevel of 27° to 30°. When working in hardwoods, a tip ground 30° to 35° will hold up longer.

REGRIND MORTISE CHISELS WITH A LONG BEVEL

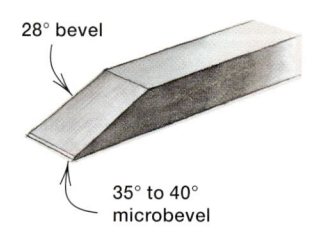

28° bevel

35° to 40° microbevel

Sockets are available on all three types of chisels. When you strike a socket chisel, the wooden handle compresses into the tapered socket, which keeps everything firmly united.

Look for a sturdy handle

The handle, not the blade, is the Achilles heel of most chisels. When chopping mortises, all the force of a hard-swung mallet strikes a spot that's 1 in. in diameter or less. Chisel handles made of wood come with and without reinforcing ferrules, which increase their strength. A lot of chisels are made with plastic handles, and I've found these to be very sturdy even though they don't have that traditional look and warm feel of wood. If you plan to use a hammer to strike them, buy ones with metal striking caps.

Wood tends to split if struck hard. To counter that, the makers of wooden tool handles taper them. The small-diameter end helps center the mallet's blow to the tool and reduces splitting. Toolmakers often add metal ferrules to the handle to keep the wood fibers squeezed tightly together. If the grain is straight and you avoid metal hammers, single-ferrule chisels are durable enough.

Many craftspeople prefer a heftier handle. A chisel handle made of wood with ferrules at both ends can take a lot of force. These chisels can be used with metal hammers or large mallets.

There's another way to strengthen a handle. Some chisels are made with a thick leather washer pressed over a tenon round left projecting from the end of the turned handle. This evens the blow around the edge of the handle and prevents splitting. These are medium-duty chisels meant to be used by hand or with a light mallet.

Mallets deliver a little or a lot of power

You can use a hammer when striking chisels, but it's best to use a wooden or hard plastic mallet. They're much kinder on handles. Mallets, with their large faces, also make it easier to deliver the force of the blow to the chisel instead of, say, the hand holding the chisel. Good mallets run from $12 to $50.

Mallets come in various weights. I find that 16-oz. to 22-oz. mallets are suitable for chopping dovetails. For heavier work, such as chopping mortises, 22-oz. to 32-oz. mallets work well. There are some woodworkers who favor 3-lb. mallets, but it certainly takes a lot of strength to handle one of these behemoths for hours on end.

Mallets also come in different shapes. The big square mallets, called joiner's mallets, are usually the heaviest of the bunch and great for use with mortise chisels. For tight quarters or for chopping at odd angles, a round carver's mallet works well. You can also use a rubber mallet or a dead-blow hammer.

Safety glasses protect your eyes from flying chips

Experience has taught me three rules for safe chisel use. First, keep all your body parts behind the tip of the chisel, well out of its path. Second, clamp down the workpiece unless it's so heavy that it won't move while chopping. And third, always wear safety glasses. Ordinary eyeglasses will do for paring on the benchtop, but when I use a hammer or work overhead, I'm partial to goggles.

One time, when I took a chisel to the underside of a teak handrail while wearing ordinary eyeglasses—not safety glasses—a grain of dirt rolled past my glasses into my eye, and it stuck. I learned my lesson.

THE BASICS OF BACKSAWS

by Zachary Gaulkin

There is an old truth buried under mountains of machine-made sawdust—the best way to sever wood is with a thin, sharp blade. This is the beauty of the backsaw. With its swaged metal spine, a backsaw can carry the thinnest of blades, allowing it to slice wood with minimum waste and maximum control. No one can deny the aggressive speed of a tablesaw or a sliding chopsaw, but for joinery (and quiet pleasure) it's hard to beat the backsaw's surgical precision.

Another great thing about this most critical hand tool is that it is a whole lot cheaper than a screaming armada of cutting machines. A backsaw is one of the cheapest tools you can buy, especially if you plan to do lots of joinery by hand. Best of all, it doesn't take much to master. True, it involves some practice, but success with a backsaw is not so much about skill as it is about choosing the right saw and keeping it sharp.

PUSH VS. PULL TECHNOLOGY
European saws cut on the push stroke, so they must be thick enough not to buckle or bend. Japanese saws can be thinner because they cut on the pull stroke, when the blade is in tension.

A sharp backsaw won't just make you a better woodworker; it will turn you into a surgeon.

EUROPEAN RIP VS. CROSSCUT

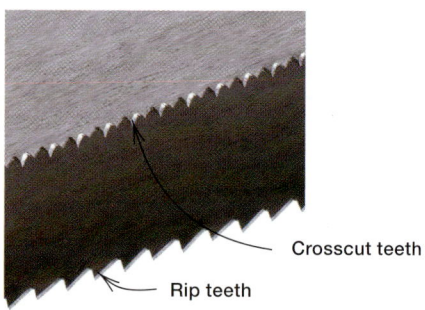

Crosscut teeth

Rip teeth

Rip teeth are usually larger than crosscut teeth, and they are filed straight across the steep leading edge. Crosscut teeth have bevels on the inside face to score and sever the grain.

A thin blade needs a strong back

The secret of the backsaw lies in its metal spine, which allows it to carry a thin blade. Whether you choose a European backsaw (left) or a Japanese dozuki (right), the backsaw is an essential hand tool for any woodworking shop.

A GOOD BACKSAW HANDLES SMOOTHLY
The handle should be comfortable, whether it's a handmade pistol-grip (left) or a rattan-wrapped handle that provides a good grip for the dozuki's pull stroke (right).

SOME BLADES YOU SHARPEN; OTHERS YOU JUST THROW OUT
Japanese backsaw blades can be removed from their handles for sharpening. Most cheaper saws come with replaceable blades, so you don't have the hassle of sharpening.

A BACKSAW HAS LIFE UNTIL THERE'S NO METAL LEFT
As long as the blade isn't bent or broken and rust hasn't invaded the steel, an old backsaw can be sharpened or retoothed to its original condition.

JAPANESE RIP VS. CROSSCUT

Crosscut teeth

Rip teeth

Japanese rip teeth are similar to European teeth, but the crosscut teeth look like tiny skew chisels with lots of cutting bevels.

SUBTLETY CAN BE PRICEY
Handcrafted dozukis can be filed, set and tensioned for different wood species and for specific applications. But they can be expensive and must be sent back to the maker for sharpening.

Get a grip

Backsaws come in many shapes and forms. Although the handles may differ, their defining characteristic is the metal back that supports and stiffens the thin blade. Unlike carpentry saws, backsaws have finer teeth and are used mainly for joinery.

TURNED HANDLE
A backsaw with a turned handle is often called a gent's saw. It can be used for dovetailing or cutting short tenons because the blades are usually narrow.

PISTOL GRIP
The wider, pistol-style handle (open or closed) provides more stability and a wider blade. These saws can be small, for dovetailing, or large, for mitering, crosscutting and cutting deep tenons.

JAPANESE HANDLE
The rattan-wrapped handles provide a secure grip for the pull-cutting action and can be used with replaceable blades that lock into a recess inside the handle.

REVERSIBLE HANDLE
The offset handle and spine on this reversible backsaw allows it to double as a flush-cutting saw. The teeth are filed on both sides to cut in either direction.

Rips and crosscuts seldom come in one package

All wood saws do two things and two things only: they rip along the grain and crosscut across it. Follow the direction of the grain and you're ripping. Cut a board perpendicular to the grain and you're crosscutting. You might think a simple saw can do both with equal ease, and sometimes it can. But the ripsaw that seemed like a scalpel cutting dovetail pins might leave a crosscut, such as a tenon shoulder, looking a little chewed up.

A saw's ability to rip or to crosscut lies in the geometry of its teeth—the size, shape and set, or the amount they are bent away from the blade. Rip teeth usually are bigger than crosscut teeth, their cutting faces are nearly straight up and down and flat across, and they have a small amount of set. The big teeth shave away material fast, and the deep gullets (the valleys between the teeth) give the shavings a place to go so the saw won't bind. The small set on a rip tooth creates a narrow kerf, making it less likely to wander.

Leave the sharpening to a professional

Using a backsaw is a pleasure. Sharpening one is another story. Some people try, but few can do it well. Most woodworkers don't even think about it until the thing just refuses to cut anymore. Sharpening your own saws is a valuable skill, but for most of us, it makes more sense to seek out professional help. A good sharpening service, though sometimes hard to find, can turn a rusty antique into a precision instrument or customize a new saw right out of the package.

If you're not sure whether your saw needs sharpening, it proba-

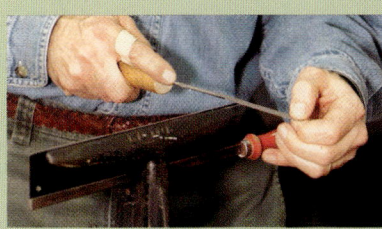

Sharpening a backsaw is a skill. A single pass will sharpen the teeth on this dovetail saw. Each stroke has to be even to keep the teeth uniform.

bly does. Even new saws need to be touched up. New backsaws generally come with punched teeth (one side of the blade is rolled over, and the other side has a slight burr) and,

therefore, cut more aggressively on one side. Filing, either by hand or machine, cleans up the edges and solves the problem.

A professional sharpener can also reduce or increase the set, depending on what kind of use you have in mind. (Many woodworkers say new backsaws come with far too much set.)

Sharpeners can file the teeth on old backsaws, or they can do much more, as long as the steel is solid and the blade isn't bent or warped. They can change the angle and set of the teeth or even retooth the saw entirely. —Z.G.

Crosscut teeth have more set, giving the body of the blade (sometimes called the plate) a wider path. The teeth are raked back (they don't have the steep leading edge of a rip tooth), and they are beveled to a point like an incisor, rather than filed straight across. These points enable a crosscut saw to score and sever the grain cleanly, without tearout.

Because backsaws are made for joinery and not for carpentry, the teeth tend to be small. The teeth still are filed for ripping or crosscutting, but the differences are not as noticeable as they are on big panel saws. So depending on your wallet and the level of perfection you hope to achieve, backsaws can be somewhat interchangeable. (In fact, most catalogs don't make a distinction between rip and crosscut backsaws; you have to ask.) It's certainly possible to rip with a crosscut backsaw (everybody does it), but it will take you longer, the teeth will probably get clogged with sawdust and the kerf might be a little ragged. You can miter or cut a tenon shoulder with a backsaw ground for ripping, but you'll probably have to clean up a shaggy edge with a plane or a chisel.

The most common backsaws you will find are European or Western in style. They cut on the push stroke, and they come in many styles: rip and crosscut, pistol grips and turned handles, long and short, brass-backed, and even reversible (see the photos on the facing page). They can have more or less set, and the teeth can be big, aggressive ones or small, fine ones. More teeth per inch (tpi) generally mean that you will get a finer, slower cut. (Backsaws range from 12 tpi to more than 20 tpi.)

Wil Neptune, an instructor at the North Bennet Street School in Boston, suggests that if you only want one European-style backsaw, it makes sense to get one that can rip well. That's because most joinery cuts—tenon cheeks and dovetails—are made along the grain, not across it. With a steady hand and sharp teeth, you can slice your dovetails without having to clean up the rip-cuts with a chisel. (You'll still have to chisel the shoulder, of course.) For crosscuts, such as tenon shoulders, you can get away with using the same saw by cutting to the waste side of the line and cleaning up the edge with a chisel. As Neptune points out, you rarely try to get a finished crosscut surface off the saw anyway.

My favorite backsaw: If you could have just one, which would it be?

Wil Neptune's orange-handled beauty is a bargain

What saw does cabinetmaker and teacher Wil Neptune reach for to cut a dovetail or tenon by hand? "That's easy," he says. "It's the cheesy one

with the blue blade and the painted orange handle." It costs $9.95 and has become a staple in the student toolboxes at the North Bennet Street School in Boston, where Neptune teaches woodworking. The saw comes from the factory a little rough. So he shows his students how to file the teeth and press out some of the set by sandwiching the blade between two old jointer knives and clamping it in a machinist's vise. "If you totally screw it up, throw it in a drywall bucket for site work, and buy a new one." The Eberle saw and file is available from J.I. Joseph Co. (617-723-2323).

A handmade *dozuki* can track a line like a bloodhound

John Reed Fox, a furnituremaker in Acton, Mass., has a simple philosophy about tools. If you are at all serious, buy the best you can afford. That's one of the reasons his favorite backsaw is a handmade *dozuki* crafted to his specifications. His *dozukis*, which he sends back to Japan every year or so for sharpening, are a dream to use. With a little camellia oil (a traditional Japanese saw lubricant), it can follow a line like bloodhound tracking a scent. Fox recently let a class of novice woodworking students use one of his *dozukis* to cut dovetails. "People were nailing the cuts right on the line, and they were

rank beginners," he says. "Everybody was astonished." A similar handmade saw is available for about $100 from Misugi Design (510-549-0805).

The antique miter saw revived for ripping

Allan Breed doesn't even know where his favorite backsaw came from. It's an old Henry Taylor, one of about a dozen backsaws he owns. After Breed reground the teeth for ripping, it has become his favorite dovetail saw, perfect for his unusual tail-

cutting technique: With the workpiece flat on a bench, he dangles the saw from his pinkie with the teeth pointing away from his body. This plumbs the saw, guaranteeing a square cut across the end grain. He plunges through each cut in two or three swipes (still hanging on by his pinkie finger) and moves onto the next one. "I can see what I'm doing, and it's more comfortable," he says. "I also wax my saws a lot, especially if there isn't a ton of set in them. It makes it a lot easier." For a good used saw, look around at yard sales and used-tool suppliers.
—Z.G.

Japanese saws give new meaning to severance pay

The variety of European backsaws is nothing compared with the Japanese equivalent, called a *dozuki*. What's the difference? There are many, but chief among them is that Japanese saws cut on the pull stroke, when the blade is in tension and won't buckle or bend. This means a Japanese saw can carry a thinner blade than its European counterpart (although the difference, again, is less apparent on backsaws than on saws made for carpentry).

There is also a dental difference: Rip teeth on a Japanese saw closely resemble a Western rip tooth. The cutting edge is nearly perpendicular to the blade, and the tooth comes to a point. But Japanese crosscut teeth are quite different from their Western counterparts. They have an angled top (the profile sort of resembles a skew chisel), and each facet is beveled. "They've got bevels all over the place," says John Reed Fox, a cabinetmaker in Acton, Mass., who uses Japanese handsaws almost exclusively.

You can go crazy choosing a *dozuki*, especially if you have an unlimited budget. A good Japanese saw smith can take into account things like wood density and moisture content, and can even tailor a saw to match the idiosyncrasies of a single woodworker's stroke. Subtlety comes at a price, though. Fox spends more than $100 for his handmade *dozukis*, which he sends back to Japan for sharpening. If you can't justify investing in a handmade saw, you can buy factory-made Japanese backsaws with replaceable blades for $50 or less. When the blade gets dull or breaks, just by a new one. According to those who swear by them, even cheap *dozukis* outperform good European-style saws.

A saw's true worth is measured in decibels

When is a whispering backsaw better than a power saw? It depends on whom you ask. Wil Neptune can cut a perfect tenon with a backsaw and chisel in minutes, leaving a thimbleful of sawdust. But he does so only on occasion. Machines are just too efficient if you have to make more than one, he says, "and when do you ever make something with one tenon?" But if he needs to miter something quickly or if an unusual joint requires lots of set-up time on a machine, a backsaw can be quite handy.

Dovetails are another story. Allan Breed, a Maine cabinetmaker, does all his dovetails by hand, racing through the cuts with an old miter saw reground for ripping. "I'll cut dovetails with anything as long as it's sharp," he says. Breed doesn't use handsaws for some romantic thrill. He does it for ergonomics and efficiency. Power saws and routers are loud, and you have to haul around a lot of metal. And on the kind of high-style reproductions that Breed makes, tooling up with machines hardly ever makes sense. For Fox, handsaws are a critical part of the work itself. With a handsaw, he can cut perfect dovetails less than an eighth of an inch apart, something no machine has yet been able to accomplish.

MASTERING THE TABLESAW

by Mark Duginske

The tablesaw is the heart of most wood-working shops. With a standard blade, you can make virtually any straight cut, and when fitted with a dado head, the tablesaw is the tool of choice for cutting grooves, dadoes and rabbets. When equipped with shopmade jigs, the tablesaw is the most efficient tool for finger joints, tenons and even dovetails.

Although undeniably versatile, the tablesaw also has its dark side. It is probably responsible for more injuries than any other

Don't dump your saw guard, adjust it

Tablesaw manufacturers spend hundreds of thousands of dollars to develop safety guards, but no tool guard is a guarantee of safety—constant vigilance is always your best safety equipment.

The saw guard: Most tablesaws sold in North America are equipped with a cage guard, which is a see-through plastic or metal guard with a sheet-metal spine that also serves as a splitter to keep the kerf from closing and pinching the blade (see the photo on p. 92). The spine is connected to the saw in two places, directly behind the blade and to the back trunnion, which allows the guard to tilt when the blade is tilted. A toothed antikickback mechanism hangs from the guard and rides on the workpiece.

This type of guard offers protection against kickback while also keeping your fingers away from the blade, but it is unwieldy in some situations. For example, it's hard to rip narrow pieces, or slide a push stick past the guard if the fence is close to the blade. And sometimes when crosscutting thick stock, the workpiece will wedge under the anti-kickback teeth. In addition, because the splitter is part of the cage guard, the entire guard must be removed when making a cut that does not sever the

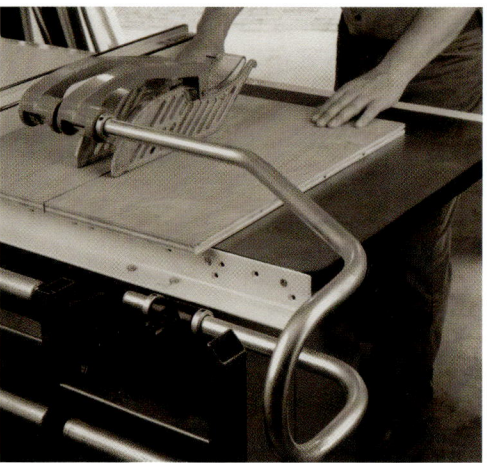

The Delta Uniguard (left), which features a retractable splitter (above) is a European-style overhead guard.

board, such as a dado or rabbet cut. The guard must also be removed when the workpiece is held vertically against the fence, such as when cutting tenons with a jig. Because these guards are time-consuming to remove and replace, they are often left off the tool, in spite of the operator's and manufacturer's best intentions.

The Delta Uniguard, as shown in the photo above, is similar to overhead guards found on many European saws. The splitter used with this type of guard is a small piece of metal that is attached to the back trunnion. Sometimes the splitter is entirely independent from the guard, and in other cases, woodworking tool. Many of those injuries could be avoided if woodworkers used blade guards and splitters (see the sidebar below) and if they took the time to set up and to align the rip fence and miter gauge properly (see the sidebar on p. 90). But above all, for safe operation of a tablesaw, you must understand the fundamentals of ripping and crosscutting.

Using the rip fence

The rip fence is a straight edge aligned parallel to the blade that slides along a bar at the front of the saw table. When the fence is locked to the bar, the distance between the blade and the fence determines the width of cut. To rip safely and accurately, the workpiece must lie flat on the table with

a straight edge against the rip fence. If the edge is not straight, joint it straight before making the cut or make a jig to hold the wood securely while making a straight cut. One option is to screw or nail a wooden straight edge to the workpiece. If the wood is not flat, face-joint it to establish a flat surface or position the workpiece so that it doesn't rock during the sawcut. Never rip a badly twisted board because it will bind and may kick back. Sometimes you can salvage a badly twisted piece of wood by cutting it into smaller lengths first.

To ensure that the fence locks parallel to the blade, always adjust the fence toward the blade rather than away from it, and then apply pressure on the front of the fence before it is locked in place. Periodically,

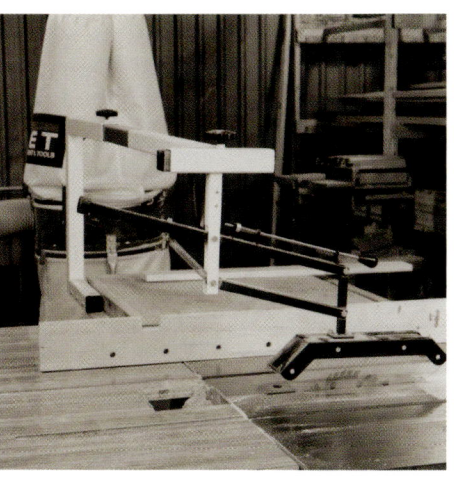

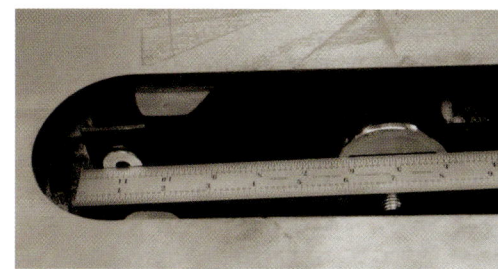

The Biesemeyer overhead guard can be installed on any tablesaw and features an alarm that sounds if a cut is attempted without the guard in place.

When mounting a North American-type guard where the mounting bracket is actually the splitter, the mounting bracket must be perfectly aligned with the arbor flange.

the guard is mounted on top of the splitter. The Delta splitter is retractable, so it can be pulled up when needed and pushed out of the way below the table's surface for partial cuts (see the small photo on the facing page). These guards can be easily lifted out of the way for cuts that require more clearance and replaced just as easily afterward.

When either type of guard is removed, you should take a few minutes and devise a method to keep your hands from coming in contact with the blade. For example, when tenoning with the workpiece upright against the fence, simply clamping a 4x4 to the saw table alongside the blade will make it nearly impossible for you to drop your hand into the blade should something go wrong.

Optional guards: **You can purchase high-quality guards to retrofit older machines. Most of these**

guards are similar to the overhead European design. The Biesemeyer guard (see the photo above left), for example, is a suspended guard with an alarm that rings if the guard is not in place during a saw-cut. The Brett guard is clear plastic and also functions as a hold-down. Either guard can be wired into the switch, so you can't start the saw if the guard isn't in place.

Adjusting the guard and the splitter: **The guard and splitter must be perfectly adjusted, or they will make the tablesaw more difficult and dangerous to operate. On North American-style guards, the flange, splitter and guard bracket must lie in the same plane as the blade, as shown in the photo above. When mounting this type of guard, leave the adjustment nut on the back support loose while you check the alignment of the blade and the guard plate (splitter) using a straight edge, then make the final adjustment of the back support and tighten the guard in place. Finally, check that the guard plate is square to the table.** —*M.D.*

Start by aligning the miter gauge and rip fence

To ensure safe and accurate cuts, you must make sure that the rip fence and miter gauge (used for crosscuts) are set up properly and in alignment with the blade and the miter-gauge slots. Because you'll be using the miter gauge to check the alignment of the blade to the miter-gauge slots and of the rip fence to the blade, you will first need to make sure the miter gauge is set up properly.

Fit bar to slot: The miter-gauge bar usually fits too loosely in the table slot to yield accurate crosscuts. To adjust the bar to fit more snugly, dimple the side of the bar with a center or prick punch. The dimples expand the metal around each indentation, effectively making the bar wider. The bar should slide smoothly along the length of the slot without hanging up. There should be minimal side-to-side play.

Square miter head: Next, square the head of the miter gauge to its bar. To do this, I lay pennies in the miter-gauge slot to elevate the bar slightly. Then I loosen the lock knob on the protractor head, butt the handle of a combination square against the bar of the miter gauge and align the protractor head with the blade of the square. Although you may be tempted to square the miter head to the sawblade, it won't do you any good until you align the blade to the miter-gauge slots.

Align blade to miter-gauge slots: To test for this alignment, raise the blade as high as it will go and clamp a 15-in.-long 1x3 to the miter gauge. Crosscut this test piece and unplug the saw. Now, slide the miter gauge with the test piece still clamped to it next to the front of the sawblade. Rotate the blade by hand-turning the belt or using a motor pulley. Don't grab the blade because your hand may deflect it. As you rotate the blade, one or two teeth will rub against the wood harder than the others and make a louder sound. Mark those teeth and slide the test piece to the back of the blade. The same teeth should rub against the blade at the back and make the same sound. If the sound is the same, the table slot and the blade are in alignment and you will not have to make any adjustments. If you get a different sound at the front and the back, the distance between the blade and the slot will have to be increased or decreased accordingly.

Realigning the blade to be parallel to the miter slot is fairly straightforward. On typical contractor saws, you simply loosen a few bolts and rotate the trunnions relative to the table. When doing so, you must be sure that the two trunnions stay in alignment. For a complete discussion of this, see "Tablesaw Tune-Up" by Kelly Mehler in *Fine Woodworking* #114, pp. 60-64, or consult your owner's manual. On larger cabinet shop saw, just loosen the bolts that hold the table to the cabinet and rotate the table slightly.

After making a slight adjustment, repeat the sound test with the saw unplugged. When you are satisfied, tighten the bolts, plug in the saw and make another test cut. It may take several attempts, but stay calm and take your time.

Rip-fence alignment: In theory, the rip fence should be perfectly parallel to the blade. In practice, however, it's best if the fence is slightly canted away from the back of the blade. This prevents the wood from binding between the blade and the fence, particularly if the workpiece warps slightly as it is ripped.

You can set the rip fence with the same test piece you used to check for crosscut alignment. First, lower the sawblade below the table, and loosen the bolts that lock your fence's angle relative to the guide rail. Then move the miter gauge with the test piece to the front of the saw, and lock the rip fence against it. Tighten the bolts, but not all the way—allow for slight movement at the back end of the fence with firm pressure. Now, slide the test piece forward until it's over the back of the saw's throat plate. There should be about 0.015 in. (about $\frac{1}{64}$ in.) clearance between the piece and the fence. To gauge the amount of clearance, slide a feeler gauge or a dollar bill folded over twice between the fence and the test piece. Finally, tighten the fence bolts and recheck the settings before making a test cut.

—M.D.

check the alignment of the fence to the blade by measuring from the fence to the front of the blade and then to the back of the blade. The distance should be no more than $1/64$ in. greater at the back of the blade. A faster and more accurate way to check whether the blade and fence are parallel is with sliding wedges, as shown in figure 1 at right. To accommodate different width workpieces, make pairs of wedges for each of the following widths: 6 in., 9 in., 12 in. and 18 in. For cutting widths wider than 18 in., you can use more than one pair of wedges.

Ripping on a tablesaw

Before making either a ripcut or a crosscut, raise the blade so that the highest sawtooth is positioned about $1/4$ in. above the work. With carbide-tipped blades, the entire carbide tip on the highest tooth should be above the work. The guard should be in place and functional.

Most woodworkers prefer to rip with the fence to the right of the blade, so the illustrations show it in that position. If you prefer the fence on the left side of the blade, reverse the arrangement. Never stand in line with the sawblade. Stand to the side of the saw opposite the fence, as shown in figure 2. This position may seem awkward at first, but it is a good habit to form because it may keep you out of the way of a violent kickback someday.

Start by pushing the work along the fence with both hands, applying forward pressure on the workpiece with your right hand and sideways pressure against the fence with your left, as shown in the photo on p. 92. As you near completion of the cut, continue to push the workpiece past the blade with your right hand, but remove your left hand from the work. It's a good idea to have your pushing hand in contact with the fence to ensure that your hand is as far away from the blade as possible.

The left hand should not touch the waste board at the completion of the cut, and you should never reach past the front of the blade with your left hand. Resist the temptation to try to control the workpiece or the waste piece at the back of the blade. If you

Fig. 1: Testing for parallelism _____

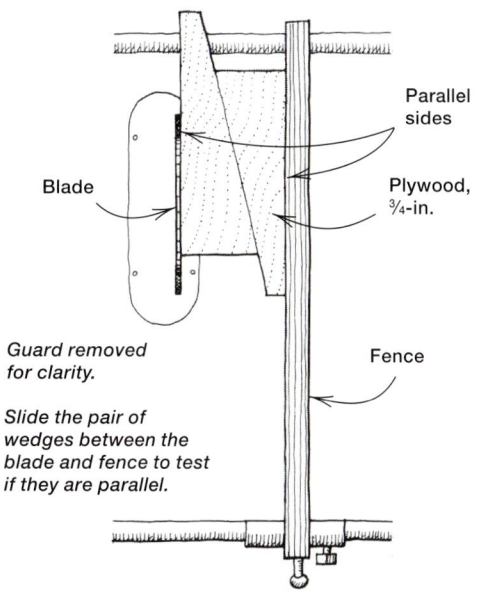

Parallel sides

Blade

Plywood, $3/4$-in.

Guard removed for clarity.

Fence

Slide the pair of wedges between the blade and fence to test if they are parallel.

Fig. 2: Techniques for ripping _____

Waste board

Workpiece

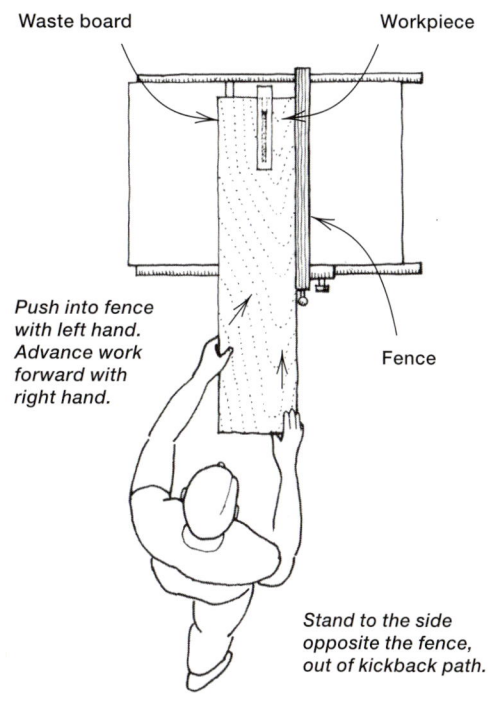

Push into fence with left hand. Advance work forward with right hand.

Fence

Stand to the side opposite the fence, out of kickback path.

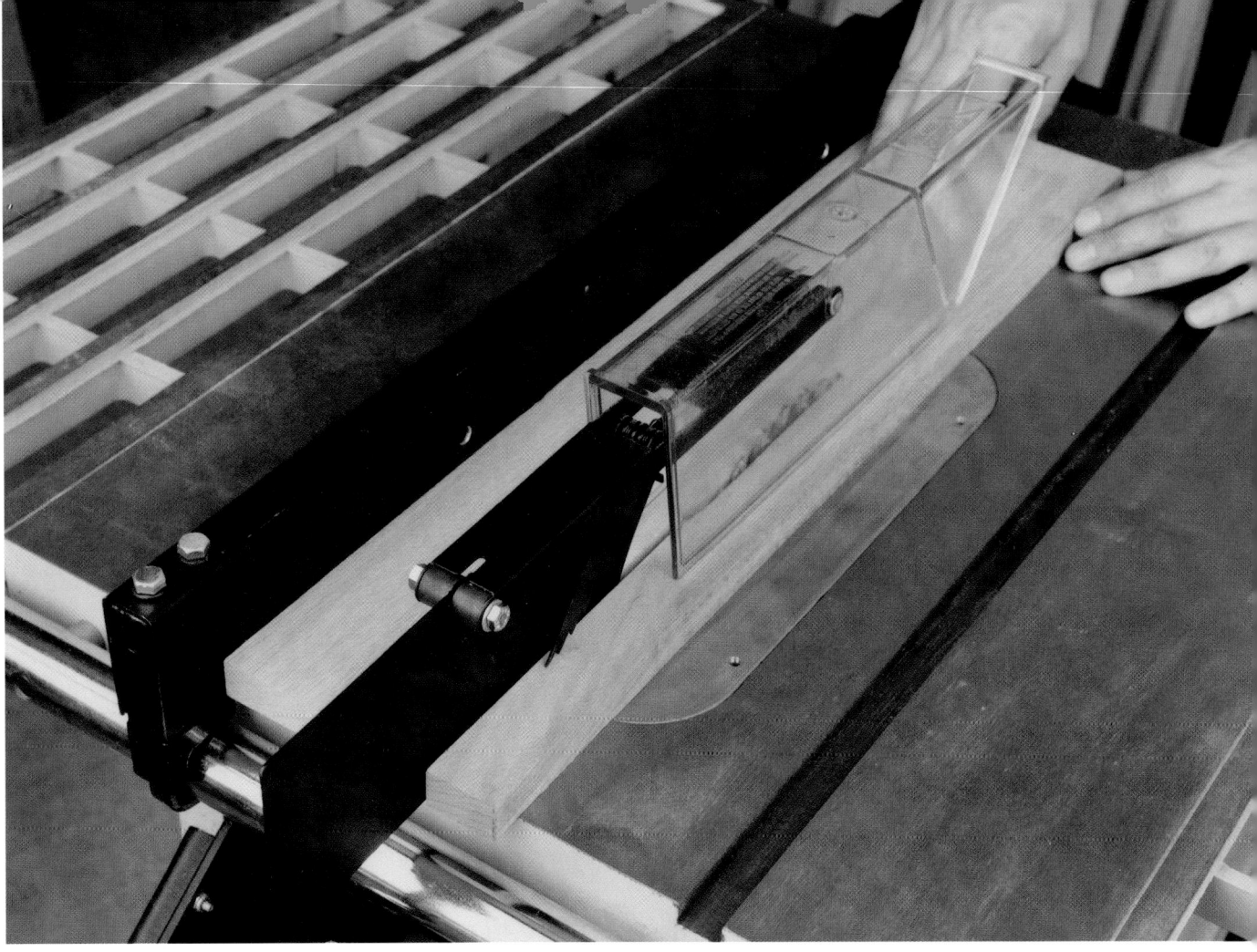

The tablesaw is both a savior and a demon. It's unmatched for accurately ripping stock to width or crosscutting pieces of nearly any size and also can be used to cut tenons, dadoes and finger joints. Unfortunately, the tablesaw also is responsible for many injuries, most of which could be avoided with blade guards and an understanding of the fundamentals of tablesaw use.

fumble with the wood at the conclusion of a cut, an accident might happen: A kickback could pull your hand into the back of the blade.

Long boards must be supported at the back of the saw. A support keeps the board from falling off the table or from binding between the blade and guard or fence. Stand-alone roller units and fold-down roller systems that attach to the back of the saw are available. An auxiliary table is a good option, too—if you have the floor space. Both rollers and auxiliary tables are commercially available, or you can build your own. The simplest solution is a sheet of plywood on a pair of sawhorses.

Sawing rabbets safely

Although a rabbet can be cut with a dado blade or with multiple passes over a standard blade, it is often faster to make two intersecting cuts to remove the waste (see figure 3 on the facing page). When taking the second cut, which separates the waste, make sure the waste piece is on the side of the blade opposite the fence. If the waste were between the blade and the fence, it could bind and eject backward with lightning speed.

Push sticks

If the distance between the blade and the rip fence is less than 3 in., always use a push stick rather than your hand to guide the workpiece past the blade. As a new push stick begins to pick up the inevitable war wounds, you really start to appreciate it. Push-stick designs are quite varied, but all have a notch that hugs the corner of the workpiece and that allows you to push the workpiece forward while also holding the back of the workpiece down on the table.

Fig. 3: Intersecting cuts

FIRST CUT

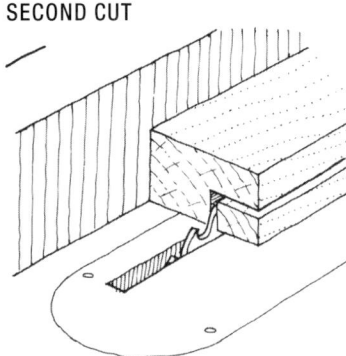

SECOND CUT

Second cut separates waste to form rabbet. Be sure waste is not trapped between blade and fence.

Fig. 4: Push-stick design

BASIC DESIGN

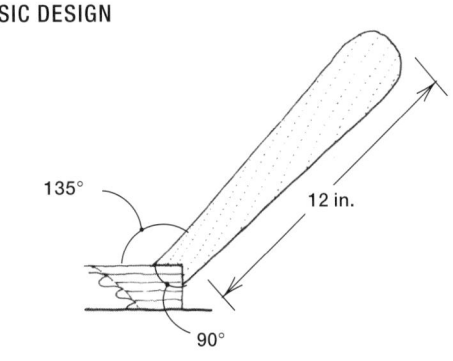

135°

12 in.

90°

LONG-NOSED PUSH STICK FOR SHORT BOARDS

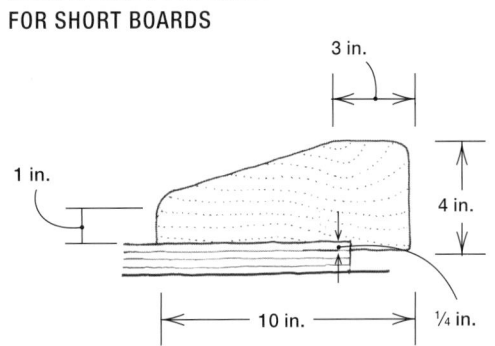

3 in.

1 in.

4 in.

10 in.

¼ in.

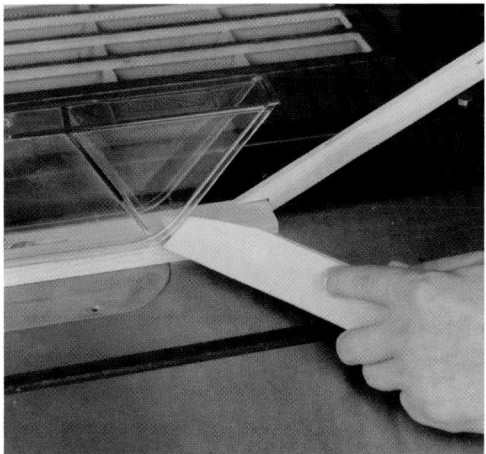

Before ripping a board, set the push stick on the saw table to the right of the fence. When there's about 6 in. left to cut, pick up the push stick with your right hand and complete the cut. However, when picking up the push stick, be sure your left hand is behind the workpiece; never let go of the workpiece with both hands, or the force of the blade will pitch it back at you.

On narrow boards, finish the cut with two push sticks, as shown in the photo at right: one stick for sideways pressure and one for forward pressure. Never allow the push stick that applies the side pressure to move past the front of the blade because you would be applying side pressure on the blade, which could cause a kickback. For short boards, you may want to make a long-nosed push stick that holds down the front of the board (see figure 4 above). This kind of push stick

Use two push sticks to rip narrow stock. To avoid kickback, don't allow the push stick that applies the side pressure to move past the front of the blade.

counteracts the upward force from the back of the blade, which tends to lift the board off the table.

Featherboards

A featherboard is a shopmade device that is clamped to the saw table or rip fence and that applies sideways or downward pressure to the workpiece. Featherboards not only hold the piece against the rip fence, or down on the table, they also prevent kickback. When used to apply sideways pressure to keep the workpiece against the rip fence, the featherboard should be clamped to the table so that light pressure is applied just in front of the sawblade. No part of the featherboard should extend past the front of the blade, or it will pinch the waste board against the blade's side. I prefer softwood featherboards with the "feather" cuts spaced about $1/4$ in. apart to provide flexibility and to allow some latitude for adjustment. You can use a featherboard and a push stick together, as shown in the photo below or two featherboards in tandem: one clamped to the table and one to the rip fence.

Wheel hold-downs

Commercial spring-loaded wheel hold-downs attach to a fence or a board mounted to the fence (see the photo below). The spring tension is adjustable for the height of the workpiece, and the wheels rotate in only one direction to provide protection from kickback. Although hold-downs are purchased in pairs, I like to install just one at the back of the saw. The single hold-down controls the wood at the back of the saw and allows me to use a push stick at the front.

Auxiliary fences

The sawblade must not come in contact with the metal fence, so it's a good idea to make a wooden fence that protects both the blade and the stock rip fence. Most standard fences are drilled so you can easily attach a wooden fence with bolts or screws. It's best if the auxiliary fence is made of plywood or another manufactured product that won't warp. If you use solid wood, choose quartersawn rather than flatsawn wood because it's more stable. Finish both

A shopmade featherboard can be used to hold the workpiece against the fence while the stock is guided past the blade with a push stick.

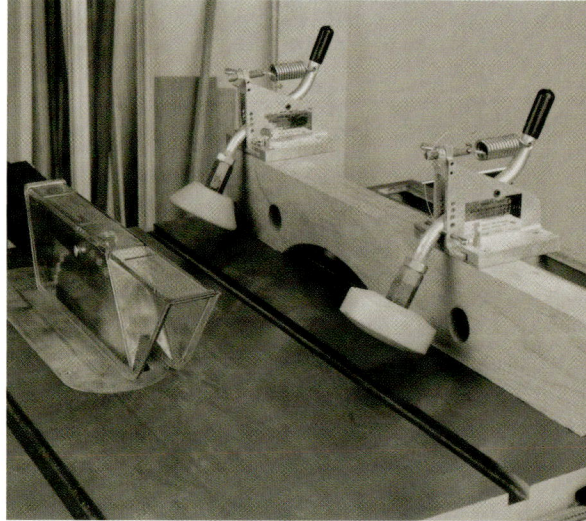

Commercial spring-loaded wheels attach to a fence or to a board mounted on the fence and hold the work both down on the table and against the fence.

sides to prevent warping, and apply plastic laminate to provide a good wear surface. Wax the fence often.

Occasionally, the metal fence is twisted. By attaching a wooden fence and shimming it with paper, you can make the setup perfectly straight and accurate. Check the relationship of the fence to the table with a square, and check its straightness with a straight edge.

A standard auxiliary fence that covers your stock fence will serve you well for most cutting operations, but there are some special cuts that require different types of auxiliary fences.

High fence

When running a board on edge through a tablesaw (such as when beveling raised panels, as shown in figure 5 at right), it's safest to use a high plywood fence to support the work. Position the fence and raised panel so that the blade tilts away from the fence. If you are making a cut that separates a small piece, it should not be captured between the blade and the fence.

Fig. 5: The high fence

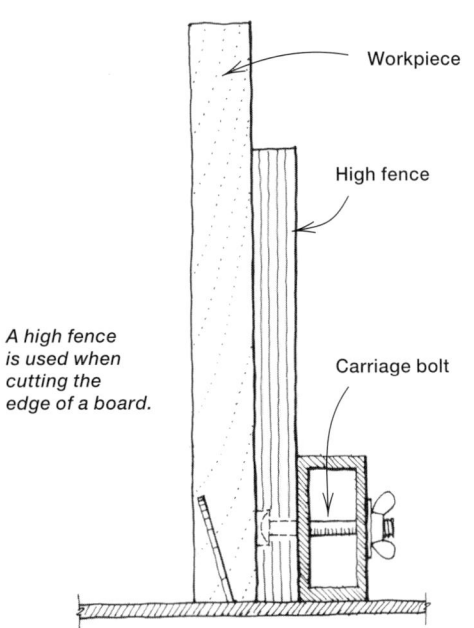

Workpiece

High fence

Carriage bolt

A high fence is used when cutting the edge of a board.

A low, L-shaped auxiliary fence provides clearance for your hand and the push stick when ripping narrow pieces and when tilting the blade.

Fig. 6: The short fence as a cutoff stop block ___

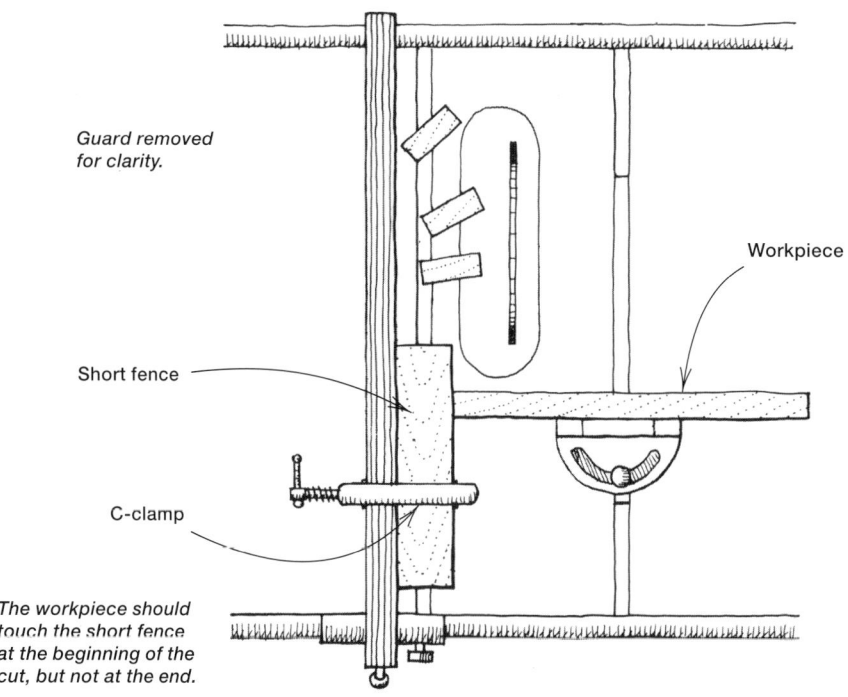

Guard removed for clarity.

Workpiece

Short fence

C-clamp

The workpiece should touch the short fence at the beginning of the cut, but not at the end.

When rabbeting or cutting molding, use an auxiliary fence that has an arc cut in it to house the unused portion of the cutter. Clamp a hold-down board to the fence.

Low fence

Although you should always tilt the blade away from the fence when ripping a bevel or a chamfer, this is not always possible. When you must bevel a piece with the blade tilted toward the fence or when ripping any narrow piece between the blade and fence, it's a good idea to use a low, L-shaped fence. This fence can be a separate two-piece fence or a board that is attached to your standard auxiliary fence. Because the workpiece is trapped between the fence and the blade, a kickback is likely, so use a long push stick to move the workpiece completely past the blade. The low fence gives you more room to maneuver your hand and the push stick past the blade (see the photo on p. 95).

Short fence

An auxiliary fence that extends the entire length of the rip fence makes it easier to cut sheet goods. Because they are dimensionally stable, pinching or spreading after the cut is not usually a problem. However, when cutting solid wood, there is always the possibility that the wood will either pinch

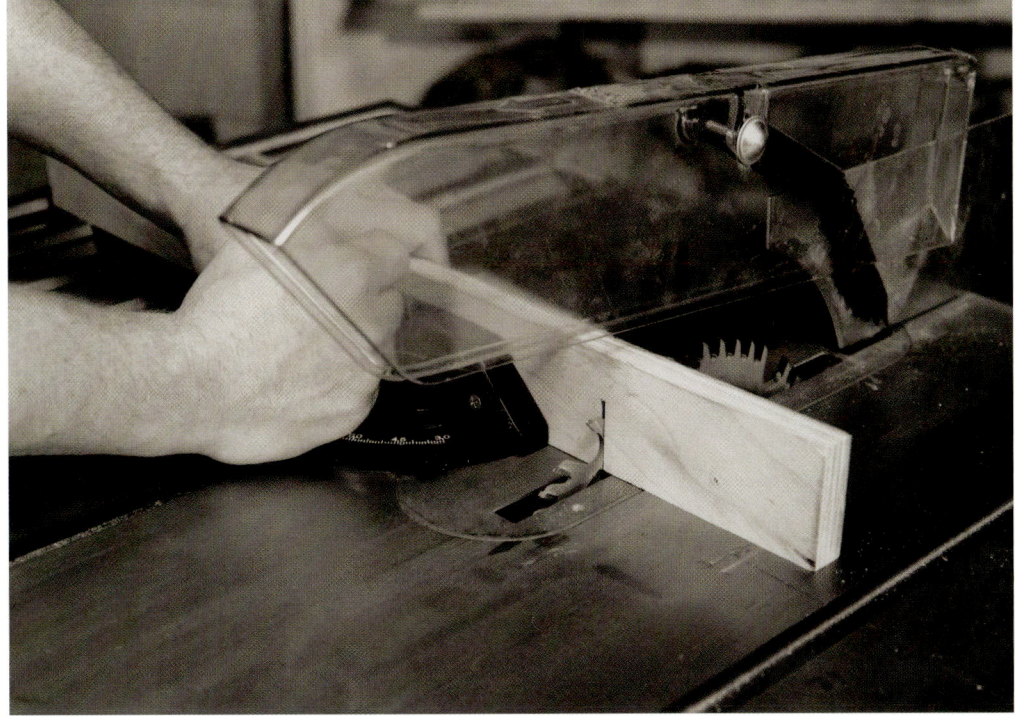

A plywood auxiliary fence screwed to the face of the miter head increases its surface area and supports the workpiece. If you let the fence extend past the blade and then cut it off as shown here, you can then use the sawkerf to align pieces that you are crosscutting.

together or spread apart during the cut. The splitter that is standard equipment on most guards is designed to eliminate the problem of the wood pinching the back of the blade. A short auxiliary fence will eliminate the problem of the wood spreading apart after it's cut. The short fence should end at the back of the blade to allow space for the wood to spread without forcing the workpiece away from the fence. A short fence also makes a good stop when crosscutting multiple small pieces to the same length using the miter gauge (see figure 6 on the facing page). In this case, the fence should only extend to the front of the blade, so you can bump the workpiece into the fence at the beginning of the cut, but not have the cutoff trapped between the fence and blade at the end of the cut.

Dado and molding fence
The dado blade and the molding head often cut the edge of a board, which means that the cutter or blade is near the fence. The auxiliary fence for these cuts should have an arc-shaped recess to provide clearance to

house the cutter. Because of the danger of kickback, you should never cut a rabbet or make a molding with the workpiece between the fence and the cutter. Molding heads and dadoes require more downward pressure than a regular blade, so it's a good idea to add a hold-down strip to the wooden fence for rabbeting and molding, as shown in the photo on the facing page. Always cut the molding profile on the edge of a wide board, and then rip the desired width of molding from it.

Crosscutting with the miter gauge
The miter gauge is an adjustable protractor that slides in the miter slot and supports the work as it is crosscut. The face of the miter gauge remains square to the bar for square and bevel crosscuts but is angled in relation to the blade for miter and compound-miter cuts.

To crosscut, press the workpiece against the face of the miter gauge and down onto the miter bar. After making sure your fingers are clear of the blade, advance both the gauge and the wood into the blade.

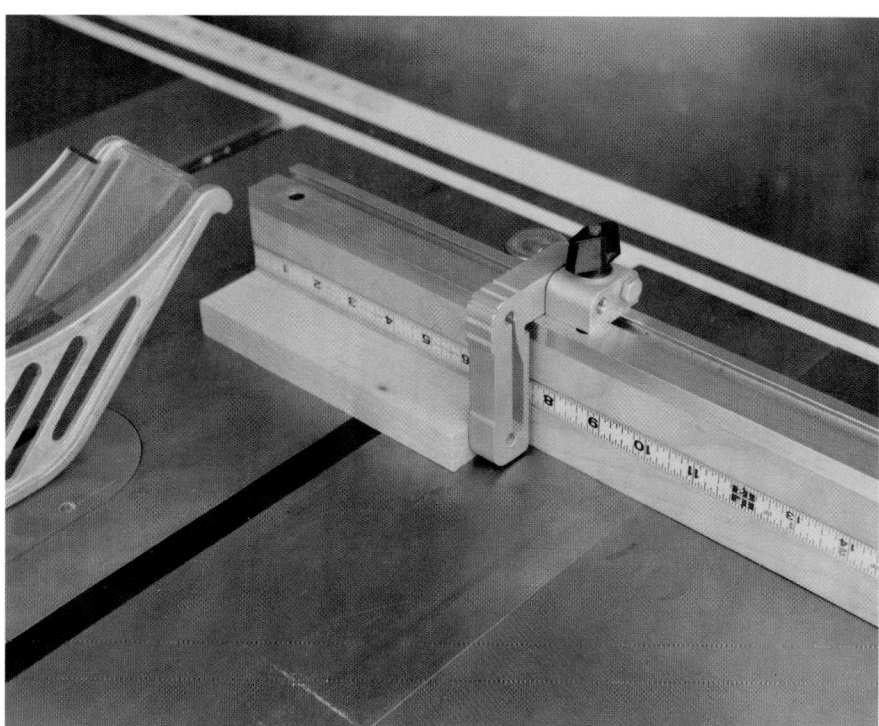

Some after-market miter gauge fences, such as the FasTTrack (shown here), have flip-up stops like those that have been standard equipment on European saws for years.

Fig. 7: Making dadoes with the two-stop system

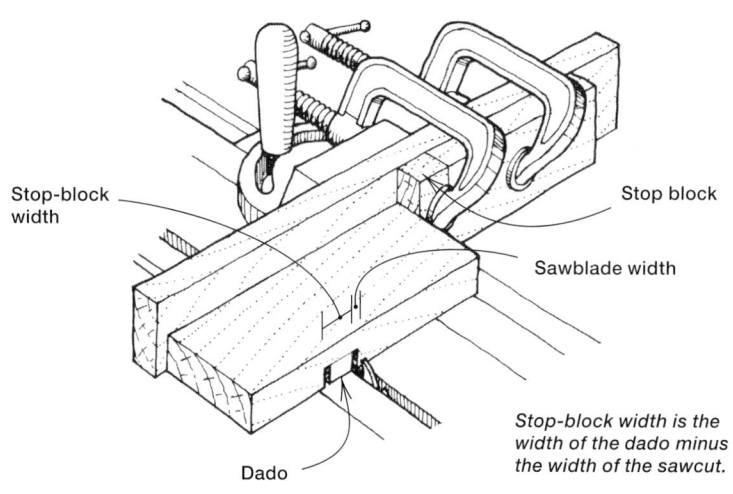

Stop-block width

Stop block

Sawblade width

Stop-block width is the width of the dado minus the width of the sawcut.

Dado

Most people prefer the left miter slot for crosscutting, but either slot works. When the blade is angled, use the slot opposite the direction of the tilt.

Use both hands to control the wood and the gauge, and hold the wood tightly against the face of the gauge so that it doesn't slip during the cut. Once the wood is cut into two pieces, stop the forward movement of the miter gauge, and pull the wood and the miter gauge backward to the front of the saw. As you back up the wood and the gauge, maintain the same pressure that you used as you cut; relaxing too soon can cause accidents. Never touch a cutoff piece while the saw is running. A safety precaution when cutting small pieces: Clamp them to the miter gauge.

The auxiliary miter fence

Most miter gauges have holes so that a wooden fence can be screwed to the face of the miter head. A longer auxiliary fence gives the workpiece more support. Use plywood for the auxiliary fence because it is more dimensionally stable than solid wood. Let the fence extend past the blade, and then crosscut it to establish the exact location of the sawblade (see the photo on p. 97).

Marking the work

When making individual crosscuts, it's best to mark the edge of the board because the edge contacts the blade first. Then the workpiece can be positioned, so the mark

Fig. 8: A shopmade microadjustable stop

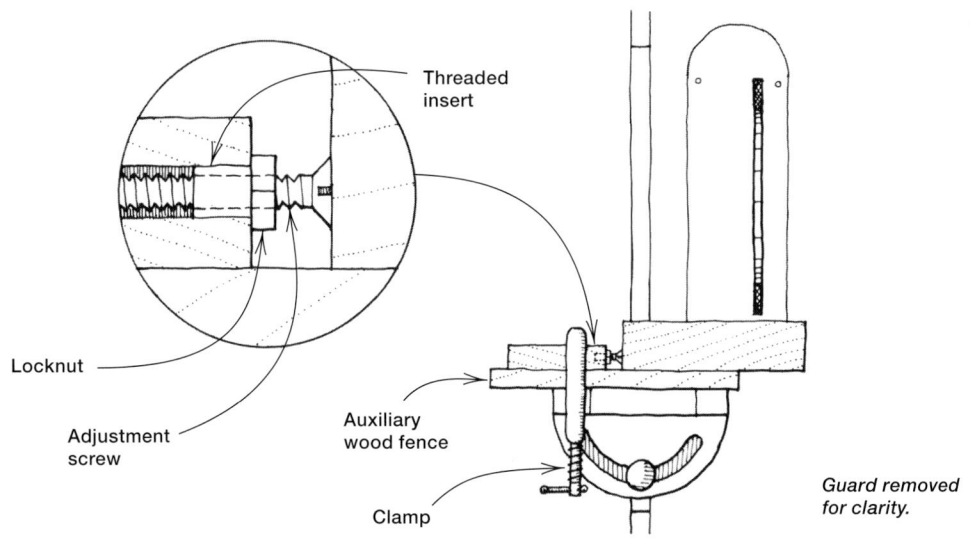

Threaded insert

Locknut

Adjustment screw

Auxiliary wood fence

Clamp

Guard removed for clarity.

lines up with an outside tooth of the saw-blade. Alternatively, you can scribe a line on the back of the board and align it with the sawcut on the auxiliary fence.

Miter-gauge stops

A stop block clamped to the wooden fence automatically measures the required length of board. This simple technique offers both efficiency and accuracy, particularly when you need several pieces exactly the same length. Keep gentle pressure against the stop as the wood is fed into the blade. After the cut is made, maintain the pressure against the stop as the wood and miter gauge are being retracted to lessen the likelihood of contact with the blade.

Dual stops

Sometimes it may be desirable to have several precise stops. For example, when cutting several boards that must first be squared up and cut to exactly the same length, two stop blocks are efficient. The stop nearer the blade is the finish stop; the stop farther from the blade is the rough stop. If your miter gauge doesn't have hinged stops, two wood pieces clamped to the fence work almost as well. Cut a piece of wood about 2 in. long for the finish stop and clamp

another piece opposite the blade for a rough stop. When you need to use the rough stop, just unclamp the finish stop block.

Another job for the two-stop system is to make the two outside cuts of a dado with a standard blade instead of a dado head (see figure 7 on the facing page). The first stop locates the right edge of the dado and the second stop, which must be as wide as the dado minus the width of the sawkerf, determines the dado's width. Once these two cuts are made, the waste in between can be removed in several passes.

Microadjustable stops

For very precise work, it's essential to be able to make very fine adjustments of the stops. One low-tech approach is to put paper shims between the rough stop block and the finish stop block. A dollar bill or sheet of typing paper is 0.004 in. thick, a dollar bill folded twice is about $1/64$ in.

Another technique is to make a block that has a threaded insert and an adjustment screw, as shown in figure 8 above. Every full turn of a $1/4$-in., 20 threads-per-inch machine screw adds or subtracts 0.05 in. to the length of the stop block. The locknut makes this measurement reliable for repeated operations.

ROUTING SAFE AND SOUND

by Pat Warner

When you lose control of a router, whether totally or just a little, it's the workpiece that most often gets messed up. Now and again, you'll chip or break a bit. And if you're really unlucky, you will get hurt. Keep this in mind: Most router bits rotate at a speed in excess of 20,000 rpm. When something goes wrong—a grab, a dig, a jolt to the machine, bad things happen fast. I have had my fingernails trimmed mighty close by a dovetail bit before I knew what happened.

Router safety is essentially a matter of controlling the router and securing the workpiece (and vice versa on the router table). Safety considerations are therefore intimately related to the quality of the cut. The safest routing technique will by and large yield the best finished surface.

Here are some tips to help you produce the quickest, smoothest and safest cuts with a router.

Trapped! Cutting a dovetail buries the bit in the work. If the router can't be pulled up and away, the bit is trapped and needs careful guidance.

Some bits bite back

Not all router bits are created equal. Some are far less capable of handling the stresses of cutting wood and will break easily. Some are prone to other problems, such as burning or catching in the cut. Recognizing bits that need particular care will help you keep them from biting you and your work.

Long, thin bits are fragile: Thin bits with cutting-edge lengths that are more than three times longer than their diameters are easily stressed and broken. Some of the thinnest bits are milled into their shank, making them even more fragile. The $3/8$-in.-dia. bit at left has less than $1/16$ in. of steel between the flutes. Cut in $1/8$-in. increments or less with these bits.

Trapped bits need precise guidance: Some bit designs, such as dovetail bits and T-slot cutters, trap the bit in the work. The slightest wavering in the cut will mess up the workpiece. These bits should be used only with jigs and fences to guide them.

Dovetail and T-slot bits also break easily. They are designed to cut while fully engaged in the workpiece, which is the most stressful kind of cut for any router bit. Most of the cutting is done at the ends of the flutes where their diameter is at a maximum. However, most of the stress is concentrated where the shank and the flutes meet, which is the thinnest part of the bit. To make matters worse, some of these cutters are ground into the shank. Just take things easy, and don't force the cut. For long T-slots and sliding dovetails, I pre-plow with a straight bit.

Many other kinds of bits cut in such a way that you can't lift the router straight up and off the workpiece freely. These bits include cope-and-stick cutters, glue- and finger-joint bits, bull-nose bits and some profile bits. To be used successfully, they should be treated as trapped bits.

Spiral bits can be unpredictable: Spiral up-shear and down-shear bits can produce impeccable surfaces. The cutting edges travel in a spiral motion and are always engaged in the work, unlike ordinary straight bits. Up-shear bits send the chips into your face, and down shears send the chips into your socks (see the top photo at right).

Large spiral-ground down-shear bits have one nasty feature: If the bit catches in the work, it will pick the router up and out of the cut. I almost lost my grip on a router with a down-shear bit that suddenly climbed up the work. Down shears are too unpredictable for this woodworker, especially on end grain. If you use them, cut very lightly, or use them in a router table with a power feed.

A twist to the left and a twist to the right. The up-shear bit (left) spins like a drill bit, with the flutes spiraling up. The down-shear bits flutes (right) spiral down.

Listen to your router whine

Routers always seem to whine, but you should listen to them. The sound a router makes while idling should not change appreciably in the cut. If it does, you may be stressing the bit and the motor.

It's all too easy to overwork a bit because it's difficult to estimate how much stress a particular cut will put on a bit. The volume of material you remove increases exponentially when you double the dimensions. This means that you remove 25 times more wood from a given length of a $^5/_8$-in.-sq. rabbet than from a $^1/_8$-in.-sq. rabbet. However, the stresses on the bit are not 25 times as great. Your best estimate will come from how it sounds in the cut. If your bit chatters, screeches or just sounds unhappy, then slow down the cut.

Jigs are safety devices in disguise

Jigs secure the work and control the path of the cut, reducing the chances of error. Consequently, they are essential to the most accurate—and the safest—router cuts.

The best jigs have a few things in common. They secure the workpiece without interfering with the path of the router. They offer a large surface for the router to run on, giving it stability. And jigs guide the router

A good jig keeps the router in line. By controlling the line of cut, jigs make mistakes less likely.

positively and completely through the cut. Avoid designing jigs that trap the workpiece between a fence and the cutter. When using an edge-guide on a router, position the bit in the fence.

It's often the simplest jigs that help the most. On a standard outside edge cut, less than half the base casting rides on the workpiece. If you rout around a corner, as little as 25% of the base rides on the workpiece, and the chances of tipping are great. I make an offset subbase that increases stability by giving the router a larger platform to ride on.

Getting away with the climb cut

The direction of cut has great bearing on the quality of the cut. If you look at a router upside down, you'll see that the bit spins counterclockwise, and when the router is on top of the workpiece, it's spinning clockwise. When the router is pushed through the cut with the bit spinning into the edge of the workpiece, it's called a climb cut (shown in the drawing below). The bit can self-feed or climb along the cut, wrenching the router forward. Running a router in the opposite direction, with the bit spinning out of the edge of the workpiece, is anti-climb cutting. Though riskier, climb cutting produces a superior edge, without the kind of tearout anti-climb cuts produce.

Use the anti-climb cut for most work, but when you need a perfect edge, use a climb cut, taking light passes. Learn to feel the speed and depth of cut when the router starts to grab and self-feed, so you don't lose control.

Keep gravity on your side

Bad accidents with routers do happen. I've heard of a carpenter who tried to rout some molding under a countertop. He didn't secure the motor in the casting. Halfway through the cut, the motor spun out of its casting and onto his leg. The lesson should be obvious: Keep gravity on your side. Hand-held routers should always be used horizontally with the bit facing down. It

Understanding climb cutting _____

DIRECTIONS FOR ANTI-CLIMB CUTTING

For the safest cuts, run the router counterclockwise around the workpiece and clockwise inside of a workpiece. Reverse this for the router table, because the router is upside down.

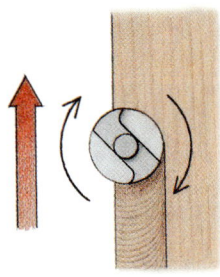

The drawing above shows a climb cut, with the bit spinning into the edge of the workpiece. Though risky, routing in this direction produces a smooth surface.

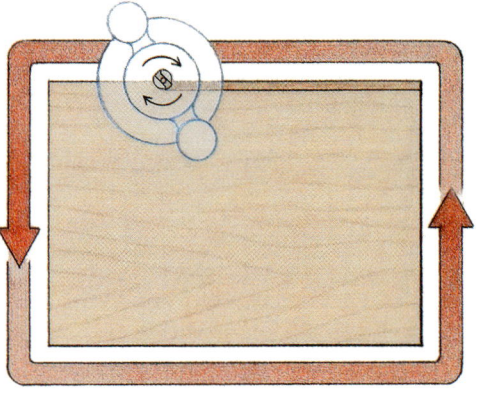

Rout counterclockwise along outside edge.

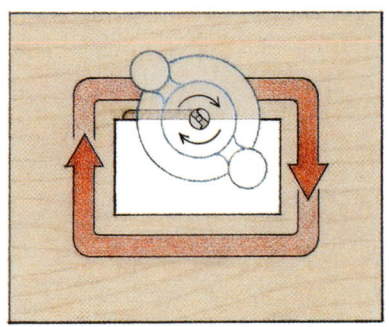

Rout clockwise along inside edge.

WRONG

RIGHT

Rabbeting the right way. The router is easier to control when flat on the workpiece. Your hands are above the bit if you lose your grip.

Rabbeting the wrong way. Routing sideways can be tempting but is always treacherous. If you lose your grip, the router will fall.

can be tempting to run a router sideways down a board, especially if the bit is oriented to cut that way, but don't do it. Find a different bit, or make a jig that supports the piece in such a way that you rout horizontally (see the photos above).

Start the router without wobble

I start a router with its base casting flat on the edge of the workpiece. I find it troublesome and risky to set down an already running router on the workpiece. However, starting the router on an edge isn't completely risk-free. Some machines will jerk from the torque of the motor and possibly push the bit into the workpiece. Worse, starting a cut before the bit reaches full speed can break the bit. I prefer soft-start machines because they don't twist on start up.

Rout comfortably

Routing at a standard bench height is difficult and tiring for me. I can't see what's going on easily, so I end up hunched over trying to see where the bit is. Being able to see the bit is crucial to keeping the router under control. To solve the problem, I made a special routing bench 40 in. high. It allows me to stand tall and see what I'm doing. I also make router jigs for my bench vise that stand at about the same height. I'm 6 ft. 1 in. tall, so 40 in. off the ground may not be the best height for you. Experiment to find your most comfortable routing height.

A special router bench for comfortable work. The author made this bench 40 in. high, so he doesn't have to lean over to see what he's doing.

FOUR

Techniques

Most experienced cabinetmakers will admit that there are at least four ways of doing any one thing. There's the right way, the wrong way, your way and his way. On occasion, the four get jumbled and reduced to two options, right and wrong, from which endless arguments arise. You have only to look in the Letters department of *Fine Woodworking* magazine to see the wide range of opinions that woodworkers have about techniques that are different from theirs. However, these arguments are healthy for the profession as a whole, because they lead to reconsideration and improved techniques among those willing to listen.

This chapter offers you the personal techniques of a number of experienced woodworkers. They will guide you through basic layout, lumber milling, basic joinery and sharpening. Each article teaches skills that can be applied to a wide range of projects. Basic layout techniques are relevant to everything from boatbuilding to instrument making and simple cabinetry. The same can be said of milling lumber four square. Even if you buy only dimensional lumber, this is essential information to know if a particular board you need has an unacceptable cup or twist. The joints described here can be applied to furniture of every stripe. But perhaps most important, the article on sharpening has absolutely universal relevance. If you don't know how to hone a blade so that it will shave hair off the back of your hand, you're really missing the boat. Dull or missharpened tools will give you more grief and frustration than any mistake you can make.

This chapter is the heart of the book, for it is here that you will see the practice of woodworking most directly. These are the ways in which woodworkers make things. They may not be perfectly right, and they certainly aren't wrong, but they are all excellent techniques.

A BASIC LAYOUT KIT

by Horst J. Meister

Layout essentials— An accurate try square and a marking knife are basic tools for laying out furniture joinery.

I was 15 years old when I built my first cabinet. Shortly before my mother's birthday, I overheard her tell my father that she would really like to have a little cabinet for her sewing room. The very next Saturday, I locked myself in the garage with a generous supply of redwood boards, a bent aluminum yardstick, a box of dowels, glue, a crosscut saw and three Snickers candy bars.

The finished piece fell a little shy of my expectations. Believing that square corners were a very desirable feature in furniture, my dad gave me a try square for my 16th birthday. Soon, my woodworking projects improved to the point that people other than my mother liked what I made.

A good try square, a ruler and a marking knife are the fundamental layout tools that few serious woodworkers can get along without. Add a marking gauge or mortising gauge, a bevel gauge, a protractor, and a set of dividers and trammels and you'll have a basic layout kit. Why spend the money? Good-quality layout tools will last a lifetime, and flawed measurements will plague a project through every stage. Even small errors are a detraction if they occur in a prominent place.

I have obtained excellent results in woodwork using some of the machinist's layout tools that are standard equipment in the tool-and-die industry. And they often cost less than comparable tools specifically designed for woodworkers. They're not as pretty as the best woodworker's tools. However, good looks don't get the job done—accuracy does.

Start with a try square or an engineer's square

The try square is a very simple device. It's just a thin metal blade permanently set at 90° to a thicker wood or metal handle. Its uses are many: You can check the squareness of milled stock, mark square shoulders, lay out joinery or check the accuracy of the miter gauge on your tablesaw or the fence on your jointer. Without a good try square, you can't make anything square. A number of companies make try squares specifically for woodworkers. They vary in price and appearance, but you don't need to spend a lot of money.

For super accuracy and durability, consider using an engineer's square with a 12-in. blade (see the top photo at right). The handle and blade are hardened and then silver-soldered together. These squares can't get out of alignment unless you subject them to serious abuse, like pounding on them with a large hammer. In the 12-in. size, most brands are guaranteed to be square to 0.0025 in. ($1/400$ in.) or less. Chinese engineer's squares are not as good as U.S., English, German or Japanese squares.

Combination squares (see the bottom photo at right) have their uses. Because the blade is adjustable, it can fit into a tight place or reach that extra inch a try square

Engineer's squares are sturdy and accurate. They're useful for checking machine fences and blades because their wide handles make them stable on edge.

Combination squares just don't measure up. The handle is shorter than that on a try square, giving less support when marking a line.

can't. Despite these advantages, they're not entirely suitable for use as a try square for two reasons. First, the bearing surface of a standard 90° combination-square head is shorter than that of an engineer's or try square's handle, which is typically 80% as long as the blade. The extra length gives better leverage against cutting pressure on the blade while marking. The relative shortness of the combination square's head makes it easier for you to push the blade off the desired line. Second, the blade and head on a combination square will wear against each other over time and eventually go out of square.

Next, an accurate metal ruler

A good ruler should have fine, crisp graduations that are cut into the metal and contrast with their background. Aluminum rulers

Choose a ruler for its longevity and accuracy. The painted graduations on the soft aluminum ruler (left) will not fare well with use, but the etched graduations on the steel ruler (right) are more precise and will last a long time.

Where exactly is 1⅜ in.? Time and use have taken their toll on this steel tape measure (top) and this folding rule (bottom). Not designed to last, the graduations have worn from the edges of both. The tape measure's hook bends easily, and the rivets wear loose. Use a precision ruler when accuracy counts.

with usable graduations are available for a reasonable price at most hardware stores. However, aluminum is a soft metal, which is easily scratched or bent. When used for scribing lines, sharp marking knives will nick the edge of an aluminum ruler.

For a few dollars more, you can buy a machinist's ruler, which is a far superior tool (see the top right photo above). Available in lengths from 6 in. to 48 in., these scales are made of hardened stainless steel and have very accurate graduations. Starrett, Brown & Sharpe, Rabone Chesterman and Mitutoyo rulers have finely cut graduations accurate to within a few thousandths per foot. A set, consisting of a 6-in., an 18-in. and a 36-in. ruler with fractional graduations, will handle most measurement tasks.

Steel measuring tapes are convenient, reasonably priced and handy. However, they're not accurate enough for cabinet work. The rivets that fasten the sliding hook to the end of the tape wear with use, making the tape less and less accurate. Most measuring tapes have painted graduations that may wear off (see the middle photo at left). And folding rules have many of the same drawbacks, most notably painted graduations and joints that can bind on sawdust or small shavings. Precision rulers have few of these limitations, but they can't measure long distances.

For marking, use a knife not a pencil

Pencil lines are too wide for accurate layout work, and the graphite tends to smear. Scoring the wood with a knife makes a precise mark that won't smudge or wear out. There are a number of different marking-knife designs on the market. I don't see much reason to choose one design over another as long as the knife leaves a clean, accurate cut, and it's comfortable to use. The blade should be thin and very sharp at its tip so it can be held tightly against the blade of a square. Then the line can be knifed right along the edge.

Strive to make your layout marks in exactly the same manner each time. Hold the marking knife at the same angle relative to the ruler and the wood each time you mark the work. A knifed line should be deep enough to see easily. Yet it should be as light as possible to keep the knife blade from following the grain rather than the ruler.

Many furnituremakers leave dovetail layout lines on drawer sides or cabinet faces as a sign the piece was made by hand. But ordinarily, you wouldn't use a marking knife on surfaces that will be exposed after assembly. Your best bet is the traditional carpenter's pencil with the lead sharpened to a knife-edged chisel point. The pencil's chisel point draws a cleaner line than the conical point on a standard pencil. And the pencil's rectangular body won't roll off your bench.

Some woodworkers prefer using an awl rather than a marking knife. Even when it's sharpened to a fine needle point, though, an awl suffers from a tendency to follow the wood's grain and crush fibers, not cut them (see the top right photo). Marks scratched with an awl tend to be fuzzy, especially in soft woods.

Marking and mortising gauges

There are different kinds of marking gauges, but they all work on the same principle. The basic marking gauge consists of a steel cutter mounted on a beam that fits in a fence. A setscrew or wedge fixes the beam to the fence at whatever distance is desired. Marking gauges can have pins, small blades, even discs for cutters. Gauges that have blades are called cutting gauges.

Marking gauges are used to scribe a line parallel to an edge. Set the pin or knife to the distance to be marked, and then tighten the fence to the beam with the setscrew or wedge. Hold the fence against the edge of the material with the pin touching the wood. Because the tool is guided by the edge of the work, any line that's cut with a marking gauge is certain to be parallel to that edge as long as the fence is held firmly against the work while the line is being cut.

The pin of a factory sharpened gauge makes a fuzzy, irregular mark. Filing the tip to an oval-shaped knife edge makes it cut better (see the center photo at right). A pin

An awl point breaks wood fibers across the grain; a sharp knife cuts them.

Good lighting, a magnifying glass and careful filing will greatly improve the performance of a pin gauge. The pin may be filed to a small knife edge, which won't tear the wood as much.

The larger blade of a cutting gauge will produce a cleaner cut across the grain.

filed to a slight angle helps draw the fence against the workpiece. For cutting across the grain, a cutting gauge does an even better job than a marking gauge (see the bottom photo on p. 109). Even when the pin of a marking gauge is sharpened as described above, it can hop or tear out when marking across the grain. The alternating rings of soft summer and hard winter wood cause the gauge to do this. A cutting gauge's knife doesn't have this problem, but it needs a light touch to keep it from making a deeper cut than you need.

I prefer a marking gauge with a small disc for a cutter. Fastened to the end of the beam, the disc is about the size of a dime and has a bevel on the side facing the fence. A disc cutter combines the advantages of both pin and knife. It will mark equally well across and with the grain. The bevel pulls the fence against the stock as you draw the tool along the work, and the line it cuts is clean, straight and sharply defined without being too deep.

A mortise gauge is simply a marking gauge with two independently adjustable cutters. It's used to make two parallel layout lines. To use one, first set the distance between the pins to the width of the mortise, and then set the beam to the mortise location on the workpiece. The two cutters outline the width of the mortise with one stroke of the gauge.

A bevel gauge or protractor for angles

A protractor is used to measure and determine angles. It has a radial scale calibrated in degrees and an arm that pivots on the center point of the scale's radius. A protractor can be set to any specified angle in its range, and the protractor's arm is then used to draw the set angle onto the stock. A good machinist's combination square set comes with a very accurate protractor that has a vernier scale that allows you to measure angles as small as $\frac{1}{4}°$.

A protractor is useful for determining exact angles, but a bevel gauge is the pre-

The author draws his shopmade disc gauge toward him. The cutter (below) does not spin freely, but when it dulls, it is easily turned to a fresh edge.

Use a protractor to scribe any angle but a right angle. Without superfine etched graduations on the head, finding an angle will be hit or miss. Cheap protractors can misguide you by several degrees.

Use a bevel gauge for layout tasks beyond 90°. With few variations, the design has remained the same for a hundred years. The Starrett No. 47 on the left has been in production since 1891.

ferred tool for checking, comparing and transferring angles (see the bottom photo on p. 111). Bevel gauges are similar to protractors in principle, having a handle and a sliding blade that can be adjusted to any angle, but they don't have a scale.

Dividers and trammels for circles and arcs

Woodworking dividers are used for scribing small circles and arcs (see the bottom right photo). The best dividers have a joint tensioned with a bow spring and a fine-pitch adjusting screw. For best results, sharpen one of the divider points to a sharp needle; this is the point you will use as the axis to pivot from. Sharpen the other point to an oval knife shape, as on the marking gauge, with the flat side of the knife shape at right angles to the main axis of the dividers. Sharpened in this fashion, dividers will cut an arc as cleanly as a marking knife (see the bottom left photo).

A trammel is nothing more than two sharp steel points (or a steel point and a pencil point) mounted in heads that slide on and clamp to a long beam. Trammel heads equipped with an eccentric point allow you to finely adjust the radius after they have been clamped to the beam. The trammel's great advantage over dividers is that the radius of the circles it can draw is limited only by the length of the beam. To draw an arc with a 10 ft. radius, simply mount the trammel heads on a beam that is as long.

Besides drawing arcs and circles, both dividers and trammels can be used to lay out complex geometric shapes with a high degree of accuracy. If you need to lay out a hexagon, for example, you can do it with dividers. Just draw a circle with the desired radius, and without changing the setting of the points, step the dividers around the circumference to divide it into six equal parts. Then connect the intersection marks with straight lines. You now have a pretty good hexagon.

Woodworking dividers, when properly sharpened, will scribe a clean line across and with the grain (above).

CREATING WORKING DRAWINGS

by Jim Tolpin

For much of my woodworking career, I dreaded the drawing stage of a project. It was always a daunting, tedious process that only put off the true fun—shaping real wood into real objects. After erasing a misplaced or poorly drawn line for the umpteenth time, I'd often think that I could have built the darn thing in the time it took to do the drawings. Considering the way I was producing drawings, I was probably right.

Today, however, I thoroughly enjoy the drawing process, and I relish seeing my ideas first come to life on paper. I've learned to appreciate the unlimited design freedom afforded by freehand concept sketching, as well as the ability to express my ideas clearly and precisely with more refined drawing

Loose concept sketching fosters creativity and allows you to refine your rough idea to the point where you're ready to create a three-view drawing and then an isometric projection. From there it's not all that far to full-scale drawings and to creating something with wood. The time spent getting a drawing right will pay for itself many times over.

techniques. The difference in my attitude came from learning to use the right tools and techniques. In this article, I'll share what I've learned about materials and techniques and explain how you can take your design ideas from rough, raw images to refined, scale working drawings. Here's an overview.

I begin the drawing process by first creating a series of concept sketches that show the object in a roughly accurate perspective view—in other words, the way the object would appear to your eyes. Choosing the sketch that comes closest to my design goal, I commit its dimensions to a scaled-down, three-view drawing—an orthographic projection. This gives me a way to see the parts of the piece in their true proportion to one another. But because this type of drawing limits me to viewing each face independently from the others, I will often go on to draw an assembled view of the drawing—an isometric projection. This drawing shows me how all the parts relate to one another, and it gives me an accurate feel for how a piece will look when it's built.

Concept sketching

This is where the fun begins. You get your first look at the project-to-be, and you can work out the bugs in the overall look of the piece without laboring over the details. Approach concept sketching by giving your hand free rein to draw and redraw any inspiration that comes to mind (see the photo on p. 113). This is not the time to worry about crisp lines, perfect symmetry, properly scaled proportions or fair curves. You can take care of all that later when you produce the mechanical drawings. Do not, however, go on from sketching to drafting until you have something you really like. It's too time-consuming to make major design changes at the drafting stage.

A ring-bound artist's sketchbook is the best place to do your concept sketching. Choose a soft (#2 or # 2¹/₂) lead pencil with a pink-tipped eraser. Avoid using harder pencils because their lines are difficult to erase from typical sketchbook paper. Keep a half-dozen or so well-sharpened pencils handy as you sketch. You don't want a dull pencil to interrupt the flow of your creative juices. Hold the pencil lightly, keeping your wrist loose and flexible. When sketching out a long line, allow your arm to move with your hand. And finally, get in the habit of turning the sketchbook to accommodate the natural sweep of your wrist when drawing angled lines.

One of the benefits of doing freehand concept sketches is that you can easily create a series of "what-if" views. Instead of redrawing the form over and over again, simply trace it onto a piece of translucent paper, leaving out the areas that will be changed in the what-if views. Or you can photocopy as many basic outlines as you'd like, and then flesh them out with your new design ideas.

From concept sketch to orthographic drawing

Once you have settled on a concept sketch that comes closest to representing your idea, it's time to assign some dimensions to the project. By setting out the design to scale in a mechanical drawing, you can see clearly how the size and shape of components relate to one another. Methods and sequences of joinery also become more obvious. These working drawings are a bridge between your freehand concept sketches and a master cut list.

Equipment: buying the right stuff

Luckily, the type of equipment a woodworker needs to produce adequate working drawings is relatively simple and inexpensive. Unless you do a lot of room-sized architectural millwork, a 2-ft. by 3-ft. board will provide plenty of space for rendering projects in a suitable scale. This board can be nothing more than a flat piece of plywood set on a desktop, but to make it more comfortable to work at, tilt up the back of

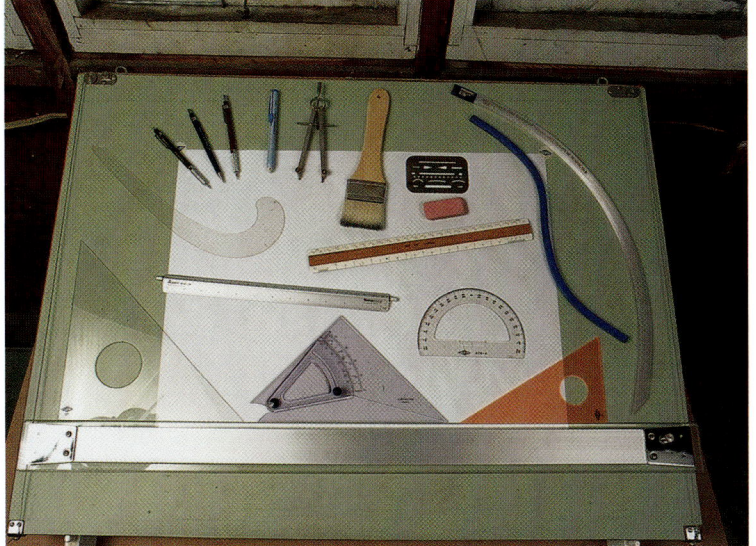

Drawing supplies used by the author include, clockwise from lower left, a 45° to 45° angle template, a metal architect's rule, a ship's curve (a large version of a French curve), mechanical pencils in three sizes (3mm, 5mm and 7mm), a pencil-style eraser, a compass, a dust brush, an eraser shield, a pink eraser, a flat architect's rule, a lead flexible curve, a plastic adjustable curve, an orange 30° to 60° angle template, a protractor and an adjustable angle template.

the board 3 or 4 in. Adding a piece of drafting-board vinyl (available through most office-supply stores) smooths the drawing surface and will allow holes left behind by compass points to self-heal. To pinch pennies, you can cover the board with a ⅛-in. sheet of corrugated cardboard, but pin holes and pencil grooves will soon telegraph through to the drawings.

You can draw consistently parallel lines and angles with templates and a simple T-square, but I highly recommend spending a bit more money and setting yourself up with a sliding parallel rule fixed to a cable run along either side of the board. These rules are widely available for well under $100—a small price for the frustration one will save you. This is supposed to be fun, remember.

You can further reduce drawing-board madness by using only high-grade (16 to 20 lb.), fine-grained vellum paper for mechanical drawings. Unlike sketch paper, vellum erases easily with a standard pink gum eraser, leaving behind a smooth, smudge-free surface. The vellum is also translucent, letting you trace over prototype sketches, speeding the drawing of repetitive elements.

Other pieces of equipment you'll need for mechanical drawing include the following:

Pencils—Forget wood pencils. They're time-consuming, messy to sharpen, and because their width changes as they dull, they make lines of uneven thickness. Instead, get a set of three mechanical pencils (3mm, 5mm and 7mm) and use an HB grade lead. It will dull quickly, but it will produce a dark line that reproduces well in a copy machine, eliminating the need to ink the drawing.

Erasers—On vellum paper, the classic pink gum eraser works as well as any. To make fine corrections, use pencil-type erasers in conjunction with eraser shields (shown in the photo above).

Ruler—I use an architect's scale rule for laying out dimensioned lines. I prefer a flat ruler with eight scales rather than the twelve-scale triangular rulers, which I find more difficult to mark dimensions from. To keep the edges of a rule smooth and clean, use it *only* to mark dimensions, never as a straightedge for drawing lines—that's what a parallel rule and angle templates are for.

Angle templates—To start out, get an 8-in. 45° to 45°, an 8-in. 30° to 60° and an adjustable-angle template. Later, you'll want to add a 4-in. version of this set for drawing small details. I like my templates in green or orange, so I can readily find them amid the papers strewn about the drawing board.

Shape templates—Circles, ellipses, squares and rectangles, as well as a variety of other shapes, are available on templates. I also use French-curve templates and their larger cousins, ship's curves, to draw in curves of progressively changing radii.

Adjustable curves—To draw curves between fixed points, I use either a flexible lead bar or a plastic slip curve. If the curve is very large, I'll bend a $3/16$-in.-sq. length of straight-grained wood to the marks while I trace a line against its edge.

Protractor—I use a 4-in.-radius protractor to draw angles from a baseline.

Compass—A pencil compass is useful for drawing circles.

Drafting basics

Unless you move on from woodworking to designing and building space shuttles, you won't need to learn more than the most basic drafting skills and conventions to produce quick, accurate and easy-to-read working drawings. The skills are mostly common sense: Make sure your board is free of lead and eraser debris before taping paper to it. Align the bottom of the paper to the parallel rule, and then secure it to the board with a small piece of tape in each corner. Keep a scrap piece of paper between your hand and the drawing to avoid smudging your work. And never wipe away eraser debris with your hand—always use a brush.

Once you establish a baseline, draw any degree angle to it using either angle templates or a protractor and straightedge. Begin the angled line precisely on a dimension mark by first holding the pencil to the mark and then sliding the template or straightedge to it. If you reverse this process, parallax can play tricks on your eyes, causing you to misjudge the placement of the pencil.

Draw out a waver-free line by tilting the pencil slightly into the corner formed between the edge of the template and the paper.

A mechanical drawing is nothing more than a happy meeting of lines that indicate the outlines of an object and where measurements are being made to. Unless these lines vary in some way, however, the drawing can be difficult to read. Figure 1 on the facing page shows how lines with different meanings are conventionally rendered in mechanical drawings. Note that dimensions are not given a unit symbol. This would only crowd the drawing. Instead, a note in the legend box tells you what units are represented by the dimension numbers.

A three-view drawing

The first type of working drawing I produce from a concept sketch (or from dimensions taken from a photo or some other source) is a three-view (orthographic) projection. I tape a copy of my final concept sketch (or a combination of sketches) to the top of my drafting board and then attach a piece of vellum to the board. I draw a thick (0.7mm) borderline around the perimeter and a legend box in the lower right-hand corner. Within this box, I record my name and a copyright symbol (©), followed by the date and the name of the client, if any. If the piece has a name, or if it is a reproduction, I will title it accordingly. Finally, I indicate the scale and units of measurement used in the drawing.

Unless the project is very large, such as a floor-to-ceiling entertainment center, I use $1/4$ in. to represent 1 in. This reduction allows me to fit the front, side and top views onto one sheet without creating a cluttered drawing that's difficult to read. I use two scales on my architect's rule to lay out the dimensions: the $1/4$ scale and the 3 scale. Although the $1/4$ scale is useful for representing full-inch increments, its divisions are

Working drawings in a nutshell

FIG. 1: LINES USED IN WORKING DRAWINGS

Lines of different thickness help to distinguish different meanings in working drawings. Here are some of the most common line types.

Border line and legend box (0.7mm)

Working line (0.5mm)

Hidden line (0.3mm)

Dimension line (0.3mm) / Extension line (0.3mm)

Centerline (0.3mm)

Cutting plane (0.5mm)

FIG. 2: SETTING OUT A THREE-VIEW ORTHOGRAPHIC DRAWING

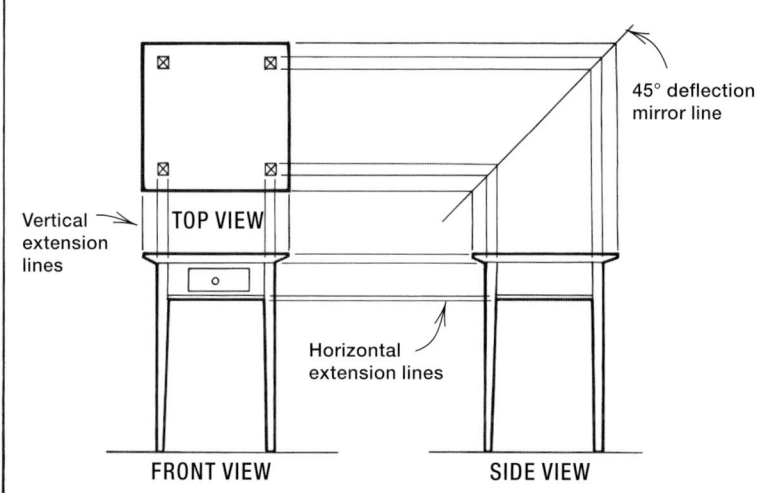

45° deflection mirror line

Vertical extension lines

TOP VIEW

Horizontal extension lines

FRONT VIEW   SIDE VIEW

FIG. 3: PRODUCING A SIDE VIEW OF AN ANGLED SIDE

Problem: You cannot use mirror line to project side of top view to baseline because distance B is foreshortened to look as though it's less than distance A.

Solution: Use an architect's rule or a compass to measure distance A and transfer distance directly to horizontal line extended over from front view. Drop lines to baseline from distance marks.

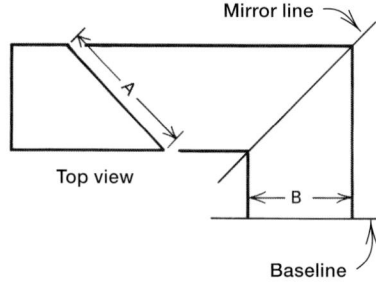

Mirror line

A

Top view

B

Baseline

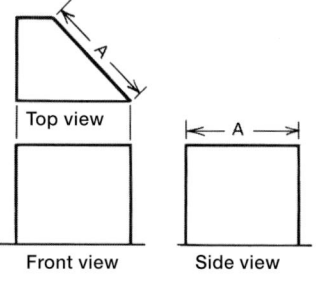

Top view

A

Top view

Front view

Side view

A

FIG. 4: SETTING IN DIMENSION LINES

Note: The overall dimension—the height in this case—is drawn to the outside of all other dimensions. In general, the smallest dimensions are kept closest to the object.

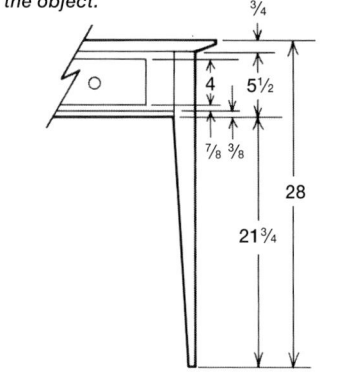

³⁄₄

4   5¹⁄₂

⁷⁄₈ ³⁄₈

28

21³⁄₄

FIG. 5: CREATING AN ISOMETRIC PROJECTION

Step 1: Create two angled baselines, each at 30° to your original horizontal baseline.

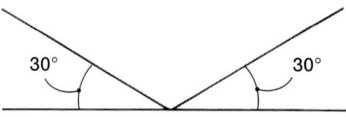

30°   30°

Step 2: Draw in the "footprint" of the top view along the angled baselines. Extend the view back into the isometric projection by drawing the back and the far-side lines. Keep these lines parallel to the angled baselines.

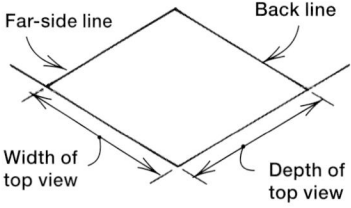

Far-side line   Back line

Width of top view   Depth of top view

Step 3: Establish the actual top view by extending vertical lines up from the corners of the footprint. Measure up along the line to the overall height of the front view. Draw in the outline of the top view parallel to the angled baselines.

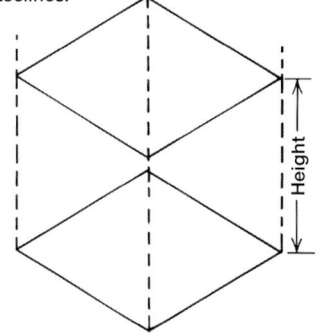

Height

Step 4: Now simply draw in the piece of furniture using the dimensions from your orthographic drawing.

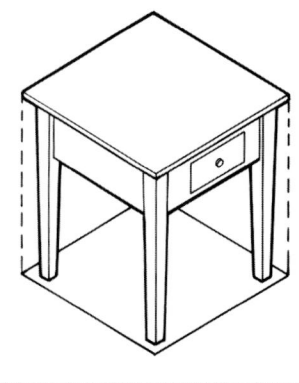

in twelfths (because this scale is designed primarily to equate ¼ in. to 1 ft.), which is not a convenient scale for fractions of an inch. For fractions, I use the 3 scale, where a ¼-in. segment is broken down into eight divisions, each representing ⅛ in.

After drawing a horizontal baseline about 2 in. up from the lower border of the paper, I lay out the rough positions of the three views with a light pencil line. As a right-hander, I find it more comfortable to draw from left to right, so I place the front view in the lower left-hand corner of the drawing, the top view above and the side view to the right (see figure 2 on p. 117).

I do the front view first, constantly referring to the concept sketch (or to dimension notes) as I draw in the outline of the form with light lines. I generally trust my eye to judge whether proportions are correct. When I'm satisfied with this light pencil rendering, I darken in the outline with 0.5mm working lines.

I draw the top view next, extending lines up vertically from the front view to define the widths. I ascertain the positions and depths of the various elements by again referring to my sketches or notes. Next I create the side view. Only one is necessary unless the piece is asymmetrical. With the front and top views already completed, the dimensions of the side view are already established in the drawing. To draw this view, I need only extend over the outlines of the other two views until they intersect over the baseline to the right of the front view. As you can see in figure 3, I reflect the top view's extension lines down to the baseline with a 45° mirror line.

A note of caution: reflecting extension lines from a top view across a mirror line works only if the side of an object is perpendicular to its front. At any other angle, reflected lines create a foreshortened view. Although this is technically correct in a true orthographic projection, it makes more sense to draw the angled side so that the length of its side remains true to scale. Skip the top view reflection and scale the depth dimensions directly from the architect's rule or with a compass (see figure 3).

I finish the three-view drawing by penciling in all my dimensions, working my way out from the smallest elements of the components, to the components themselves, to the overall size of the structure (see figure 4). Then I draw in the fine details shown in my concept sketches: curved or molded corners or edges, knobs, pulls and the like. I rarely bother with cross sections or detail blowups in my three-view drawings. Instead, I wait to do these on a full-scale rendering. If I need this kind of information, I want it actual size, so I can transfer the information directly onto a story pole, or measuring stick. I do label all the parts on the three-view drawing, so I can refer to them in the bill of materials and cut lists.

From three-view drawing to isometric projection

The advantage of an isometric projection is that it shows you how the various faces of an object will relate to one another. And because an isometric doesn't diminish or foreshorten dimensions as does a vanishing-point perspective drawing, all the views of this working drawing remain true to scale, making it simple to draw and easy to take off scaled dimensions (see figure 5).

Developing a three-view drawing from a photograph

It's possible to develop scaled views of a piece of furniture from nothing more than a photograph. It helps, of course, if you know the overall dimensions of the piece, but some detective work—such as scaling dimensions from familiar objects in the photo—can often provide enough clues. The picture should be as free from distortion as possible (no wide-angle shots) and should offer a three-quarter

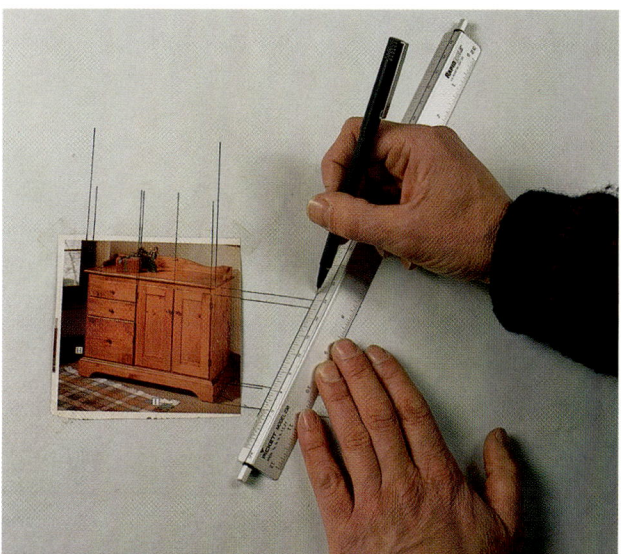

view, which lets you see the front, side and top of the piece.

To determine the dimensions of doors, drawers and other elements of the piece, affix the photo to the center of a piece of vellum paper with double-faced tape. Use a straightedge to extend lines out from the overall width and height of the piece. Then lay an architect's rule between the two lines that represent the overall dimension of the piece (see the photo at left). Usually, you'll have to angle the rule to get the scaled dimension to fall between the lines. Use whatever scale allows you to correlate the overall dimensions of the piece to a reasonable, divisible section of the rule.

Draw this angled reference line, and then extend over the outlines of the internal elements. To find their dimensions, simply consult the same scale on the rule. Repeat this procedure to find the dimension of elements within the other planes of the photograph. Once you've established all the dimensions for all elements of the piece, use this information to create a three-view drawing of the piece from which you can create a cut list.   —J.T.

Once I've created the isometric cube that establishes the perimeter of the piece of furniture I'm drawing, I fill in the three views by transferring scaled measurements from the three-view drawing, being careful to orient the lines parallel to the 30° baselines. You may find it helpful to place isometric grid paper under the vellum as an aid to sketching in some details. When you're finished filling in the details of the piece, erase the extension lines used to raise the structure, and you're done.

SIMPLE MILLING SEQUENCE YIELDS FLAT, STRAIGHT AND SQUARE LUMBER

by Peter Korn

If wood were a stable, homogenous, man-made material like metal or plastic, how much simpler the woodworker's task would be! Instead, we pay a price for our love of natural beauty. We work with a biological medium that reacts continuously to the environment, changing dimension and shape as it breathes moisture in and out.

If you've ever attempted to dovetail cupped boards or to build a frame-and-panel door from bowed lumber, you know how frustrating it is to work with poorly prepared stock. Fine craftsmanship occurs one step at a time, and the first step is preparing (milling) stock foursquare—straight, true and accurately dimensioned.

Boards are almost never flat enough to use directly from the lumberyard. Even S2S (surfaced two sides) lumber is milled only with thickness planers, which create boards of uniform thickness but do little to iron out cup, bow or twist. In any case, wood's propensity for continuous movement dictates milling only when you're ready to use

The thickness planer is an essential tool for milling wood. It will quickly and accurately give you a second flat face, parallel to the jointed face.

Ripping rough stock on the bandsaw is far safer than on the tablesaw because there's no danger of kickback if a warped or twisted board shifts as it's going through the blade. The author rips to about ¼ in. more than finish width to allow for jointing an edge and then ripping parallel to that trued edge.

it. Stored wood will often warp between milling and joinery.

I begin every project with a cutting list specifying the exact measurements of all the parts, including allowances for tenon length. If there are curved parts, I usually mill foursquare blanks and then bandsaw the curves later. Before cutting, I lay out the lo-cation of each part on the rough lumber with chalk or a crayon, trying to minimize waste and make the most attractive use of grain. Laying out the parts right on the milled stock also prevents embarrassing mistakes.

When the cutting list calls for several parts of the same dimension, you must weigh time against conservation of material. It takes less time to mill long pieces to thickness and then cut shorter parts from those

long boards than it does to crosscut smaller pieces and then mill them. Longer boards tend to be more twisted and/or bowed along the length of their faces. If you mill a long board whole, however, you'll lose more material in making it flat than if you'd cut it into shorter rough blanks. The right approach is always a judgment call, depending on how straight your rough lumber is and how much thickness you have to spare between rough lumber and the dimension of your finished stock.

When I cut rough lumber into blanks for milling, I leave the blanks at least ¼ in. wider and 1 in. longer than the final pieces I'll need. I crosscut to rough length with a radial-arm saw, circular saw or handsaw depending on what's handy and where I am. For the initial rip to rough width, I prefer the bandsaw (see the photo on p. 121) because it's quieter, less dust-producing and safer than the tablesaw. Where the cups, bows and twists endemic to rough lumber increase the likelihood of tablesaw kickback, a bandsaw purrs right on through. I bandsaw by eye to the lines I have marked.

If you prefer to rip rough lumber to width on the tablesaw, make sure the edge against the rip fence is straight. If it's not, run it over the jointer first.

Six steps to foursquare stock

These are the steps I use to prepare stock from rough lumber:

Step 1: Flatten the first face of the board.

Step 2: Make the second face of the board parallel to the first face at the desired thickness.

Step 3: Square an edge. (Steps 2 and 3 are often reversed.)

Step 4: Rip the second edge square and to the desired width.

Step 5: Cut one end square.

Step 6: Cut the other end square and to length. (Usually, I leave stock an inch or so long until the joinery is cut.)

Before power tools existed, the entire milling process was done exclusively with hand tools, but milling is one job that machines do much more efficiently than hand tools with no sacrifice in quality.

Generally, I joint the face of a board and square a perpendicular edge (steps 1 and 3) on the jointer, plane the board to thickness (step 2) with a planer, and rip the board to width and crosscut it to length on the tablesaw (steps 4, 5, 6). If I have to flatten the face of a board wider than the 8-in. capacity of my jointer, I'll use handplanes for that step (see the sidebar on pp. 124-125), but I still use machines for the rest of the sequence. If I didn't want to have to flatten a wide board with handplanes, I could rip the board in half, mill each half foursquare and then glue the pieces back together. Handplaning avoids the extra glueline, and it's also one of the great pleasures of working with wood. There's nothing quite like unveiling a board's beauty with a well-tuned handplane, shaving by sinuous shaving.

Flattening the first face

The setting of a jointer is critical to its performance. The outfeed table should be set at the highest point of the knives' rotation. A slightly high outfeed table will cause a board to become convex along its length. A low outfeed table causes snipe—the rear end of a board drops as it leaves the support of the infeed table, making the last few inches thinner.

The height of the jointer's infeed table determines the amount of wood removed with each pass. Take thin passes to reduce the possibility of tearout as well as wear on the machine. I never take off more than $1/16$ in. per pass.

The first step in stock preparation is to create one flat face, which becomes the reference face. So long as your jointer's capacity is greater than the width of the board you need to flatten, it's a quick operation. Whenever you joint, maintain pressure on the outfeed table just past the cutterhead. Always use a push stick.

Whenever you joint or plane wood, you should check grain direction and ensure that you cut with the grain to avoid tearout. Where the grain is contrary, feed wood slowly and steadily and be sure the knives are sharp. *Always* use a push stick when using the jointer to flatten a face, so your fingers don't pass right over the cutterhead (see the photo on the facing page). If a board is cupped and/or bowed—as most are—joint the concave side so that the board doesn't rock.

Making the second face parallel to the first

A thickness planer's infeed roller, outfeed roller, pressure bar and knives should be set according to the machine's manual. Also, the knives must be sharp and the table parallel to the cutterhead. I vary the setting of the table rollers in the planer's bed to suit the occasion. If I have hundreds of board feet to plane, I'll raise the table rollers a bit above the bed to help the lumber along. This causes a bit of snipe at the boards' ends as they are lifted by the table rollers, but I live with it because of the time and effort saved. When I want finer, more accurately machined stock, I lower the table rollers beneath the surface of the bed, which I keep waxed to help the boards slide along.

Snipe can occur even with the table rollers lowered. On a planer with an adjustable table and a fixed head, the table may be rocking, in which case the gibs that hold the table in place need to be tightened. On a planer with a fixed table and an adjustable head, the head assembly may need to be tightened in place. Check the manual for your particular machine if you have a problem.

To prevent tearout, thickness plane with the grain as much as possible. If a board has very squirrelly grain that has a tendency to tear out, feed the board through as slowly as your planer allows, and take thin passes. Never plane more than $1/16$ in. at a time, in any case, to avoid stress on the machine.

Removing wood from the surface of a board will often upset its internal stress equilibrium and cause the board to warp.

When jointing an edge, choose whichever edge looks as though it will be less prone to tearout. Make sure the fence is square to the jointer beds and that the face against the fence is snug up against it. As when face jointing, transfer downward pressure from the infeed to the outfeed table as the board passes the cutterhead.

To maximize stability and flatness, I often stop planing when a board is between $1/16$ in. and $1/8$ in. from final thickness and let it readjust itself overnight. The next day, I reflatten one face with the jointer or handplane and take the board to final thickness with my planer.

Squaring the first edge

Unless there are other considerations, the first edge I square is the one that can best be cut with the grain (see the photo above). Here is where the advantage of flattening both faces before truing an edge becomes apparent because I can now choose either face to run against the jointer fence. I always check the fence for square before jointing any wood, but I usually also make a test pass and check the board with a try square.

Ripping to width

A rip blade in the tablesaw works well for ripping stock to width, but I prefer a combination blade when preparing stock so I won't have to change blades to crosscut the ends. Set the blade square to the table and just a tooth's height above the wood for safety. Then set your fence for the exact width of your cut by measuring from the rip fence to any sawtooth that inclines toward the fence.

There are two schools of thought about rip fences. One holds that the fence should be exactly parallel to the sawblade. The other believes that the fence should tilt a hair away from the back of the blade as extra

Flattening the face of a board with a handplane

Like most other woodworking skills, handplaning wide boards is daunting only until you give it a serious try. All you need are one or two well-tuned planes, some elbow grease and a couple of days of practice.

The two planes I use are a scrub plane and a bench plane. The bench plane alone would be sufficient, but the scrub plane saves time and effort by removing wood quickly from seriously cupped boards. Scrub planes are made for rough work, and there is no trick to tuning them beyond sharpening the curved blade.

A bench plane is a more precise instrument, which requires greater attention to get optimum performance. The sole should be flat and polished, the blade sharp enough to shave with and the frog adjusted by trial and error for the best result. (For more information on choosing and tuning bench planes, see pp. 69-75.) Bench planes come in a wide range of sizes. For flattening boards, I prefer a 14-in. jack plane, but I know other woodworkers who like to work with a longer, heavier plane, such as a 22-in. jointer plane.

To set up for planing, I clamp the work on a flat benchtop, making sure that nothing extends above the board's surface. A bench with dogs and a tail vise is best, but you can

Sighting along winding sticks tells the author that the board doesn't twist. He also uses a long straightedge to check flatness along and across the board's length.

A scrub plane makes quick work of high spots on the rough board. Korn planes across the grain diagonally to prevent tearout and then planes on the opposing diagonal, removing the ridges created with the first passes. A bench plane is the next step.

also wedge a board between stops that are either clamped or screwed to the bench. I usually place the convex side up, so the board sits securely on the bench. Also, I find it easier to take down a center hump than to attack raised edges.

Using winding sticks and a long straight edge, I locate and

mark the board's high spots and determine the degree of twist. Winding sticks are simply sticks of uniform width placed across each end of the work, parallel to each other. Sighting along their tops reveals the exact degree of twist in a board, as shown in the top photo on the facing page. Once I've marked all high spots with a pencil, it's time to plane.

I set my scrub plane's blade so that it protrudes about $1/16$ in. beyond the sole. I plane diagonally across the grain in parallel strokes, removing wood quickly and minimizing the chance of severe tearout, which would most likely occur if I went with the grain. Then I go back and plane on the opposing diagonal until I've covered the board (see the bottom photo on the facing page). If I didn't have a scrub plane, I would begin flattening the board by using the jack plane in the exact same manner, but the process would just take longer.

When the work is more or less flat across, I switch to my bench plane, planing with the grain along the length of the board (see the photo at right). I check for cup, bow or twist every once in a while and again mark any high spots with a pencil. It's important to avoid planing low spots because they'd just become that much lower. If my plane starts to make dust instead of shavings, I resharpen

Taking a bench plane and planing with the grain, Korn takes out the scrub plane's marks and smooths the face of the board flat, readying it for the thickness planer and further milling.

the blade. I find that rubbing paraffin on the sole of a metal plane cuts down on friction tremendously.

My straightedge and winding sticks tell me when a board is flat, but it's evident, too, when

I'm able to take long, lovely shavings over the full length of the board. —P.K.

When ripping on the tablesaw, safety should be foremost in your mind. Use a guard, splitter and push stick, and make sure you stay out from behind the board you're ripping: Kickback happens faster than you can react to it.

insurance against kickback. I used to believe it was best to angle the fence away from the blade, but now I try to get the fence exactly parallel. Whichever you believe, just be sure the far end of your rip fence doesn't angle in toward the blade. At best, the wood will pinch and burn from friction; at worst, stock will catch and fly back at you faster than you can react.

Tablesaws are inherently dangerous, so here are some oft-repeated tips to take to heart: When ripping, keep the board firmly against the fence at all times, and push it with a smooth, steady motion (see the photo above). Never let go of a board until it is entirely past the blade. Use a push stick rather than pass your hand by the blade. Don't hold wood with a hand placed beyond the blade—your hand could be drawn back through the blade by kickback. Avoid standing directly behind the board being cut, and make sure no one else is in the path of potential kickback either.

Crosscutting the ends square and to length

After stock has been flattened on both sides, jointed on one edge, and ripped to the designated width, it's time to cut the board to length. There are a number of tools with which you can crosscut. I prefer a tablesaw

Crosscutting one end square and the other end both square and to length can be done on the tablesaw with either a sliding table or a miter gauge with a wooden extension fence (below). The author lines up his cutoff mark with the inside edge of the sawkerf in the miter fence, ensuring an accurate cut.

equipped with a combination blade. Crosscutting on the tablesaw is done with the aid of a sliding table or a miter gauge with an add-on wooden extension fence (see the top photo). Never crosscut with the end of a board against the rip fence.

After the first end is cut square, you can either measure out the desired length on the stock and pencil a cutoff mark, or you can attach a stop to the fence of your sliding table or miter guide at the desired distance from the sawblade. The quickest way to cut to a pencil line is to align it with the edge of the kerf the blade has left in the fence—as long as you always use the same blade (see the photo above).

From the moment wood is milled, movement should be minimized by careful handling. To promote even exposure to air, I either leave boards on edge or stack them horizontally with spacers between them. I also keep wood away from direct sunlight and any other heat source that could affect one side of a board more than the other. I also try to cut all joinery right away while the wood is as square and straight as it will ever be.

RABBETS AND DADOES

by Sven Hanson

Judging by the attention that dovetails get, you'd think every craftsman cuts 200 of them a week. In reality, the rabbet, a joint with a single shoulder cut at the edge of a board, and the dado, a groove plowed inside the edge, are what many cabinetmakers use to join everyday case work.

On the evolutionary scale of joinery, the rabbet is a step above the butt joint, but it's a big step. The shoulder of a rabbet adds additional glue surface to the joint and supplies mechanical support. A dado has two shoulders, adding even more strength. The shoulders of rabbets and dadoes aid in the assembly of case work. They align the pieces when dry-fitting a case. You can check for size and fit before applying glue and clamps, which is a real boon in a one-man shop. In addition to their many applications in case work, these two joints also can be combined to produce simple but very sturdy drawers.

You can use hand tools to cut rabbets and dadoes, but these joints are usually machined with a router or a tablesaw. Each tool has its advantages. By choosing the right tool and using a few shopmade fences and jigs, you can cut these joints accurately and quickly. The techniques are as straightforward and uncomplicated as they are useful.

Case joints

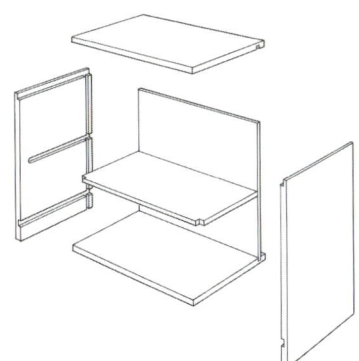

THE RABBET

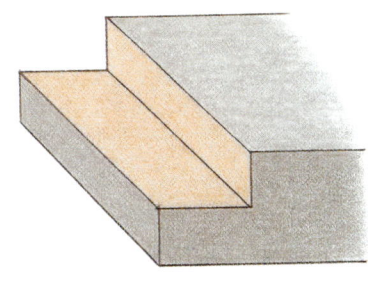

A block of wood and two clamps make a fence. An auxiliary fence helps create a clean rabbet by spanning dips that a bearing would follow.

The router reigns for case work

For joining the tops, sides and backs of most case work, I prefer the rabbet joint. It's strong and simple to cut, and rabbets help with the alignment of parts during assembly. Most of the time, the rabbets go across the grain at the ends of vertical cabinet pieces (or ends of the drawer sides). I prefer using a router to cut this joint because the bit leaves a cleaner cross-grain cut than a dado blade would.

The rabbet

Maneuvering components smoothly over a tablesaw or a router table can be difficult when building large cases. Additionally, any slight cup of the workpiece will prevent the blade or bit from cutting to its full depth. That's why I like using a hand-held router for cutting rabbets in the tops and bottoms of cases (see the photo at right). A router bit cuts cleanly and leaves a sharp, square inside corner that gives a very good surface for gluing.

Rabbeting bits come with guide bearings, but I usually remove them and guide the tool with an auxiliary fence. Bearings follow every dip in the wood, which could round the corner at the start or end of the cut (see the photos on p. 130).

My fence, which is nothing more than a straight block of wood clamped to the router base, provides a secure surface from start to finish, and it gives me an infinite range of adjustment. A fence also gives me the option of using straight bits to cut rab-

Router bits with bearings have limitations. A bearing-piloted bit (right) will dip into voids and round corners. The result is a sloppy rabbet (below).

Two dadoes

DADO

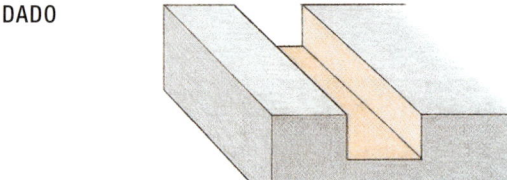

STOPPED DADO

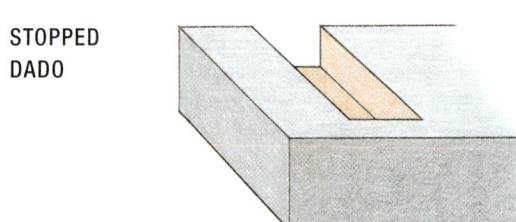

bets. When I make case goods, I usually make the depth of the rabbet half the thickness of the stock.

A cut begins with the bit well away from the work. I wiggle the router to check that the fence is snug to the edge of the board, and then I take a slow, steady pass. At the beginning of the cut, I press the front of the fence against the workpiece. Near the end of the cut, I push on the rear of the fence.

If there's no block clamped to the far side of the workpiece to combat tearout, I stop the cut an inch from the end, lift the router past the end of the board and carefully back the cutter in to complete the cut. A second pass along the rabbet ensures a good cut.

The dado and the stopped dado

Tall cabinets, such as entertainment centers, require internal structural support to prevent racking. Here's where I use the dado joint. A fixed shelf or panel dadoed into the sides near the center of the case adds a lot of rigidity. I cut the dadoes as deep as the corner-joint rabbets. For a snug fit, use a straight bit whose diameter matches the thickness of the panel that will be captured by the dado. If you're using sheet goods, you can order slightly undersized bits. They come in odd sizes such as $^{23}/_{32}$ in., which is the actual thickness of most $^3/_4$-in. plywood.

To guide the router, I use a shop-built T-fence (see the photos on the facing page) clamped to the workpiece. A dado slot in the top of the fence provides a reference

Shopmade T-fence for cutting dadoes— Screw two strips of plywood together at right angles to make a guide fence for cutting dadoes with a router.

point for positioning the jig. When using it, I install a square base on my router. Round router bases tend to plow sawdust into the fence and then ride up on the dust bank. I prevent tearout on the far side of the cut by clamping a backer block of hardwood where the bit will emerge.

A dado plowed right through the edge of a case side is not a pretty joint. I usually stop the dado before it comes out the front edge. Cutting a stopped dado with the T-fence and router is easy because I can see the layout marks.

The tablesaw dominates for drawers

Nothing cuts a dado faster than a tablesaw equipped with dado blades. Dado blades can be of the stack variety (see the photo at left on p. 132), with two outside cutters and various-sized internal chippers and shims, or wobble-style (see the photo at right on p. 132), with one or two blades and a hub that allow you to dial in different settings. Stack dadoes tend to cost more but usually give you a smooth, flat-bottomed cut.

The drawer joint

Around the time the tablesaw was invented, woodworkers figured out how to make this strong joint without the fuss and time required for dovetails. The simplified version of the drawer joint combines dadoes cut in the drawer sides with tenons cut on the front and back pieces.

Before beginning, make a custom throat plate for your tablesaw. It will reduce tearout by supporting the wood fibers on the edges of the cut. I create the opening in the plate by lowering the blades below the insert, turning on the saw and raising the dado blades through the insert to a predetermined height. Instead of starting and stopping the saw to measure the blade height, I mark the depth of cut on my rip fence and slowly raise the blade to that mark.

I begin this joint by first crosscutting a dado on the insides of the sides using the tablesaw's miter gauge and rip fence for guides (see photo 1 on the facing page). I position the dado so that when the drawer is assembled the sides will be proud of the front by just $1/32$ in. That way, when you fit a false drawer front, it will fit snugly against the ends of the sides. For the drawer to end up nice and square, I make sure the rip fence is parallel to the blade and the miter gauge is square to the rip fence.

To make a matching tenon on the drawer front, I set up my saw for a rabbet cut. I set the rip fence so the dado head is partly buried in it. Because that's incompatible with hardened aluminum extrusion, I keep surplus $3/4$-in. melamine-surfaced particle-board on hand for making disposable fence faces. I set the fence so the exposed portion of the dado head equals the width of the rabbet. The exact width of the dado head doesn't matter as long as it's wider than the intended rabbet. The depth of the rabbet is set by the height of the blade. The stock is again guided by a miter gauge and a rip fence (see photo 2). It's a good idea to run some scrap stock the same size as the work-piece to check settings. The joint should be snug. If it's too tight, the short-grained sections of the mortises could break off during assembly.

The drawer joint

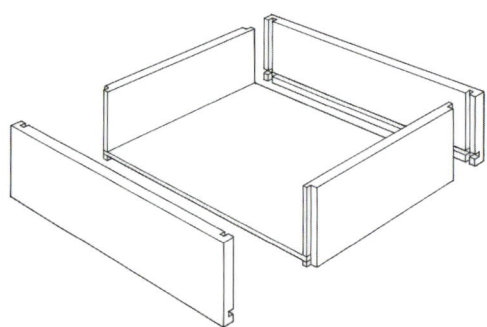

1. Cut the mortise first. Guide a drawer side against the rip fence using a miter gauge when cutting the mortise.

2. Next cut a rabbet to create a tenon. Make this cut in a piece of scrap first, and check the fit.

3. You want a snug, not tight fit. You should be able to squeeze the joint together by hand.

THE SLIP JOINT

by Frank Klausz

Some years ago, I went to see a show at the Metropolitan Museum in New York that featured artifacts from the tomb of the Egyptian king Tutankhamen. On display was a chair built around 1350 B.C., on which I could see a slip joint. There are rea-

sons this joint has been in use for so long. Also called an open mortise and tenon, the slip joint is hard to beat for ease of assembly. And because of the large gluing area where the pieces meet, a slip joint holds up to a lot of stress.

I build and repair furniture for a living, so I'm interested in not only doing a job well but also doing it efficiently. Unless an architect or designer has supplied me with very detailed drawings, it is often up to me to decide what joinery to use for a given job. The slip joint is one of my favorites. A doweled butt joint may go together faster, but it's not nearly as strong.

Where to use it? If I have a cabinet that calls for simple frame-and-panel doors, where rails and stiles are square-edged and the doors are inset, I don't have to think twice about which joint to use. For overlay

A jig for making slip joints

This jig makes both mortises and tenons. A channel, sized to your tablesaw fence, keeps the jig running smoothly and safely.

Mount clamp with hanger bolt and wing nut.

Hanger bolt, washer and wing nut

18 in.

24 in.

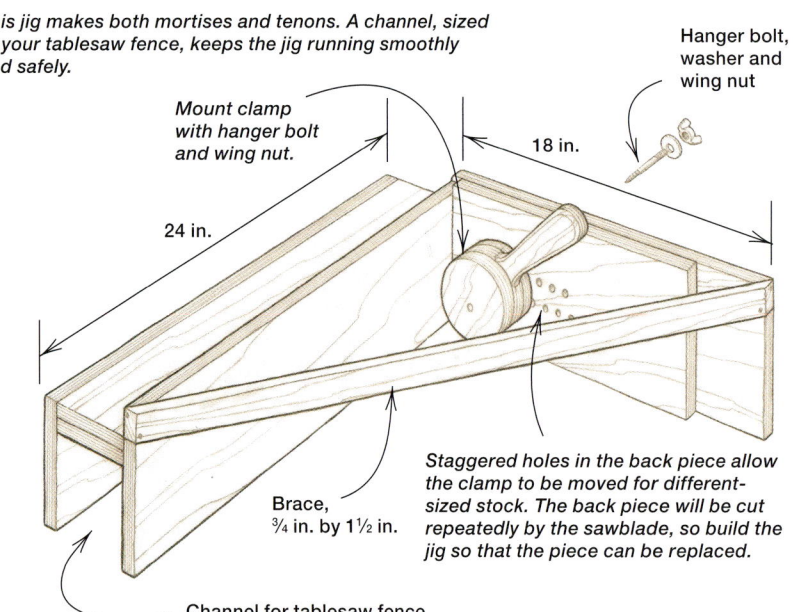

Brace, ¾ in. by 1½ in.

Staggered holes in the back piece allow the clamp to be moved for different-sized stock. The back piece will be cut repeatedly by the sawblade, so build the jig so that the piece can be replaced.

Channel for tablesaw fence

QUICK CLAMP

The eccentric clamp holds any thickness of stock tightly. The offset hole makes the clamp act as a cam.

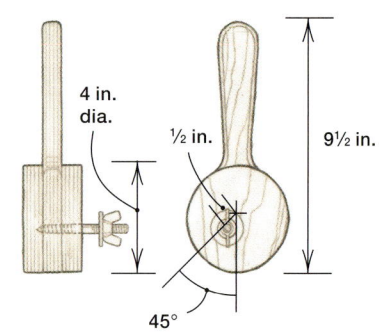

4 in. dia.

½ in.

9½ in.

45°

doors, where the edges will show, I'd still use a slip joint, although I'd ask the clients first whether they had any objections to seeing end grain on the outside of the stile.

When I make a chair, I use this joint for the slip seat that gets upholstered and secured within the chair rails (see the photo on the facing page), because it's the best and most appropriate joint for the job. I don't do a lot of millwork, but if I were making window sash, I'd use a slip joint for the stiles and rails, even if the inside edges were shaped to a cope-and-stick profile.

What I really like about the slip joint is how fast it is to cut and assemble. I use a jig that I designed several years ago for use on my tablesaw (see the drawing on the facing page). If you don't have a tablesaw, you can cut this joint by hand or with a bandsaw, as I'll explain later. With either of these methods, take your time. If you use a bandsaw, make sure that the blade doesn't wander.

Cutting mortises on the tablesaw

Whether you build a jig similar to mine or use a system of your own, start with the mortise when cutting this joint on the table-saw. The beauty of this system is that you don't have to spend any time marking all the pieces with a gauge or pencil. The setup for the mortise is done by eye, and the tenon cuts are taken directly from the mortise.

When I was an apprentice, I learned to determine the thickness ratios of the mortise and tenon by dividing the stock into thirds. So a board $3/4$ in. thick would have a tenon $1/4$ in. thick, give or take. You can estimate the mortise dimensions without having to measure them. All that matters is that the pieces fit together well when you're done. I always make sure to keep some scrap pieces of wood on hand for setting up and testing

Start with the mortise _____

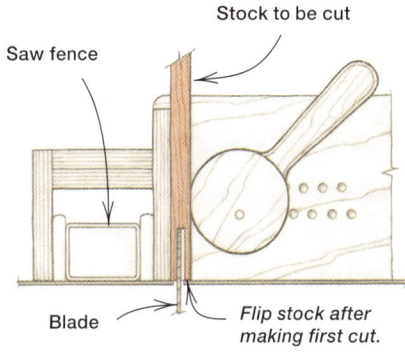

Stock to be cut

Saw fence

Blade

Flip stock after making first cut.

MORTISE
With the clamp, secure the piece of stock to be cut firmly into the back corner of the jig. Make the first cut. Remove the stock, flip it around, reclamp it and make the next cut. Depending on the size of your slip joint, two passes are usually enough to complete the mortise. The one shown at left took three passes at two fence settings.

the joints before I use the stock I've milled for the job. Test pieces should be of the same thickness and width as the stock you'll use later.

I make the first setup by cranking the saw-blade up to the width of the stile. I place the jig over the top of the saw fence, which serves as a guide track, and clamp in a piece of scrap. I adjust the saw fence so that it's cutting into the middle third of the thickness of the wood. Then I push the piece through, flip it in the jig and push it through again. The first mortise is done. With the mahogany frame shown in the photos, my first setup left me with a sliver

of waste between the first and second passes. I decided to leave it like that—making the tenon a little fat of one-third—and to make a second fence adjustment later to clean out the mortise (see the photo on p. 135). Once I'm satisfied with the setup on the test piece, I can go ahead and cut all the mortises.

One important point: Keep your saw table free of debris that would prevent the wood from riding flat on the table. Also, be sure to clamp the wood firmly in the back of the jig. Losing track of either of these details will cause the mortises to be cut too shallow and out of square.

TENON
Use the mortised piece to reset the fence for the tenon cuts. Set the blade to cut on the other side of the cheek line. Always use scraps to test this fit. Once the fence is set, cut one side of the tenon, flip the piece in the jig and cut the other. Cut off the waste at the shoulder line later, using a miter gauge and a stop block.

Change the setting for the tenon ___

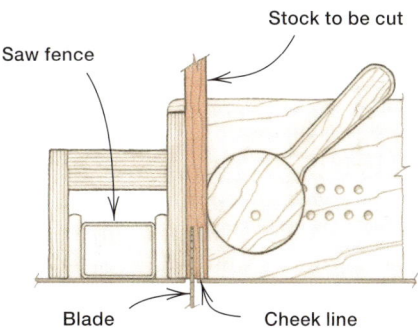

Saw fence

Stock to be cut

Blade

Cheek line

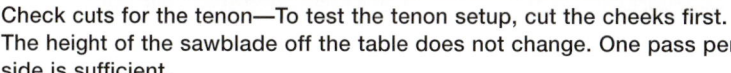

Check cuts for the tenon—To test the tenon setup, cut the cheeks first. The height of the sawblade off the table does not change. One pass per side is sufficient.

Shoulder cuts for the tenons are best done with a miter gauge. A scrap clamped to the fence acts as a stop. Self-stick aluminum carbide sandpaper on the miter gauge keeps stock from slipping.

Cutting the tenons

After cutting all the mortises, I turn off the saw, leaving the last mortised piece clamped in the jig. I loosen the fence and tap it light-ly toward the blade by the amount of the blade thickness ($\frac{1}{8}$ in. for most saws), as shown in the photo on the facing page. With this setup, the cheek line of the mor-tise is cut on the inside of the sawblade, closest to the fence; the cheek line of the tenon is cut on the outside of the blade. Once the jig is at the new setting, I remove the workpiece and clamp in a fresh piece of scrap for a test tenon. I run the piece through the saw, turn it around and run it through again (see the photo at left above).

At this stage, I usually chop off the waste around the tenon, without marking it, to see if the tenon fits snugly into the mortise.

Making the slip joint by hand

Cutting mortises and tenons by hand is neither as fast nor as accurate as the tablesaw method. But if you don't have the equipment or just prefer the look of handwork, this may be the way for you.

I start by looking over my milled pieces, deciding which will be the show faces and indicating that with a pencil mark. I save some marking time by ganging pieces together when I lay out the joints (see the photo below left). I pencil in the shoulder line on the edges of four pieces at the same time and transfer those lines all the way around all the pieces. I then set my marking gauge to scribe the cheek lines (see the photo below right). Mortises and tenons are marked with the same gauge setting. I just cut on different sides of the line—inside for mortises, outside for tenons. When I'm shaping this joint by hand, I always start by doing all the sawcuts first.

For the long cuts starting on the end grain, I prefer to use a wide-blade bowsaw (one of several my father made for me years ago when he came from Hungary to visit me). I clamp pieces in the vise in pairs to stiffen them and to make the process go a little faster. Remember to cut along the waste side of the marking-gauge line. I start the bowsaw at about a 45° angle to have a better view of what I'm doing. I cut straight down the marked lines to the shoulder lines drawn in pencil (see the photo at left on the facing page).

To finish cutting the tenons at the shoulder line, I use a fine dovetail saw while holding the pieces against a bench stop, as shown in the top right photo on the facing page. I am very careful to cut precisely to the waste side of each shoulder line. This is important. Otherwise, I may end up with uneven tenon shoulders and a joint that will have to be adjusted later.

After the sawcuts have been made, mortises must be chiseled from both sides. I keep the flat of the chisel true to the marked pencil line as I remove the material. I cut halfway through the first side and then flip the piece over and work in from the other edge. A good size chunk will often pop out in one piece when working the second side. When all the mortises are done, I begin fitting the pieces together. This process takes a while.

Handwork is handwork—it's just not as precise as machined joinery and you're bound to have some adjustments to make. You may have to remove some material from a too-fat tenon or from the inside of one of the mortise cheeks, depending on how the joint fits together. Rasps and paring chisels will perform well for those tasks (see the bottom right photo on the facing page). If you cut the tenons too thin and the mortises too wide, you can add shims of

Mark the shoulder line. All pieces cut by hand must be marked on every side and end.

Mark mortises and tenons at the same setting. Fill in the scribed lines with pencil marks, so the lines are easier to read.

(A handsaw or bandsaw works well.) I once asked my grandfather how tight this joint should be. He said, "If you need a mallet to force it, it is too tight and will split, but if you can use your hat instead of a mallet, it is too loose."

After these cuts have been made, the waste on either side of the tenon must be removed. I do that with the stock flat on the table. I remove the jig and dial the sawblade down to the right height to trim off the waste. I always clamp a stop block against

Cut the shoulders with a dovetail saw. For well-fitting joints, make sure that you cut to the same line on all the pieces.

The bowsaw is Klausz's tool of choice for cutting this joint by hand because the long, wide blade tracks well and cuts quickly.

Fine-tune the fit. Rasps and chisels are good choices for removing material from either the tenon or the mortise. Hand-cut frames need many test runs before you can call them done.

veneer (preferably of the same species) as gap fillers when you reach the glue-up stage.

Assembly and glue-up: I use a white PVA glue, applying it with a ½-in. acid brush. After I've dry-fit and adjusted the frame, I apply the glue evenly on all sides of all pieces. Then I put clamps loosely on each corner, using the scraps from cutting the tenons to protect the frame pieces. After that, I check the frame for squareness and make sure all the shoulders are tight. Then I tighten the clamps all the way, make a final check for squareness, wipe off any excess glue with a wet rag and put the frame aside to dry. Later, I'll clean up the edges with a plane, working in from the corners to avoid chipout.

I remember once as a young man watching my father work, asking him, "How can you do that so fast?" He replied, "Don't worry. After five or 10 years, you're going to be a good beginner yourself." And now, after 35 years, I'm still learning.

—F.K.

the fence to serve as an index for trimming the cheeks to the exact shoulder line. The stop block also prevents the waste from being pinched between the fence and the blade. The miter gauge works well for this operation (see the photo at right on p. 137).

Getting this setup tuned correctly may take a few tries with scrap pieces, but the final trimming goes quickly. One tip—save your cutoff scraps as protective pads for gluing up the frames.

CUTTING THROUGH DOVETAILS

by Vincent Laurence

I was trying to explain to someone years ago why I'd just taken a job as an apprentice woodworker after spending four years and $70,000 on an English degree. Suddenly, in the midst of my explanation, his eyes lit up. "You mean," he asked, "you're going to learn how to make dovetails?" He understood.

There's good reason for the lofty esteem accorded the dovetail joint. Even without glue, dovetails are very strong. And they've proven their reliability for well over three millennia. Much of their contemporary allure, though, has nothing to do with strength or reliability. Finely executed, hand-cut dovetails are a testament to the skill of the craftsman who made them.

PINS FIRST
Tage Frid immigrated to the United States from Denmark in 1948. A furniture-maker for 67 years, he also taught wood-working for nearly four decades.

Pin board

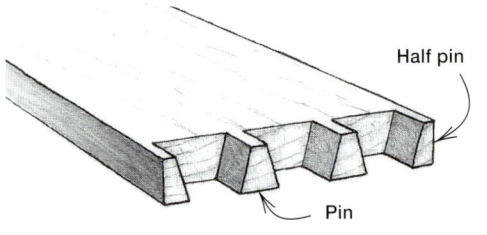

Half pin

Pin

Set the marking gauge 1/64 in. wider than the stock, so the pins and tails will protrude slightly.

It takes practice to cut a dovetail joint well, but the joinery is relatively simple. Two pieces of wood are connected with interlocking pins and tails. There are only two methods of cutting dovetails by hand: cutting the pins first and cutting the tails, or pin sockets, first. Both methods work. But advocates of each method tend to be passionate about the advantages of their approach and the obvious flaws in the other. With this in mind, we asked two of our contributing editors, a pair of woodworkers with 99 years of cutting dovetails between them, to tell us how and why they cut dovetails the way they do. Their methods and tools may differ, but both cut flawless dovetails that will last generations. Here's what they had to say.

TAGE FRID: I cut pins first

I started my apprenticeship in 1928, at the age of 13. At first, I drove a push cart, delivering furniture around the city of Copenhagen. After a year, I told the master to whom I was apprenticed, "All right, I know how to drive the push cart. I'd like a bench now, so I can learn some woodworking." Within a month, I was cutting dovetails. I've cut quite a few since then and have taught hundreds of students.

Cutting the dovetail pins first makes sense. It's easier to hold the pin board in place to mark the tails than it is to hold the tail board against the end of what will be the pin board. Also, the walls of the pins provide a good surface for the awl as you mark the tails. And by marking from the inside of

Gauge the baseline on both sides of both boards being dovetailed together.

Use a bevel gauge to extend pin and half-pin marks across the end of the board. A 1:6 ratio is about the right angle for most hardwoods.

Mark pins and half pins on the end of the board. You can space them by eye, or use a ruler for more consistent spacing. A pencil mark is plenty accurate at this stage, because the pins are the first parts of the joint to be cut.

Extend the pin marks down to the baseline using a combination or try square.

Cut to the gauged baseline. Split the line with the sawblade on the waste side.

Deepen the baseline with the corner of a chisel (near right), and then chop a slight bevel to the baseline from the waste side (far right). This will prevent fibers from tearing out beyond the baseline when removing the waste between pins.

Alternate chopping from the face of the board and the end (photos right). When chopping on the face, hold the chisel in at a slight angle so that the tail slot is undercut. Chop just about halfway through the board. Flip the board over and repeat.

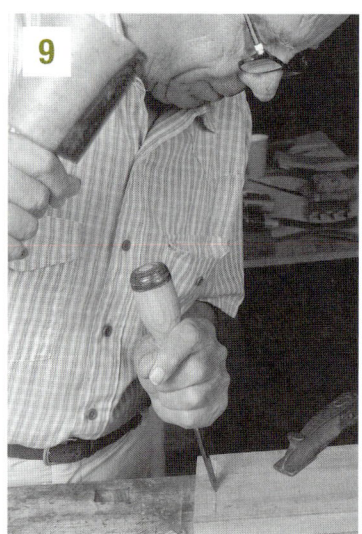 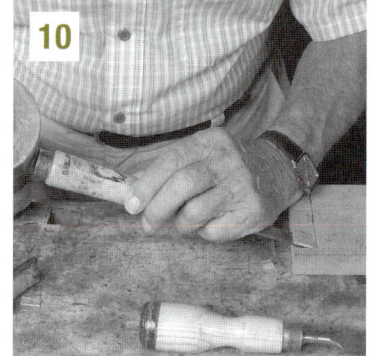

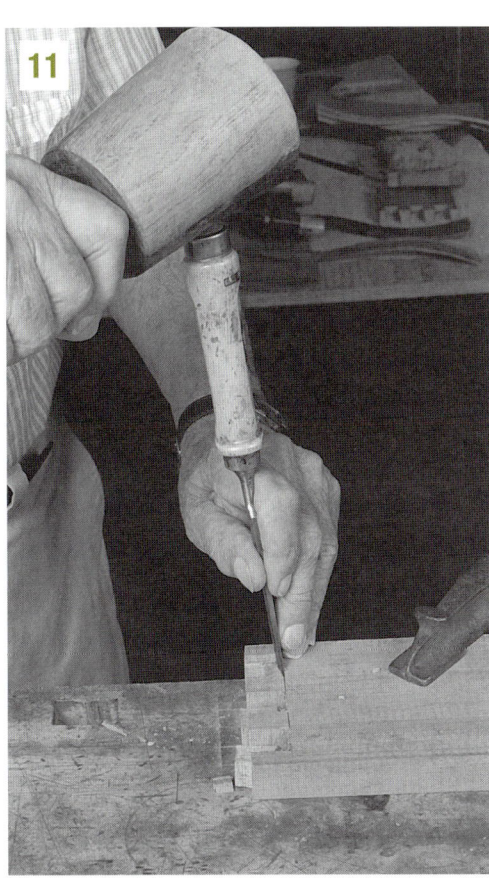

Continue chopping the board until the remaining waste drops out.

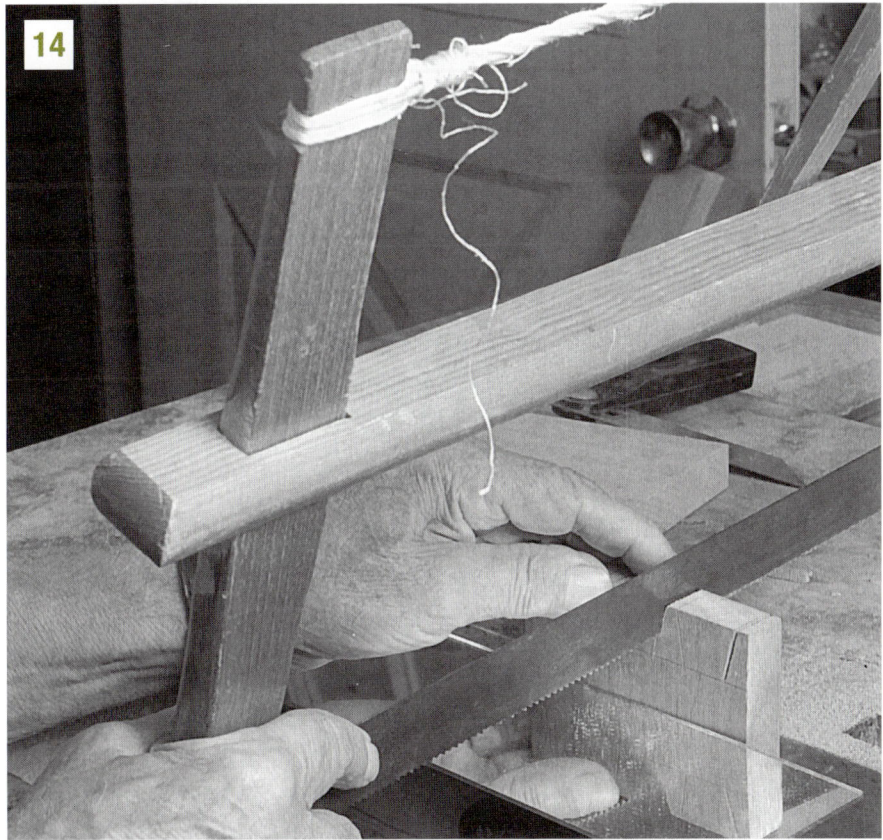

Mark the tails from the pins (top). Hold the pin board securely in place on the tail board. The edges of both boards should be flush with each other and the inside face of the pin board should rest on the baseline of the tail board. Scribe the tail layout from the inside of the joint so that the awl follows the pins, not the grain. Extend the marks across the end of the tail board (above). Then cut the tails down to the baseline (left). A mirror makes the layout lines easier to see. Split the line on the waste side.

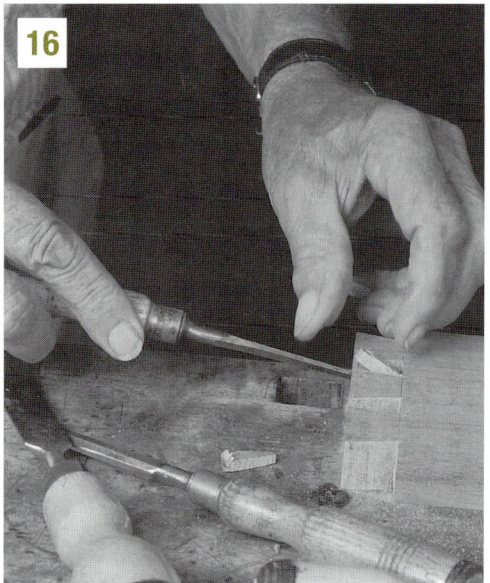

With an awl, connect the baselines from both sides of the board (above left). Chop away the waste between the tails, first creating a little bevel to prevent tearout at the baseline. Alternate chopping from the end and face until you're halfway through the board (left). Then flip it over and repeat. Clean out the corners (above right). The little bit of wood remaining at the base of the tails often prevents dovetails from closing.

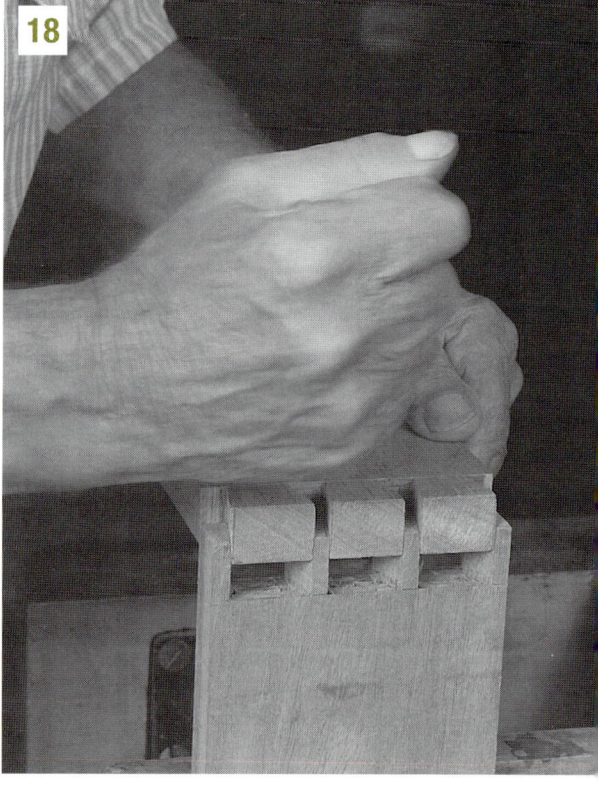

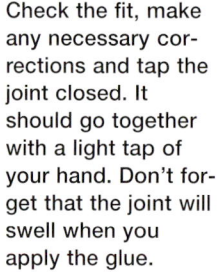

Check the fit, make any necessary corrections and tap the joint closed. It should go together with a light tap of your hand. Don't forget that the joint will swell when you apply the glue.

the joint, the angle of the pins will cause the awl to cut cleanly across the face grain of the tail board rather than follow the grain.

Another reason to cut the pins first is that when accuracy counts—when cutting the second half of the joint to fit the first—you're cutting to a line on the face grain, not on the end grain. It's easy to split this

line right down the middle (but be sure the sawkerf is on the waste side of the line). Doing that in the end grain is almost impossible. It's easy to lose the line in the end grain with the first sawcut. By cutting the pins first, I don't have to worry if the saw bounces around a little on the end grain—I just cut the tails to fit.

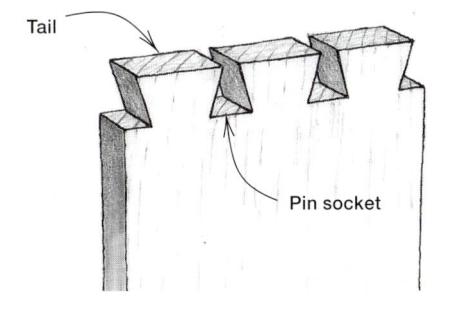

Scribe a baseline on both sides of all the boards you're dovetailing. For boards that are the same thickness, you need only one setting—the thickness of either board. When the pin board and tail board are different thicknesses, the thickness of each determines the baseline for the other.

Tail board

Tail

Pin socket

TAILS FIRST
Chris Becksvoort builds custom furniture in New Gloucester, Maine, and does restoration work for the Shaker community at Sabbathday Lake, Maine.

CHRIS BECKSVOORT: I cut tails first

The first time that I made dovetails, I consulted a woodworking book. It stated, in no uncertain terms, that the pins had to be cut first. Also, my father, a European-trained cabinetmaker, insisted that dovetails must be cut pins first.

But because I was a teenager with an attitude, I took these stern pronouncements as a challenge. I made the tails first, and I have been doing it that way ever since.

I find that this approach is more efficient because I can cut the tails for a pair of boards at the same time by taping them together. And because I'm not trying to match tails to

Lay out center lines for the pin sockets on the tail board. For a board with two pins, I divide the board into thirds, as shown. There's also a half pin at each end.

Use a chisel to determine the width of the pin sockets. This makes chopping the sockets much more efficient. Place the chisel over the centerline, and use a pencil to mark each side. Then mark out the half-pin sockets on the ends.

Mark the angles of the pin sockets with a dovetail gauge or a bevel square. Transfer these lines across the end grain. Now tape the two tail boards together, so you can cut pin sockets on both at the same time.

Cut the tails. You can use a handsaw, a scroll saw or a bandsaw with a fine blade to make cuts to the baseline. Remember to cut on the waste side of the line. Also, cut the two half-pin sockets now.

pins, the cut isn't critical. When it comes time to mark the pins from the tail boards, accuracy *is* critical. And that's another reason I prefer cutting the tails first.

I think a knife is the most accurate tool for transferring position, more accurate than an awl and far more accurate than a pencil. But a knife will tend to follow the grain on the face of a board, which is the surface that

6

7

Chop out the waste. Start by creating a small groove on the waste side of the baseline. Then chop alternately in at a sharp angle (left) and downward at a slight angle (below). Don't chop in from the end of the board yet. Keeping the corner intact prevents tearout when the waste is removed from the center of the socket. Once you've chopped about halfway through the joint, flip the boards over and repeat. This time, though, chop from the end.

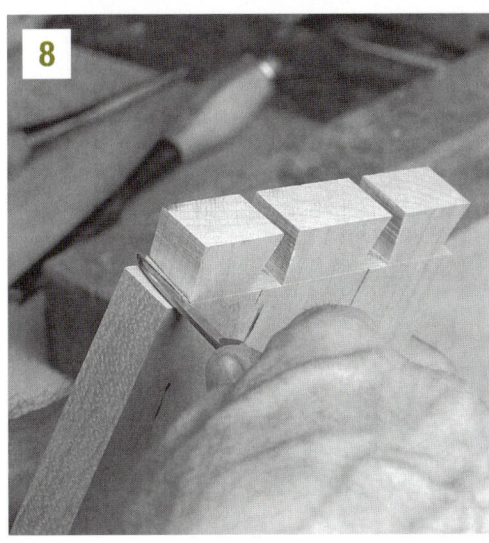

8

Use a chip-carving knife to clean the corners.

you're marking if you use the pins to lay out the position of the tails.

When cutting the tails first, I end up marking out the pins on end grain. The knife doesn't drift or wander with the grain; it marks out the pin locations with great precision. Then I saw just outside the line and pare to the line. The result is a tight, strong, attractive joint every time.

Mark out the pins from the tail board. Clamp the pin board into a vise, and set the tail board perpendicular to it. Make sure the edges of both boards are flush, and be sure the inside edges of all the sockets align perfectly with the inside corner of the upright board. Apply pressure to the top board, and mark the dovetails with a sharp knife (top left). Extend the pin marks down the side of the pin board using a small square (top right). Cut down to the baseline on the waste side of the line (right).

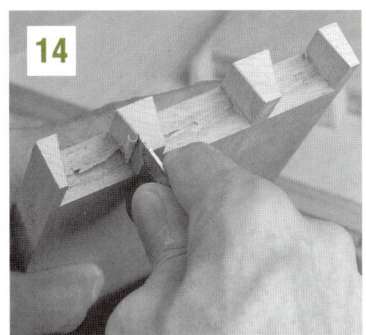

Chop out waste between pins. Clamp the boards so their inside faces are up (top left). This prevents the chips from becoming wedged between the pins when you finish chopping out the waste from the other side. When you're about halfway through, turn the boards over and re-clamp (top right). As with the tail boards, once you've flipped the boards over, you can chop in from the end. Pare to the line with a chisel (left).

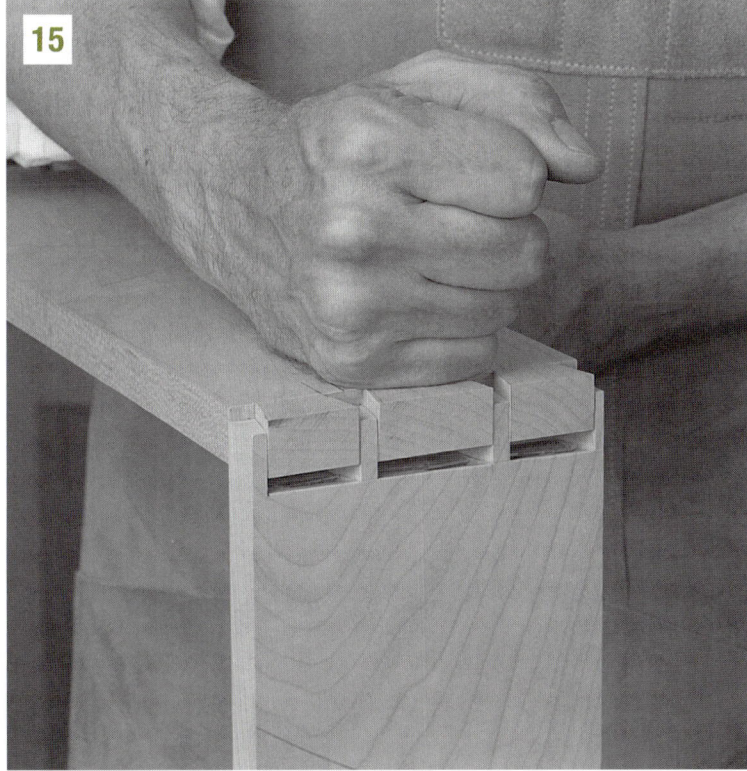

Test-fit the joint. If you've cut and pared right up to the lines, the parts should fit like they were made for each other, a snug friction fit that comes together with a light tapping of your fist.

OILSTONES AND WATERSTONES

by Gerald Polmateer

Oilstones have been the choice of American and European woodworkers for centuries for honing a keen edge on their cutting tools. The only conflict was whether a natural white Arkansas stone produced a sharp enough edge or whether the harder and finer black Arkansas stone was needed. But, about 15 years ago, waterstones began finding their way to this continent from the Far East in quantities large enough to create a new controversy. Although the brouhaha has settled somewhat, many woodworkers are still confused as to which sharpening stones would work best for them. To help resolve the issue, this article takes a look at the care and use of oil and waterstones and the advantages and disadvantages of both.

Whetstones and how they work

The purpose of a whetstone, whether oilstone or waterstone, is to sharpen an edged tool, such as a plane or chisel, by abrasion. When sharpening, you actually grind away the two faces of the blade to make them meet precisely at the cutting edge. The smoother the intersection of these two faces, the sharper and longer lasting the cutting edge will be. The process of obtaining the smoothest edge is much like sanding: You start with a coarse grit to quickly remove excess material and then switch to ever finer grits to refine the surface and remove the larger scratches of the previous grit.

When sharpening, metal particles can quickly fill the pores of the abrasive surface

Waterstones vs. oilstones—Typical synthetic waterstones are shown in the top row, ranging in grit from 800 to 8,000. Waterstones are fast cutting and leave a finely polished edge. The oilstones in the bottom row include man-made silicon carbide and aluminum oxide stones (left) and natural white and black hard Arkansas stones (right). Natural oilstones are capable of producing razor-sharp edges but are slower cutting than the waterstones.

and reduce the cutting action unless they are removed. That's where the oil and water come in. Water and particularly oil are frequently and mistakenly referred to as lubricants. But a lubricant is the last thing you want when trying to abrade a surface. Both the oil and water actually increase the cutting action by holding the metal particles in suspension to prevent them from clogging the surface of the stone.

Oilstones

Oilstones are whetstones that use oil to float away the metal particles. Man-made stones generally cut faster than natural stones, but natural stones produce the finest edge. Some of the best natural stones are made of novaculite, which is mined primarily in Arkansas, and hence, they are called Arkansas stones. Arkansas stones are slow cutting and are categorized by name according to coarseness and hardness. Included are the Washita, the coarsest stone, which is comprised of several colors; the soft Arkansas, gray with green specks; the hard white Arkansas; and the hard black Arkansas, sometimes referred to as a surgical stone because of its ability to impart razor-sharp edges to medical instruments (see the photo on the facing page). A stone that performs as well as the black Arkansas is a white translucent Arkansas stone, but this stone costs a great deal more than the very expensive black Arkansas and is even more brittle.

As technology developed, manufactured oilstones became a satisfactory, cheaper alternative. (Although white and black Arkansas stones remain unsurpassed in the field of oilstones for producing a keen edge.) The man-made stones are formed by compressing an abrasive, usually silicon carbide or aluminum oxide, with a bonding agent (such as ceramic, resin, shellac or sodium silicate) into a brick. The bricks are then fired in a kiln at a high temperature.

Silicon carbide and aluminum oxide stones come in three different grits: fine, medium and coarse. Silicon carbide cuts faster than aluminum oxide, but aluminum oxide produces a finer edge.

Flattening an oilstone is a difficult task because of the hardness of the stone. It requires lapping the stone on a flat steel plate with a silicon carbide abrasive powder. Because this can be an arduous task, stones should be checked regularly to prevent them from becoming excessively cupped.

Storage and care of oilstones

Oilstones should be kept clean and moist. I store mine in a wooden box with a piece of felt under the stone to help keep it moist and a lid on top to protect it from dust. After each use, I wipe off any metal particles and apply a clean coat of oil before shutting it in its box.

To get a true straight edge on your cutting tools, the sharpening stone must be flat. Because oilstones are very hard and wear slowly, their flatness is often taken for granted. But they should be checked periodically and flattened if needed before they become excessively worn.

Flattening excessively worn oilstones is difficult, but the process is easy with regular maintenance. Probably the easiest way to flatten a stone is by lapping it on a flat plate of soft steel or cast iron with a loose abrasive powder or grinding compound. The lapping plate should be thick enough to remain rigid against pressure and large enough to accommodate your largest stone. I use a 3-in.-wide by 14-in.-long piece of $1/2$-in.-thick mild steel that I flattened using a 100-grit sanding belt placed on a tablesaw top. Mounting the plate on a wooden block with a space underneath, as shown in the photo above, helps keep the back side from rusting, prevents the base from warping the plate and makes it easy to clean.

To use the lapping plate, spread oil on the surface, sprinkle some silicon carbide abrasive powder on top, and then move the sharpening stone back and forth with a medium amount of pressure, much like sanding a board with a sanding block. Once the stone is flattened, it should be conditioned by rubbing a piece of iron across the stone a few times to return it to its normal coarseness.

The abrasive powder, which is also used for polishing stones, is available from lapidary supply stores in several grits. (It may also be available at auto supply stores as valve grinding compound.) I prefer 90-grit because the particles break down as it's used and effectively act as a finer grit.

Using oilstones

To keep the stone from glazing over or clogging, the proper oil must be used to float the metal particles to the surface. For coarse and medium stones, I use an oil of the consistency of 3-In-One or Smith's honing oil (see the sources of supply box on below). The finer the stone, the lighter the oil I use. For the white and black Arkansas stones, I prefer kerosene, but some people use water. Just a few drops of kerosene spread evenly over the surface of the black stone is enough; the white stone will require a little more.

If your man-made stone seems to continuously absorb oil, it means your stone wasn't filled. Filling is a process of baking in a petroleum jelly-like grease, which makes it easier to keep a coat of oil on the surface of the stone. If your stone isn't filled, you can let it soak in an oil bath until bubbles stop rising from the stone, or you can try baking some petroleum jelly into your stone in your own oven. Immerse the stone in petroleum jelly and then heat it for about an hour at 200°F. Remove the stone and let it cool. Don't try this with a natural stone because the heat will destroy it.

When the honing oil turns black from metal particles as you sharpen tools, wipe it away and apply fresh oil. When using the finer stones, apply a little less pressure and constantly check for particles because they can chip the finely honed edge.

Waterstones

Waterstones are whetstones that use water to float away the metal particles and also are available in man-made or natural stones. The natural stones usually contain quartz, sericite and/or volcanic ash that have been compressed over the eons through natural stratification. The natural stones have been mined in Japan for more than 2,000 years and because of the natural compression process, can have varying degrees of hardness within the same stone. These stones have become scarce and thus very expensive.

Synthetic stones were developed less than 100 years ago in response to the shortage of natural stones. The manufacturers of waterstones are more secretive than their oilstone counterparts; therefore, it's hard to determine the exact composition of these stones. They are, however, usually made of silicon carbide or aluminum oxide with various kinds of clay bonding agents. They are pressed into bricks and fired in an oven just as man-made oilstones are. The clay is a softer and looser bonding agent than used in oilstones, so the stone wears away easily. The fast-wearing stone continuously exposes new and sharp abrasive material for fast cut-

SOURCES OF SUPPLY

Most mail-order companies and even some home centers or hardware stores now offer both oil- and waterstones. In addition to these sources, the following companies manufacture or supply sharpening products:

OILSTONES

Smith Whetstone, Inc., 1700 Sleepy Valley Road, Hot Springs, AR 71901; (800) 221-4156. Catalog available.

Norton Co., 1 New Bond St., Worcester, MA 01606; (508) 795-5000. Catalog available.

WATERSTONES

The Japan Woodworker, 1731 Clement Ave., Alameda, CA 94501; (800) 537-7820. Catalog available.

Hida Inc., 1333 San Pablo Ave., Berkeley, CA 94702; (800) 443-5512. Catalog available.

HONING OILS

3-In-One is available from any hardware store.

Smith's honing oil is available from Smith Whetstone, see address above.

Waterstones cut quickly and are great for flattening the backs of plane irons and chisels. Here, the author uses a stick to apply pressure as he flattens a plane iron. Using the side of the stone saves the face for working on the bevel and increases its life. The plastic containers in the background store the stones in water, so they're always ready to use.

ting. This high performance, combined with reasonable cost, makes the synthetic stone a good choice for almost any waterstone application.

Waterstones come in a variety of grits, including very coarse (80- to 220-grit), coarse (600- to 1,200-grit), medium (1,200- to 2,000-grit) and finishing (4,000- to 8,000-grit), as shown in the photo on p. 150.

Storage and care of waterstones

Before use, most waterstones need to be soaked for about 20 minutes or until air bubbles stop rising from the immersed stone. I store most of my synthetic waterstones in plastic containers full of water with lids so that the stones are continuously soaking, as shown in the photo above. The stones are protected from dust and dirt but ready to use whenever needed. Whether stored in water or dried after each use, waterstones should be protected from freezing, which could split the stone into small pieces.

Storing each grit stone in its own box will keep the grit from a coarser stone from getting on a finishing stone and ruining that finely polished edge you've been honing. If different grit stones are stored in the same container, they should be thoroughly washed before use.

Submerged storage works for all stones except those that are permanently mounted on a base. Generally, only the finishing stones are mounted and these stones can be sprayed with water on the surface as needed during sharpening.

Natural stones should be allowed to dry between uses. Immersing natural stones for long periods of time may cause fractures along naturally occurring fault lines in the stones.

Like oilstones, waterstones also need to be flattened before use. Because waterstones are soft and wear quickly, flattening needs to be done frequently even during sharpening. Unlike oilstones, flattening a waterstone is a relatively easy process. Even badly worn stones can be salvaged by rubbing them on the face of a concrete block using plenty of water. Less severely damaged stones can be flattened with a piece of 220-grit wet-or-dry sandpaper laid on a sheet of glass at least ¼ in. thick. Add a little water, rub the stone across the sandpaper for a couple of strokes and then look at the surface of the stone. The surfaces that are rubbing on the sandpaper will be a different color from the low spots that aren't yet hitting the sandpaper. Keep rubbing until the stone is a uniform color over its entire surface. After flattening, a quick pass or two along the edges will prevent chipping the stone during sharpening.

Using waterstones

Before using the stones, you may want to make a base like the one in the photo on p. 153 to hold the stone and prevent it from slipping during sharpening. A wedge holds the stone in the base, making it easy to change stones for a finer grit. Another alternative is a flat piece of plywood or lumber with stops screwed at each end of the stone. Clamping the flat piece to the workbench keeps it from sliding around.

Sharpening with waterstones can be a messy proposition. I protect my benchtop with newspaper, so I can just roll up the mess and throw it away when done.

During sharpening, the surface of the stone should be kept wet enough to keep the tool moving smoothly, but it should not be flooded. Add more water as the stone starts to dry up, but do not wash away the slurry that builds up on the surface of the stone, as shown in the photo below. The slurry speeds the cutting process.

Check the stone frequently for flatness by rubbing on the wet-or-dry sandpaper and note the high spots. Try to work the tool evenly over the stone to eliminate these high spots.

As with oilstones, start with the coarse grits and work through to the finishing stone to remove the previous grit's scratches. After honing on the finest stone, allow the slurry to dry out, and continue honing. The slurry acts as an even finer grit to further polish the edge.

Alternative sharpening stones

Although water and oil stones are the primary choices for honing cutting edges, there are a couple of other alternatives worth at least a mention: diamond stones and ceramic stones.

Diamond stones aren't really stones. They are a piece of steel with industrial diamond particles bonded to it. The hard diamond particles stay sharp and cut fast, but a diamond stone won't produce a polished finish. Another problem I've encountered with diamond stones is the bases are too flexible. If the sharpening stone is not rigid, it will produce a convex surface on the tool being sharpened.

Ceramic stones are almost as hard as diamonds and resemble conventional whetstones in size and shape. Ceramic stones wear very little, require no honing fluids and clean up easily with water, a scrubbing pad and cleanser. However, for sharpening plane irons and chisels, ceramic stones have a serious flaw: they are not flat and they're almost impossible to flatten by hand. They work great for carving knives and tools where a flat stone is not a prerequisite.

Keep the surface of the waterstone wet enough to let the tool slide smoothly over the stone. Add more water as the stone starts to dry, but don't wash away the slurry that develops. The slurry speeds the cutting process and helps polish the edge.

Mixing water and oil

For some reason, people have an either/or attitude about selecting water or oil stones. However, I've had great success using both types. I prefer waterstones when first sharpening a tool because they cut fast. But in the middle of a job, I like the convenience of making a couple of quick passes on my Arkansas stone with just a couple of drops of oil to touch up a dull tool.

Whatever you buy, seek out a reputable supplier and buy good quality stones. I don't recommend stones that share a common oil or water bath because the coarser grit particles always seem to find their way to the finer stones. I like the thicker stones because they remain rigid. The stone should be wide enough to accommodate plane irons and long enough for smooth strokes without worrying about the tool dropping off the end of the stone. I buy 1-in.-thick stones that have a 2-in. by 8-in. working surface.

Use the chart at left to help weigh the pros and cons of water and oil stones. Keep in mind a dull edge may not be the fault of your sharpening stones or technique. Poor quality tools are difficult to sharpen and won't hold an edge, even if sharpened with the best stones. Buy quality stones and tools; they'll last longer, give better service and you'll never regret it.

The pros and cons of oilstones and waterstones

Waterstones

Advantages

1. Cut very quickly
2. Easy to flatten
3. Inexpensive (synthetic)
4. Uses cheap and readily available water
5. Uniform size and grit (synthetic)
6. Large sizes available
7. Quickly develops slurry, which aids in honing

Disadvantages

1. Water can be messy
2. Water can cause rust
3. Water evaporates quickly
4. Soft stone easily damaged by tools
5. Algae can form in water storage tubs
6. Wears quickly
7. Must be protected from freezing

Oilstones

Advantages

1. Convenient and ready to use
2. Oil won't rust tools
3. Easily stored in box
4. Hard and resistant to gouging by tools
5. Won't freeze
6. Uniform size and grit

Disadvantages

1. Slow cutting
2. Lapping plate must be used to flatten
3. Expensive (Arkansas stones)
4. Oil can stain wood

FIVE

First Projects

Although the first project you ever make should be simple in design and construction, it will be the trickiest. It will also be the most fun. For every detail and task you can foresee, there will be five you can't. For every problem you noodle out, two more will come up as a consequence. Even something as simple as how to clamp the project firmly in place without marring it while you sand can seem an almost impossible proposition. But for every problem, you'll find a solution—and therein lies the fun.

This short chapter offers three good first projects: a bookcase, a wall shelf and a kitchen table. None of them will demand too many seasoned woodworker tricks to get together, yet when you're done you'll have a beautiful, lasting piece of furniture that looks as if only a professional could have made it. Who says you can't have your cake and eat it too? Simple and easy does not have to look cheap or badly made.

These projects can be read and used like recipes. Following step-by-step, you can produce exactly what's in the picture. However, you don't have to follow them that way. Cooking off the menu is perfectly acceptable; in fact, it's probably inevitable as woodworkers tend to be independent minded. Shorten the table's overall length a few inches to fit your kitchen, or change the detail on the side of the wall shelf to something you like better. Almost any change is fair game. After all, it's your project.

For that matter, you don't even need to cut the sliding dovetails on the wall shelf according to the author's technique. Perhaps you've got a different and better setup for cutting them. And if you prefer a simpler dado, that will work too. While you're at it.... Pretty soon, perhaps before you realize it, you're a woodworker with your own preferences, ready to offer other woodworkers a better way of doing something.

BOOKCASE MADE WITH BISCUIT JOINERY

by Peter S. Turner

A small bookshelf—
This V-shelf book-
case is made of
solid cherry, joined
with No. 10 biscuits.

Furniture with few design flourishes benefits from wood that has lots of figure. When
I build simple bookcases like this one, I look
for cherry with bold grain patterns, which
I often find when sifting through stacks of
No. 1 and No. 2 common grades. Using
lumber with beautiful figure, selecting and
matching all the stock, is really my favorite
part of furnituremaking. I modeled this
bookshelf after one that once belonged to
my great grandmother. It's a small, easy-to-
build piece whose few design details are
quite simple. For the joinery, I use No. 10
biscuit joints for everything. All the pieces
are $1/2$ in. thick, which gives the bookshelf a
light and delicate look.

Roughing out all the pieces

When picking lumber for this project, I
select stock that's at least 7 in. wide, so each
half of a V-shelf requires only one plank (see
the drawing on the facing page). You can
edge-join two boards for the sides and
bottom shelf, or you can use single boards
if your stock is wide enough. If I edge-join
two boards for the sides, I make sure that
the glueline ends up in the exact center.

I begin by flattening, edge-jointing, then
thickness-planing all my stock down to
$9/16$ in. Then I pick through the boards and
find the best matches to make up the two
sides and bottom shelf. I glue up the sections using pipe clamps. After the glue is
dry, I clean up any squeeze-out and joint
one edge of each side and the bottom shelf.
Then I select the boards for the two
V-shelves, joint one edge and rip them
slightly oversize on the tablesaw.

At this point, I run the lumber through a
thickness sander until everything is $1/2$ in.
thick. I prefer a sander because on highly
figured woods, my planer produces tear-out.
You could, of course, thickness-plane the
boards, and take care of any blemishes with
handplanes and scrapers. Once all the stock
has been sanded to $1/2$ in., I rip it to final
width on the tablesaw.

Using the sliding crosscut sled on my
tablesaw, I cut the sides and shelves to
length. It's critical that the shelf components
all be square and exactly the same length.

Bookcase with V-shelves

All parts of this bookcase are made from ½-in.-thick material. The shelves are joined to the sides with No. 10 biscuits. The lengths of all three shelves should be the same and the ends of the V-shelves dead even.

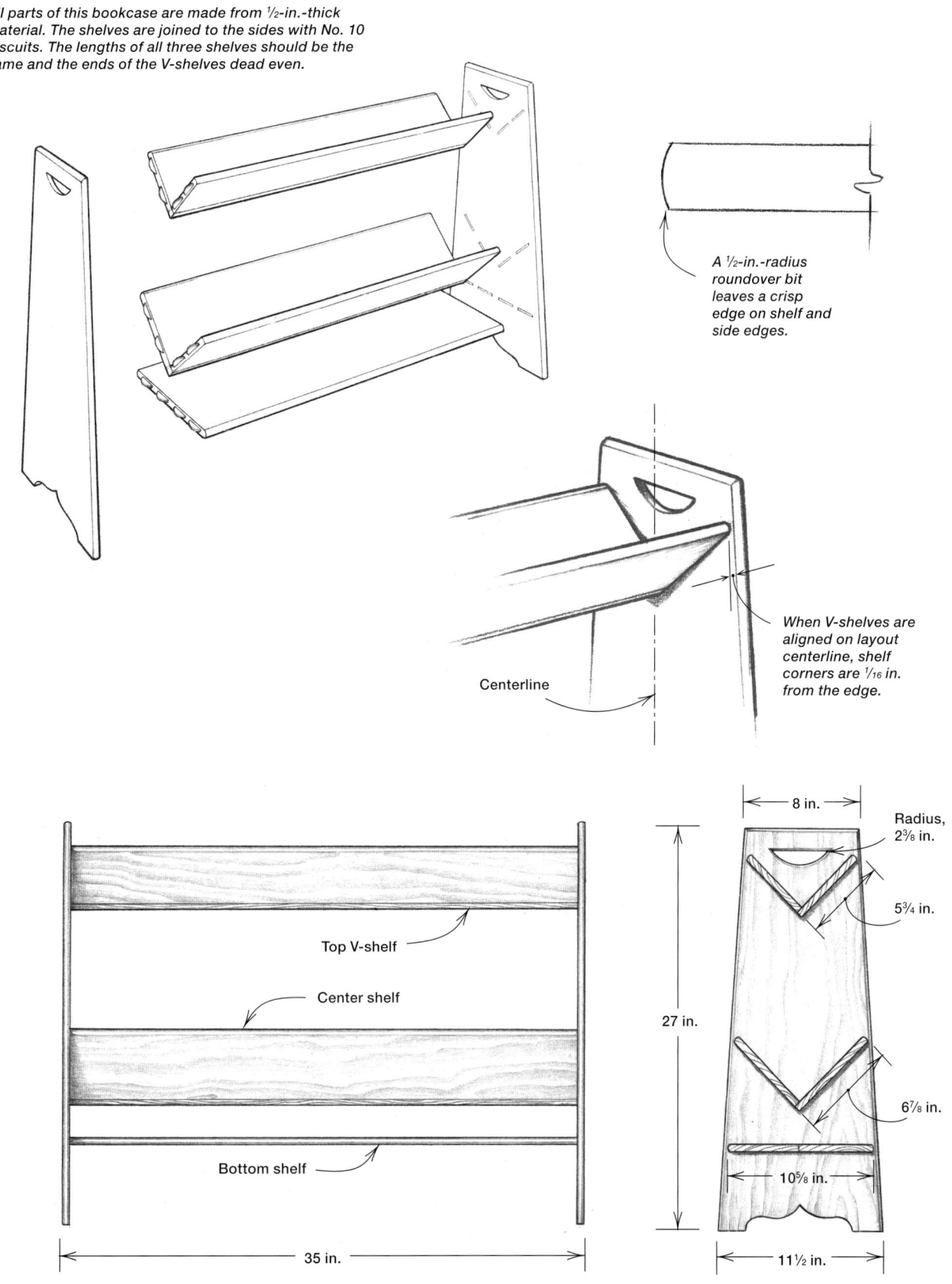

A ½-in.-radius roundover bit leaves a crisp edge on shelf and side edges.

When V-shelves are aligned on layout centerline, shelf corners are ¹/₁₆ in. from the edge.

Centerline

Top V-shelf

Center shelf

Bottom shelf

35 in.

27 in.

8 in.

Radius, 2³/₈ in.

5³/₄ in.

6⁷/₈ in.

10⁵/₈ in.

11½ in.

Simple jig for cutting tapers

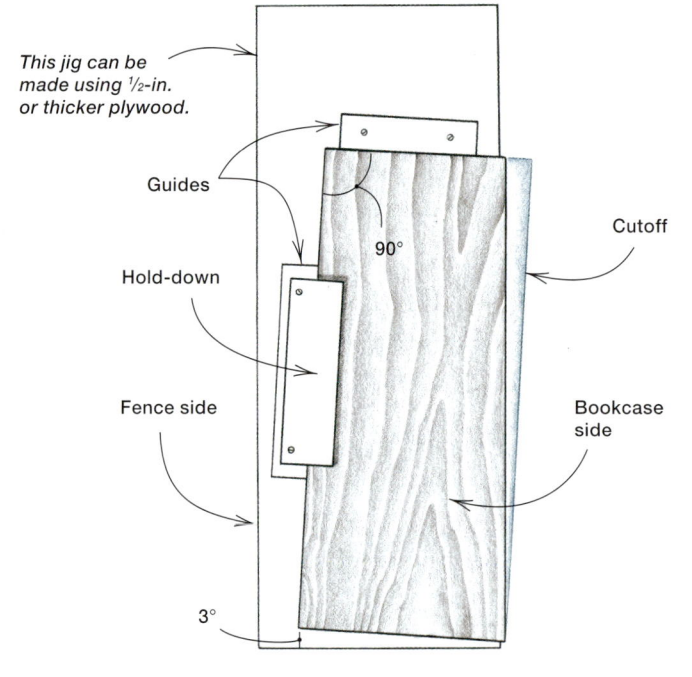

This jig can be made using ½-in. or thicker plywood.

Guides

Hold-down

Fence side

90°

Cutoff

Bookcase side

3°

The joint between the shelves and ends are what will make or break this piece, so be sure your crosscut sled is right on.

I taper the sides using a homemade jig on my tablesaw (see the drawing at left). The jig is just a piece of plywood with a few guides screwed to it at an angle. To use the jig, I place it flush against the tablesaw's fence and nudge the fence toward the blade until the left side of the jig just touches the blade. I lock the fence, place one of the sides in the jig and screw a piece of scrap-wood onto the right-side guide to act as a hold-down. I cut the taper by pushing the jig along the tablesaw fence (see the photo at left below).

To cut the opposing taper, I flip the work-piece on its other face, place the cutoff against the right edge of the workpiece and, finally, place a shim the same thickness as my tablesaw blade between the cutoff and the jig guide (see the photo at right below). I make sure all the pieces are snug, attach a hold-down and cut the taper.

Rip one side. A hold-down screwed to the right guide of the jig keeps the workpiece snug when sawing.

Cutting the opposite taper—Place a shim the thickness of the sawblade against the right guide, then the cutoff and, last, the workpiece, which is turned over on its other side.

Join V-shelves, and shape edges

With all the pieces cut to size, it's time to join the V-shelves and cut the biscuit slots in the sides that will fasten the shelves. First I join the V-shelves. I use four biscuits per shelf, evenly spaced. For each V-shelf, one set of slots is cut in the edge of one board, and the mating set is cut into the face of the other board.

To glue up the V-shelves, I use scrap along the faces where the clamps are positioned to protect the wood. I'm not worried about the edges because they get shaped later. When I tighten the clamps, I use a try square to check that the pieces stay 90° to each other (see the top photo at right). I use four clamps for each shelf, each clamp positioned over a biscuit joint. The ends of each V must be dead even. When the glue is dry, I rip each wing of each V-shelf to its final width on the tablesaw.

The long edges of both V-shelves and all edges of the sides, excluding the feet and cutouts, are rounded over leaving a crisp edge where the roundover meets the edge of the board. To get that shape, I set my router-table fence slightly past the outside edge of the pilot bearing on a $1/2$-in.-radius roundover bit. I use hold-downs and feather-boards to make sure the stock passes firmly and squarely over the bit. Because all the stock for this project is $1/2$ in. thick, I only have to set up once. When all the edges are machined, I lightly scrape and sand them to get a fair roundover, being careful not to soften the edges.

Slots in sides and shelves need to match

I first cut all the slots in the shelves with the biscuit joiner. The shelves have four slots cut on each end. After I cut these, I'm careful not to get carried away and erase the layout marks until I have transferred them onto the sides.

To mark the location of the mating slots on the bookcase's sides, I use the V-shelves as layout guides. First I draw a vertical centerline on the inside face of each side. To locate a V-shelf, I place it on end against a side, keeping the apex of the V on the centerline, and slide it along the centerline

These joints hold the case together. The V-shelves are joined at 90° to each other. Biscuit slots cut in the ends of the shelves join them to the case sides.

until both edges are inset $1/16$ in. from the case side. I hold the shelf in place and trace along the bottom edge with a pencil. I also transfer to each side the layout marks showing where the biscuit slots should be cut.

To cut the slots in the sides, you need something to register the biscuit joiner against because you can't use the tool's fence as you did on the shelves. I clamp a straight block of wood parallel to the lines I traced off the shelves. I offset this straightedge to make up for the fact that I'm registering the base of the biscuit joiner, not its adjustable fence, against the straightedge. Here's how I figure out the offset: I measure the distance from the bottom face to the bottom of a V-shelf slot. On my biscuit joiner, I measure the distance between the bottom of the blade (I use a raker tooth) to the base. I subtract the first number from the second;

Use V-shelves as layout guides

Mark the inside faces of the sides. Transfer the biscuit slot marks from the shelves to the sides.

Mark the offsets from the lines just traced. These new marks are used to position a straightedge for the biscuit joiner.

A straight board guides the biscuit joiner. The author places the base of the tool against a board clamped to the side to cut the slots for the shelves.

that's the offset, which I lay out on the side. I use two clamps each time I reposition the straightedge, and then I cut all the slots.

Template routing the cutouts and shaping the edges

I made up a template for the cutouts in the sides using a piece of $1/4$-in. hardboard. It's easy to work with, and if you don't like the look of a template you've just shaped, it's cheaper and faster to make another template than another bookcase side. If you add a router with a guide bushing, a template also makes quick work of cleaning out the cutouts. When I made my template, I used a compass to draw the curve of the handle and a French curve to draw the whale tail. I

faired out the curves by sanding and filing.

I mark the cutouts on both ends and remove the waste with a jigsaw, staying at least $1/16$ in. off the line. Then I clamp the template over a cutout and go over the area again using a router fitted with a $5/16$-in. guide bushing and a $1/4$-in. straight bit. The bookcase's handles get one more run past the router. After removing the templates and guide bushing, I chuck a $1/4$-in. roundover bit in the router and ease the edges of the cutouts.

The final shaping of the sides is accomplished using hand tools. Using a file and chisel, I shape the corners of the handles and the sharp junctures where the curves of the whale tails meet.

Assemble the bookcase on end. Cauls, a squaring jig and backer boards ensure that the case is clamped tightly and won't be marred.

Assembly, cleanup and finish

Before final assembly, I dry-fit the case to make sure that everything lines up. To avoid marring the piece and to make sure I get even clamping pressure, I use cauls and backer boards. The backer boards are two pieces of scrap plywood slightly larger than each side. To these, I attach a pair of cauls with double-faced tape.

I also use a shopmade squaring jig that's nothing more than a right-angled triangle made of scrap. I clamp this jig to the bottom shelf and one side to keep the case properly aligned during glue-up.

When I assemble the case, I stand it on its side. After clamping it, I check whether all the shelves fit flat against the sides (see the photo on p. 163). I mark any that don't and after unclamping the case, plane them to fit.

Prior to finishing, I sand all the pieces through 180-grit. Then I wipe everything down with a damp rag to raise the grain. When the pieces are dry, I continue sanding up to 320-grit. When I sand the edges, I'm careful not to lose their definition.

I lied earlier when I said that selecting and matching the stock was my favorite part of building furniture. I forgot about applying the first coat of oil. It's nice to see the grain and figure pop out when oil is rubbed into the wood.

I use three coats of Kaldet finish oil, which is made by Livos, a German company. It is a linseed oil-based product that contains citrus solvents. The oil is available from The Natural Choice (800-621-2591). I prefer Livos products because of their low toxicity, nice satin sheen and pleasant lemony scent.

BUILD A WALL SHELF

by Peter S. Turner

My wife, Colleen, occasionally asks me to build a piece of furniture for our home. I would love nothing more than to honor these requests, but there never seems to be time. But a hanging shelf is one project that I figured I could finish quickly.

I got the inspiration from a drawing of a peg-hung Shaker shelf in Ejner Handberg's book, *Shop Drawings of Shaker Furniture and Woodenware, Vol. II* (Berkshire Traveller Press, 1975). The shelf sides in Handberg's drawing are curved on top, but the bottom is straight. I added another curve at the bottom, experimenting with different curves until one satisfied my eye. Handberg's Shaker shelves also hung from a wall-mounted peg rail. I don't have a peg rail at home, so the first time I made this piece, I used brass keyhole hangers. In later versions, including the one shown at right, I used simpler brass hangers mortised into the second shelf from the top. These are less expensive, easier to install and make hanging the shelf a snap. We use one hanging shelf as a spice rack. The varying heights and sizes of our spice jars helped establish the shelf spacing and overall width.

Consistency is the key to this piece. If you start with flat stock of uniform thickness and length, the joinery follows smoothly. To ensure consistency, do all your milling at once (all the stock is 1/2 in. thick), and use a plywood pattern and flush-trimming router bit for making identical curved and tapered sides.

The trickiest parts of this piece are the sliding dovetails. Routing the grooves is easy, but the long tails on the ends of each

Shake up your wall with a shelf. This simple wall-hung shelf, perfect for a spice rack or sea shells, was adapted from a traditional Shaker design. The shelves are joined to the sides with sliding dovetails.

shelf take some patience and finesse. I use a router setup in which the router is mounted horizontally; it seems to make it easier to get a straight, even cut (see the drawing on the facing page).

By holding the pieces flat on the router table, I have more control as I slide the piece past the bit. I make test pieces out of

Shaker shelf updated

Traditional, peg-hung Shaker wall shelves often have a slight curve at the top and taper from top to bottom. This shelf has a curve at the bottom also, and only the top half is tapered. The piece can be modified by changing the width or the shelf arrangement.

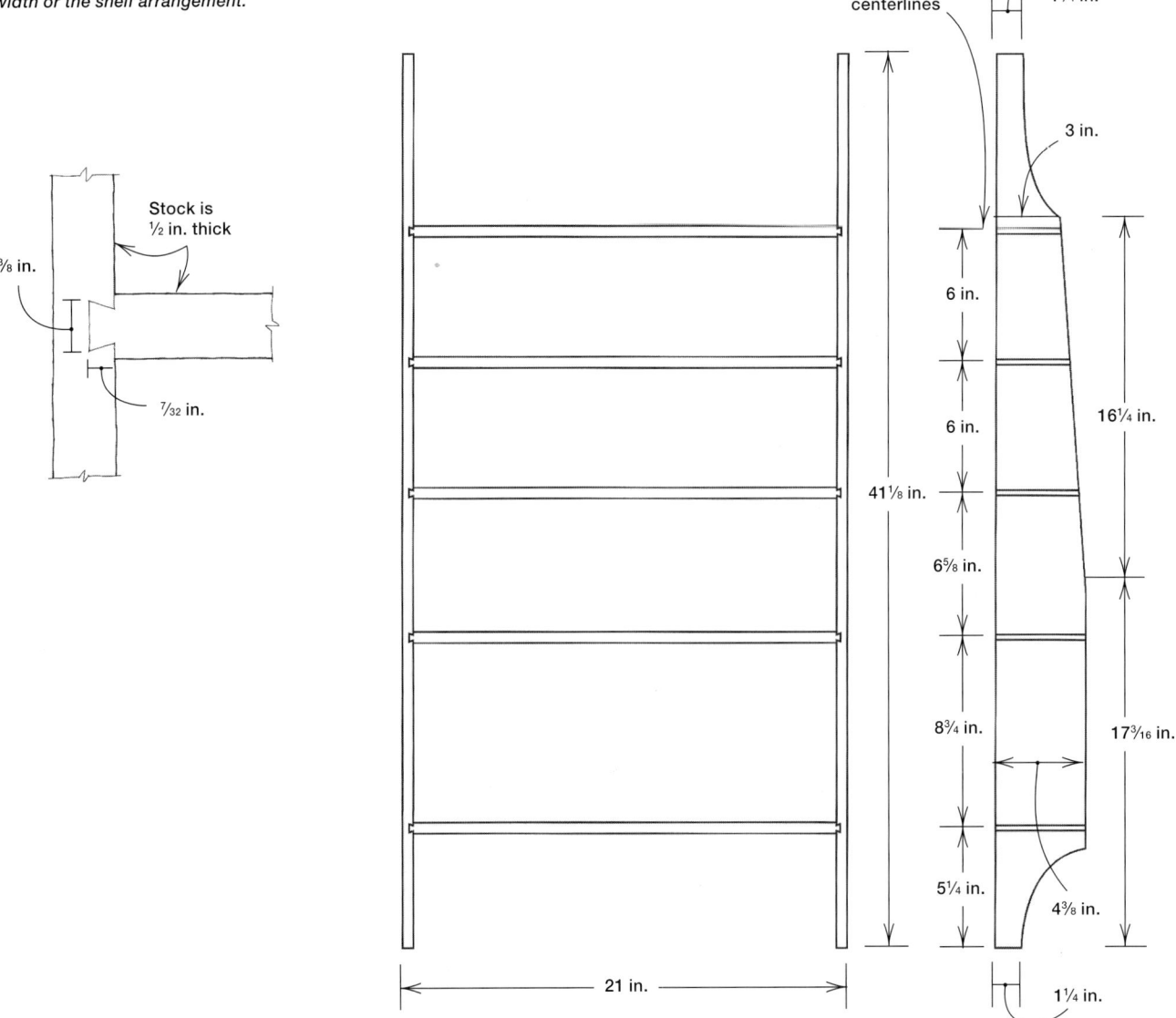

scrap, which I milled at the same time as the final pieces.

The Shakers housed the shelves in dadoes, rather than sliding dovetails, and you can do the same. It won't be as strong, but if you're worried about the shelves, you can toenail them from the bottom with finish nails or brads.

Horizontal dovetailing fixture makes a difficult joint easy ___

Cutting sliding dovetails can be tricky. To get a long tail to slide snugly into its groove requires a uniform cut. Rather than holding the shelves vertically to cut the dovetails, you can mount the router horizontally on a standard router table, as shown. Holding the workpiece flat on the table, cut one side of the tail; then turn the piece over, and cut the other side. Use a scrap of the same thickness to establish the exact height and depth of the dovetail bit, and then fit them in a test groove to prevent marring the final pieces.

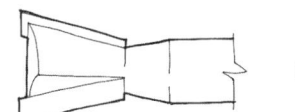

Dovetail bit, ⅜ in.

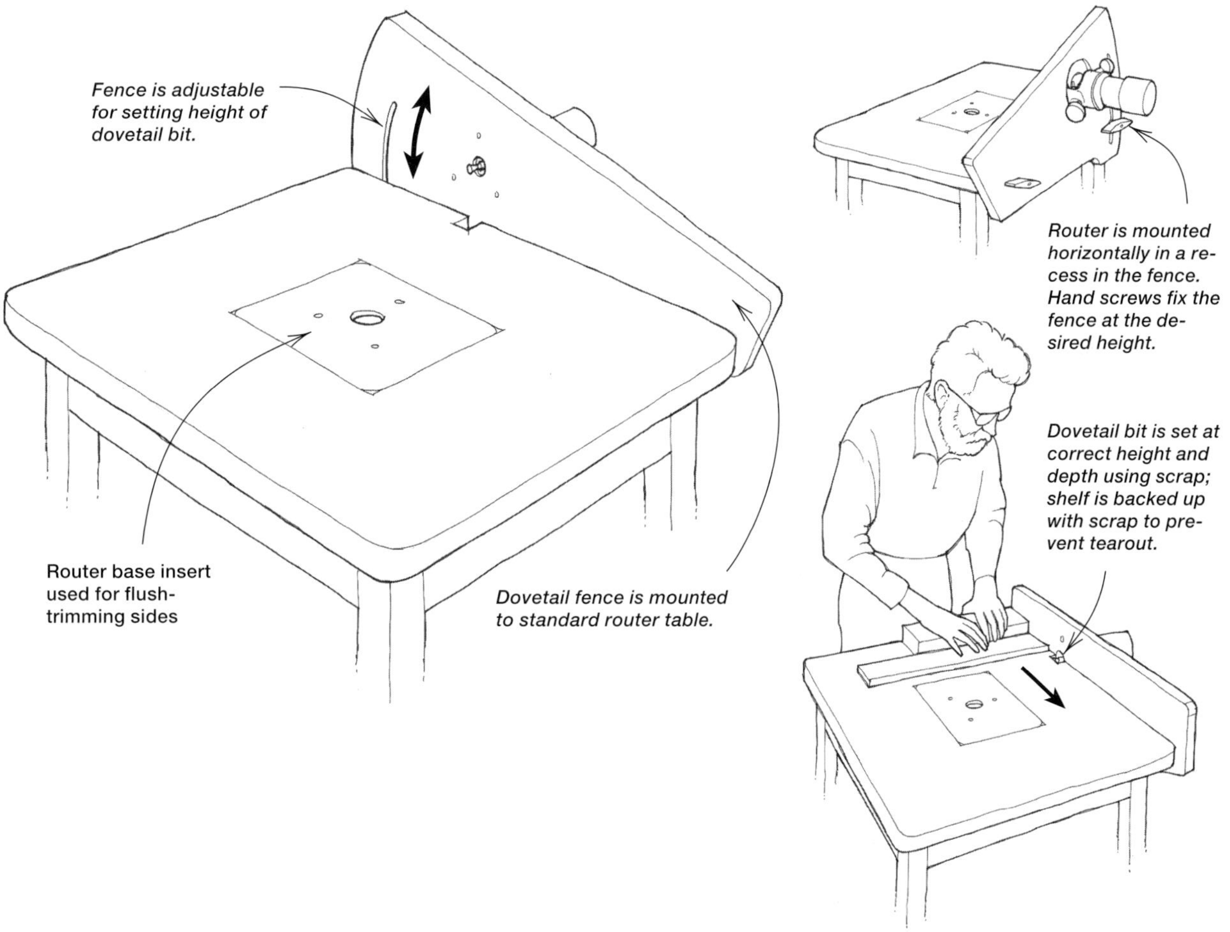

Fence is adjustable for setting height of dovetail bit.

Router is mounted horizontally in a recess in the fence. Hand screws fix the fence at the desired height.

Dovetail bit is set at correct height and depth using scrap; shelf is backed up with scrap to prevent tearout.

Router base insert used for flush-trimming sides

Dovetail fence is mounted to standard router table.

Wall shelf step-by-step

STEP 1

Routing dovetail grooves in the sides: After milling all the material to a thickness of ½ in., cut the sides to length, but leave them at least ¼ in. wider than the widest dimension (4⅜ in.). Then mark the centerlines for each shelf on both pieces. Using a slotted piece of plywood to guide a ½-in. router template insert, cut the dovetail slots. First rough the slots with a ¼-in. straight bit, and finish them off with a ⅜-in. dovetail bit.

STEP 2

Trace the pattern, and bandsaw the sides: With the grooves routed, cut the curved and tapered sides. First make a plywood pattern matching the shape of the sides of the shelf, trace the pattern onto the back of each side and bandsaw the shape close to the line.

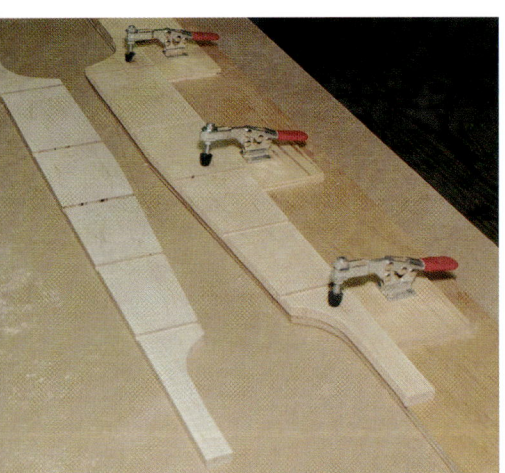

STEP 3

Flush-trimming bit makes both sides identical: After roughing out the sides on the bandsaw or jigsaw, clamp each side into the plywood pattern using hold-down clamps fastened to the plywood. Then rout the edge with a ½-in. flush-trimming bit, either using a router table (see the drawing on p. 167) or a hand-held router setup. This step will remove any tearout created when you routed the dovetail grooves, and it makes each side identical.

STEP 4

Routing the dovetails on the shelves: To cut the dovetails, mount your router horizontally on the router table (see the drawing on p. 167). This makes it easier to adjust the height of the cut. It also lets you hold the workpiece flat on the table rather than against a fence. Adjust the depth and height of the router bit to match the depth of the slots. I cut the tails to fit by trial and error, testing on scrap stock milled at the same time as the shelf parts.

STEP 5

Cut shelves to width and assemble: Don't cut the shelves to width until after you cut the dovetails on the ends, so you can remove any tearout caused by the router. The front edge of the top three shelves is angled to match the tapered sides, which you can do by transferring the angle to the jointer fence. After sanding all the pieces, slide each shelf into the sides, starting at the bottom and clamping each shelf as you go.

MY KITCHEN TABLE

by Tim Gilchrist

I built my first kitchen table a number of years ago when I was still in college. My intent was to create a stylish yet indestructible platform capable of withstanding all potential abuse. I also wanted a piece of furniture that I could take apart and move at the end of the school year. That solid red oak structure bears its battle scars well. The table could support seven full kegs of beer at once, withstand the deeds of careless room-mates and then be taken apart and moved with ease.

Now that I have a real job, a house and drink beer out of bottles, I decided to build a new table. I wanted something more stylish but with the same stalwart presence and convenient mobility of my trusty red oak table. I spent some time in furniture stores looking at tables for design inspiration before I found a style I was happy with.

This table was made to be taken apart. The author wanted sturdy and easily transportable furniture. A solid maple top and a knockdown design answered those needs.

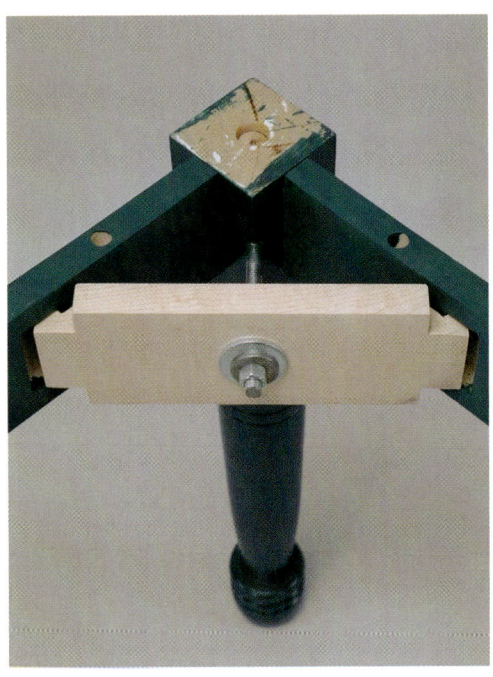

Let your lumber supplier do some of the work

I work in a really small basement space. The dominant feature of the workspace is a large cast-iron oil burner, so I don't have room for a lot of equipment. I do all my work on a Shopsmith combination tablesaw, bandsaw, lathe and drill press. Because I don't own a jointer or a planer, I buy most of my lumber already surfaced. It costs a little more, but I don't have any other choice, short of dressing it all by hand.

For this table, I chose 5/4 maple for the top and the apron, dressed to a full 1 in. thickness. For the turned legs, I got a good deal on some 8/4 Eastern white pine, clear as a winter's day. So I had it dressed to a finished 1¼ in. thickness and laminated each leg from three thicknesses for a full 3¾ in. dimension. I'd never turned pine

A collapsible corner joint

Wooden gussets hold leg-to-apron joints together. By tightening the nut on the threaded rod, the aprons are pulled tightly to the legs. Apron tenons are not glued into legs.

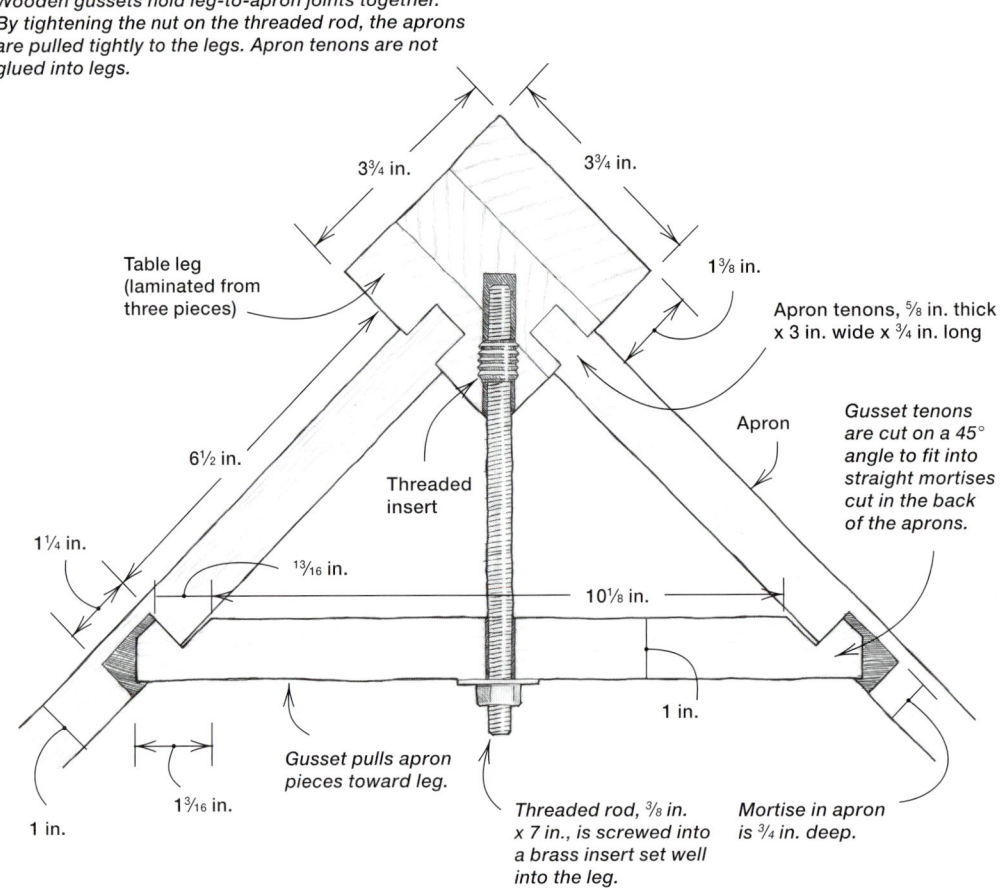

before. With this job, I learned that you have to keep your turning tools extra sharp to cut the pine cleanly.

Knockdown joints

My job may require me to relocate from one coast to the other, so I wanted to be able to take this table apart easily for the move. I've seen the stamped metal corner braces held in with wing nuts on hanger bolts on a lot of mass-produced furniture, but they looked too flimsy for my taste. So I designed a wooden corner gusset that would do the same thing (see the photo on the facing page). The ends of all four gussets and all four apron pieces were cut into tenons. The gussets fit into mortises cut into the inside of the apron pieces. The apron tenons slip into regular blind mortises cut into the legs (see the drawing on the facing page).

I cut all my mortises the same way, using the drill press. First I drilled a series of holes with a flat-bottomed bit, and then I cleaned them out by hand with a chisel (see the photo at left below).

I cut the tenons for the ends of the apron pieces with my miter gauge on the tablesaw, making all the necessary adjustments first on a scrap of the same thickness. I don't own a dado blade, so I just made a lot of repetitive cuts with a regular sawblade and cleaned up the tenons with a chisel.

Tenons for the gussets were a little more complicated because the corners had to be cut on an angle. That way, the gussets draw the apron pieces tightly into the corner joint with the leg. I made all the cuts for the gusset tenons with the bandsaw. I started by marking all the corners with a pencil, using a combination square, and then cutting the

Gusset mortises—After boring holes on the drill press, the author cleans out the mortises by hand.

Tenons for the gussets, cut to size and shape with the bandsaw, pull the apron pieces tightly to the legs.

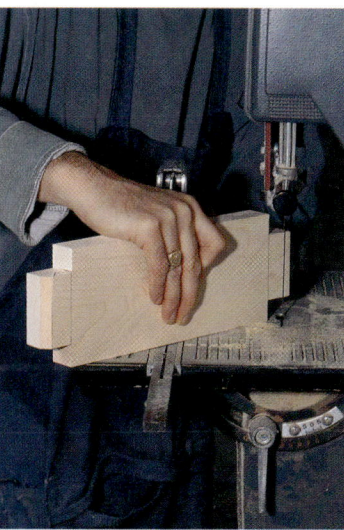

Angles in the tenons, marked in pencil, are cut freehand to the right profile. The gussets are held on edge to make the cuts.

Sturdy knockdown connection—A length of threaded rod is screwed into a threaded insert in the leg to provide a post for the gusset. When a nut is tightened against the outside face of the gusset, the table aprons are cinched tightly against the leg.

tenons to shape with the gussets held flat on the saw table (see the middle photo on p. 171). After that, I turned each piece on edge and made the angled cuts for the tenons (see the photo at right on p. 171).

In place of the hanger bolt on the stamped metal corner braces, I used a length of ³⁄₈-in. threaded rod screwed into a brass threaded insert driven deep into the corner of each

leg. I used the drill press to make the pilot hole for the threaded insert. Once I'd marked and drilled a hole for the threaded rod in the first gusset, I used that one as a master. I made a mark for the holes in the other gussets by placing them underneath the first one and twisting a brad-point bit through the existing hole.

Turned legs—copy the first one

The legs were turned from laminated blanks, 3¾ in. sq., cut to length at 28 in. Even in pine, this size was asking a lot of my little lathe, so I ripped some waste off the corners with the bandsaw before doing any turning. I made a jig to cradle the stock as I trimmed it on the bandsaw. The jig consists of several plywood scraps cut in a V-shape in the tops and held together with two lengths of ⅜-in. dowels.

Because of the length of these cuts, I clamped a scrap of wood over the bandsaw tabletop to serve as a temporary extension. That way, the jig could move in one even and continuous run. To indicate where to stop the cuts, I marked the tops of the legs with a pencil.

To give me a good idea of the profile, I laid out the turned shape in pencil on one edge of the first leg. Then I scribed pencil lines for all the reference points that defined the shape—grooves, beads and so forth. When I was happy with the way the leg looked once it was turned, it became the master for the others.

A solid top built to take abuse

Because of my limited shop space, I had to use the floor to lay out and mark all the pieces for the top. I used six boards ripped to three different widths to arrive at a finished width of 32 in. for the tabletop.

I usually work alone, and I don't own a biscuit machine. So when I have to join a lot of boards, I glue up one joint at a time—it's easier to maintain control over the results. Even then, with this top, there were several joints in which one board sat 1/32 in. or so proud of another. That didn't bother me. I planed those areas out by hand and sanded the surface to clean them up a little. A little gouge or a mark from a handplane can give character to a country-style design like this one.

To join the top to the apron, I drilled and countersunk pilot holes through the bottom edges of the apron pieces. After fitting the top in place, I marked for threaded inserts in the underside. The holes through the apron were drilled out larger than the screws that would hold the table in place, to make some room for the top to move.

Finishing up

I chose to prime and paint the legs and the apron pieces with a good quality oil-based paint because I knew that it would stand up well to the rigors of daily use. I picked the hunter green color because it seemed to go so well with the clear maple top. For the top, I used several coats of Homer Formby's tung oil mixture. After about a week of drying time, I waxed the top for additional protection.

I was happy with the results—a rugged table I can take with me if I'm forced to make a career move—a table I can use to pay bills, fix odds and ends around the house, even prepare and eat food. As my college buddy from Memphis would say, "That dog can hunt."

SIX

Finishes

Finishing has long been, and probably always will be, the great bugbear for woodworkers. It's not that woodworkers don't want to make their completed projects beautiful, it's that they don't want to destroy all their hard work with a finish gone wrong. The problem is that finishing really isn't woodworking. It's an entirely different set of skills. You're dealing with the uncertainties of liquids and powders, not the (relatively) firm ground of solid wood. Remember, finishing is chemistry. And we all know how hard chemistry classes were in high school.

Many woodworkers start out with penetrating-oil finishes, which are by far the easiest. You brush them on. A while later, you wipe them off. You wait until the piece is dry and presto—a finished project. Unlike other finishes, they're almost foolproof. They don't run, blotch, peel, crackle or cloud. And you don't need much more than the directions on the can or bottle to get it right. A fair number of woodworkers, not unreasonably, stick with penetrating-oil finishes all their lives. One of those woodworkers might just be writing this introduction.

This chapter aims to give you some sense of what's possible if you ever decide to take the training wheels off your brush. And there are good reasons to consider it at some point in your woodworking career. Having only one finish in your repertoire is as limiting as knowing only one way to join wood. The right finish can transform a good piece of furniture into a spectacular one.

One article surveys every kind of finish and compares their attributes. Another runs through some basic brushing techniques essential to all finishes except penetrating oil. Finally, the last one gives a simple recipe for a versatile and easy oil and varnish mixture. This finish has the advantages of more complicated finishes but still retains the simplicity of a penetrating oil.

But beware: Finishing is a skill that's almost as rich and diverse as woodworking itself. Some woodworkers get so caught up in the finishing aspect of woodworking that they become finishing and refinishing specialists who make furniture only rarely. There could be worse things.

CHOOSING A FINISH

by Chris A. Minick

Ask ten woodworkers what they like best about woodworking. I'll bet a truck-load of walnut that finishing isn't at the top of the list. Most woodworkers hate finishing—and with good reason. Finishing requires you to work with stinky chemicals rather than shaping wood. Because finishing is the last step in a long process, a mistake could ruin the whole project. Or the error could mean spending hours stripping off the finish with more smelly chemicals. Furthermore, there

are so many types and brands of finish to choose from (see the photo on the facing page). It's no wonder why many woodworkers get accustomed to applying only one kind of finish to every project. While that approach may be efficient, it could lead to a visual sameness to your work. More important, your old standby finish may not be the most suitable treatment for your project's intended use.

Comparison of translucent finishes

Finish type	Tung, linseed oils	Danish oil	Oil-based (alkyd) varnish ❤	Polyurethane (uralkyd) varnish ❤	Nitrocellulose lacquer ❤
Finish description					
Surface penetration	In	In	In & on	In & on	In & on
Stain resistance	Poor	Poor	Good	Excellent	Very good
Moisture resistance	Poor	Poor	Very good	Excellent	Good
Relative color ◆	Dark amber	Amber	Amber	Amber	Light amber
Relative luster	Dull	Satin	High gloss	High gloss	High gloss
Best applicator ✖	Wipe on	Wipe on	Brush	Brush	Spray
Repairability	Excellent	Excellent	Poor	Poor	Good
Dry time (hours)	18-24	6-12	2-6	2-6	¼ - ½

Notes: ◆ 3 coats of finish were used to achieve these colors on cherry.

✖ Many finishes can be applied (less effectively) by other methods.

Picking finishes and applicators—Along with the most common wood finishes, author Chris Minick displays the applicators he prefers for each. From left: paste wax, linseed oil, Danish oil and mineral oil—all applied with a rag; semi-gloss interior paint—applied with a polyester brush; shellacs—applied with an ox-hair brush; polyurethane varnish—applied with a foam applicator; water-based acrylic—applied with a nylon/polyester brush; and nitrocellulose lacquer—applied with a spray gun.

Acrylic lacquer ❤	Shellac (orange)	Bees, carnauba waxes	Water-based acrylic ❤	Water-based polyurethane ❤
In & on	On✶	On	On	On
Very good	Very good	Poor	Fair	Fair
Very good	Good	Poor	Fair	Fair
Clear	Amber	Clear	Clear	Bluish
High gloss	High gloss	Satin	Medium gloss	High gloss
Spray	Brush	Wipe on, buff	Spray/ brush	Spray/ brush
Fair	Very good	Excellent	Poor	Poor
1/2	1/2	1/4	2	2

❤ Most manufacturers add flatting agents to create a "satin" option.

✶ Shellac can be considered "in and on" for dilute solutions.

I consider three things when choosing a finish: the application equipment I have, the appearance I want and the protection I need for a project (such as film hardness and moisture resistance). To sort out the most common finishing-product options, it helps to know about their properties. I use the comparison chart below to weigh the strengths and weaknesses of each finish.

Penetration and application

The most important factor affecting how a finish performs is whether it penetrates the surface. Based on where the finish resides, woodworking finishes can be divided into three general classes: "in the wood," "in and on the wood" and "on the wood."

Good surface preparation and Danish oil do wonders for this piece of macacauba (a relative of rosewood). The rich colors of the dense tropical wood also come alive when the surface is sanded to 600-grit and waxed, as the back part of the board shows.

In-the-wood finishes

Penetrating finishes like tung, linseed and Danish oils are easy to use. Just wipe them on, and wipe off the excess. Because easy repairability is their biggest advantage, I often use oil finishes on projects that take abuse. A periodic reapplication of oil hides any scratches. The lack of a surface film allows oil finishes to be re-coated anytime without fear of adhesion loss.

Oil finishes darken wood but leave it natural-looking. That chocolate-brown color of the walnut box on the left in the photo below was achieved with three coats of linseed oil. I like the appearance of an oil finish on dark woods, but I find the yellow color of tung oil objectionable on light-colored woods like birch. In addition, tung oil tends to obscure subtle figure.

Not all so-called oil finishes are purely oil. Danish oils, for example, which add a rich, satin luster to certain hardwoods (see the photo at left), are usually dilute varnish solutions to which oils have been added for increased penetration.

In-and-on-the-wood finishes

Oil-based varnishes and lacquers have the unique ability both to penetrate the wood and to form a protective coating on the surface. This class of finish produces that wonderful illusion of depth associated with fine furniture. Some woodworkers steer away from polyurethane varnishes, fearing they will give projects a plastic-coated look, but I've found an easy way to avoid the plastic look. Because I don't have a good touch at spraying on an oil-based varnish, I usually brush on three or four coats of thinned varnish to a piece. Then I burnish the final coat (after it has dried) with a soft cloth to kill the plastic look. The key to getting a nice finish with oil-based varnish is to apply thin coats and then rub out the last. The walnut box on the right in the top photo on the facing page has a brushed-on varnish finish.

Nitrocellulose lacquer is an in-and-on-the-wood finish that exhibits marvelous depth, high luster and is quick-drying. These attributes make it the preferred finish of professional furnituremakers. Brush-on formulations of nitrocellulose lacquer are available, but I've found them difficult to apply.

Spraying is the most practical way to apply nitrocellulose lacquers. Unfortunately, I don't have a spray booth or the other explosion-proof equipment needed to safely apply highly flammable finishes. As a consequence, I only use solvent-based lacquers on small projects.

On-the-wood finishes

As the name implies, on-the-wood finishes lay on the surface and do little to accentuate the grain or color of wood. The shellac finish on the center walnut box (see the photo at right) has the typical satiny look of this class of finish. Wax is an obvious on-the-wood finish, too. And aside from its easy repairability, one of the best things about wax is its nontoxic nature (see the sidebar on pp. 180-181).

Same wood, different lusters—These three boxes were made from a single piece of walnut (a strip is shown at bottom), but finished differently: The left box was coated with linseed oil to give a dull look; the center box was wiped with shellac and waxed to a satin sheen; the right box (with the reveal on the lid) was brushed with polyurethane varnish and burnished to a low gloss. The finishes also bring out variations in color and grain contrast.

A layered finish adds depth. This spruce soundboard stock shows what effect an under layer of super-blond shellac (the top horizontal band) has. From the left, the vertical finish strips are nitrocellulose lacquer, acrylic lacquer, water-based acrylic and water-based polyurethane.

Nontoxic finishes

While browsing through my hardware store, I picked up a can of interior oil-based varnish. Plainly printed on the label was "nontoxic when dry." This statement surprised me because I knew the finish must contain metallic driers to function properly. Although lead compounds are no longer used as driers in varnish, manganese, zirconium and cobalt are used, and their low-level toxicity effects have not been fully explored. So why risk putting heavy metals on your salad bowl or breadboard?

Current research about food-preparation surfaces indicates that wooden cutting boards are better than synthetic ones. And the study suggests that if you finish the wood, you may actually impede some of the wood's beneficial effects (the tannins may deter bacteria). However, if you decide to finish the wood, there are several superior nontoxic finishes.

Safe to apply—To add a nontoxic finish to his maple cheese board, the author rubs on mineral oil, also known as paraffin oil, which is prescribed as a laxative.

Mineral and linseed oil: My first choice for finishing wooden kitchen items is mineral oil, which is a petroleum-derived hydrocarbon. Sold as a laxative in my pharmacy, the bottle of mineral oil I use recommends "one to three tablespoons at bedtime." I feel pretty safe using this finish on a cheese board (see the photo at left). A few coats of mineral oil help protect against food stains and dishwater, and an occasional re-coating keeps the board looking new. Another laxative, raw linseed oil (not the boiled kind which may contain metal driers), imparts a yellow color to wood and also makes a fine nontoxic finish.

Tung and walnut oils: Pure tung and pure walnut oil dry without metallic driers. As long as their container says "pure," both walnut and tung oil are considered nontoxic. Products labeled tung-oil finish or tung-oil varnish may contain resins or metallic driers. One source for drier-free oils is Wood Finishing Enterprises (1729 N. 68th St., Wauwatosa, Wis. 53213; 414-774-1724).

It may surprise you to learn that the new water-based finishes also lay on the surface of the wood. The chemical composition of a typical water-based finish prevents the resin from penetrating the wood. This accounts for the no-depth look that these finishes impart to bare wood. However, I've found water-based finishes look great when applied over sealed surfaces (see the bottom photo on p. 179) rather than directly to the wood. A fair amount of practice is needed to acquaint oneself with the idiosyncrasies of applying water-based finishes. But because water-based finishes are nonflammable, have little odor and are easy to clean up, I find the benefits are worth the application effort.

Surface preparation

Of course the final finish you achieve is only as good as the surface you prepared. In some instances, sanding to 600-grit is all you need. In other cases, you may want a scraped surface. If you do sand, it's best to work your way up through the grades of grit, as described on pp. 56-63. I often use my random-orbit sander to smooth a surface because I can sand cross-grain without scratches or swirls. Smoothing between coats and after the topcoat will further improve the look and feel of your finish.

Waxes and shellac: Carnauba wax (made from Brazilian palm trees) or paste furniture waxes that contain beeswax (secreted by honey bees) give a nice shine to a smooth piece of hardwood. Both waxes are approved by the Food and Drug Administration (FDA) as nontoxic food additives. I apply paste furniture wax to cutting boards fairly often because its protection against water is low.

Shellac, a nontoxic resin made from insect secretions, is also recognized by the FDA as a food additive. Used as a candy glaze (hence the name confectioners' glaze) and as a timed-release coating on oral medications, shellac makes an excellent choice for baby cribs and other pieces requiring a film-forming finish. Shellac has a short shelf life once dissolved in alcohol. So it's best to prepare your own solutions from fresh, dry shellac flakes. I've found the pre-mixed variety is often too old to dry properly.

Watch paints and water-based finishes: Most children's toys look best when painted. Don't use common house paint—oil-based or latex! These paints often contain pigments, biocides and fungicides that may be harmful if ingested. Instead, use one of the specially developed nontoxic paints, which are available at most arts and crafts stores. Look for the seal of The Arts and Crafts Materials Institute or the words "conforms to ASTM D-4236" on the label. Either designation indicates the product meets government and industry standards for a nontoxic paint.

Similarly, don't assume water-based finishes are nontoxic just because they contain water. A clear, water-based finish can contain up to 15 separate additives, some of which are harmful if ingested. Also, be careful if you apply a clear finish over stain. It's best to read the can and call the manufacturer if you're unsure.

Material Safety Data Sheets: No discussion of finish toxicity is complete without mentioning Material Safety Data Sheets (MSDS). These sheets include information for the safe handling and disposal of a product, and they list most of the hazardous ingredients it contains. But except for special cases (carcinogenic and certain highly toxic materials), hazardous ingredients at concentrations of less than 1% of the formulation do not have to be listed on the MSDS. Just because a material doesn't appear on the MSDS does not mean it isn't in the finish. Metallic driers, for instance, typically fall below the 1% rule and do not have to be listed. If you have concerns about a particular finish, call the manufacturer. You'll be provided with the product's MSDS and other safety information. —*C.M.*

Appearance: color and luster

Clear finishes are far from colorless. While the color of a finish is not usually my primary consideration when selecting a finish, color can have a profound effect on the final appearance of the project. The samples shown in the photos above the chart are all cherry with three coats of finish. Paints were not included in the chart because of their wide variety.

Solvent-based acrylic lacquers (commonly found in auto supply stores) are clear and make good coatings for light-colored wood or as a clear coat over whitewashed, stained or painted pieces. Water-based acrylic finishes are just as colorless as their solvent-based kin, but they look hazy over dark stains. Oil finishes are on the other end of the color spectrum. These deep-colored finishes drastically alter the hues of wood. But because oils don't form a surface film, the dark yellow tint is only noticeable on light-colored wood. Standard alkyd varnishes, polyurethane varnishes and nitrocellulose lacquers impart an amber glow, often called "warmth," as displayed by the lacquered Queen-Anne highboy in the photo on p. 182. By contrast, the bluish tint of a water-based polyurethane coating gives stained wood a cold cast, an effect that is even more pronounced on walnut. I prefer

Highboy gets a high-end finish. Andrew Davis of Santa Fe, N.M., hand-rubbed layers of lacquer to finish this mahogany Queen Anne highboy. Aniline dye and japan colors were used to add tint.

French period piece. Yet we prefer a more rustic look on a Shaker-style bench. A hard and glossy polyurethane varnish looks out of place on either piece.

Layering different finishes on the same piece

Finishes can also be layered for special effects. The spruce guitar soundboard in the photo on the facing page has a double-layer finish along the top. First I brushed on fresh, super-blond shellac to enhance the grain and chatoyance of the stock and to add an amber color to the finish. Next I applied the vertical bands of water-based finish, so I could compare each against the look of acrylic and nitrocellulose lacquers. When undercoated with shellac, the color and depth of the water-based finishes closely matched the lacquers.

My favorite finish for black walnut is a three-layer finish. I apply linseed oil to deepen the brown color; two coats of shellac seal in the oil and enhance the wood's highlights. Finally I apply a topcoat of water-based lacquer to add depth. Layered finishes can produce unusual effects, so always test a layered finish on scrapwood before committing it to your project. Keep in mind, too, that not all finish combinations are compatible. Generally, I've had good luck layering water-based finishes over solvent-based ones if I seal in between them with shellac.

Protection

Durability is an important consideration when I'm choosing a finish. Along with film hardness and adhesion, a finish often has to resist abrasion, distortion, heat and solvents. Generally, the higher the molecular weight of a finish, the more protection it offers. Oil finishes, although easy to repair, offer little protection from water or food stains. The varnish component of Danish oil increases the protection level of the finish only marginally. Likewise, paste wax performs rather poorly at resisting stains or moisture. By contrast, the superior protection of polyurethane varnish makes it my first choice for kitchen tabletops and other pieces that must

warmer finishes, so I rarely use water-based polyurethane in my shop.

Aside from color, there's another quality of finishes that affects appearance—luster. A finish's formulation, thickness and method of application cause a surface to be either dull, satin or glossy. It's usually the style of a furniture piece that dictates which looks best. For example, we're accustomed to seeing a hand-rubbed finish on an 18th-century, stand hard use. Oil-based varnish, shellac and both acrylic and nitrocellulose lacquers protect wood against stains and water, but not quite as well as polyurethane. Water-based finishes are slightly less protective than a nitrocellulose lacquer.

So while certain finishes provide excellent stain and water protection without repairability, others repair easily but don't provide much protection (see the chart). Do you settle for protection or repairability? You may not have to make that choice. Combining different finishes on the same project provides a way to take advantage of the strong points of each.

Applying separate finishes on the same piece

I often use different finishes on the same project. Vertical and horizontal surfaces in a piece will wear differently, so you may want to finish them differently. And because of the effects of dust and gravity, you may want to apply the finishes differently as well. The top of my dining room table is finished with a polyurethane varnish, which is practically bulletproof—protecting against food stains, water and abrasion. Because the table's legs are subject to chair bangs and kicking feet (three teenagers live in my house), I oiled the legs with linseed. By occasionally re-coating them, I hide the scratches. The stool in the photo at right was also treated with a combination of finishes. With a multi-finish approach, I like to finish the components separately. Before finishing, I mask off the surfaces that will be glued. Once the finish is dry, I assemble and glue up the components.

One last test of a finish comes when I stand back to admire a project. The finish should enhance the wood. If all I see is the finish, then I chose the wrong one. A close friend summed it up best, "You never see a perfect finish, you only see the bad ones."

Separate treatments: Minick chose five finishes for this stool. The seat was coated with water-based acrylic; the legs were shellacked, painted and waxed; and the rungs were Danish oiled. Similarly, a guitar's body and neck may be finished differently.

FURTHER READING

To learn more about:

Brushing on a finish, see *Fine Woodworking* #98, p. 54, *Fine Woodworking* #95, p. 46 and *Hand-Applied Finishes*, by Jeff Jewitt, The Taunton Press, 1997.

Finish durability, see *Fine Woodworking* #82, p. 62.

Finishing hazards, see *Fine Woodworking* #92, p. 80 and *Fine Woodworking* #80, p. 58.

Spraying a finish, see *Fine Woodworking* #82, p. 56.

Water-based finishes, see *Fine Woodworking* #89, p. 52, *The Woodfinishing Book*, by Michael Dresdner, The Taunton Press, 1992, and *Water-Based Finishes,* by Andy Charron, The Taunton Press, 1998.

BRUSHING ON A FINISH

by Chris A. Minick

Brush a complicated surface in several stages, working from the deepest surfaces, like the bevel on this raised panel door, to details, like the molding the author is brushing here with a sash brush. Apply finish to the panel field and door frame last.

If you learned to use a brush by painting your house, the clear finish you brushed on your latest woodworking project probably doesn't look too good. Why? Because paint and varnish are very different materials. Paint needs to be vigorously brushed back and forth to get it to lay out thin because it's *thixotropic*, meaning that it's thicker when at rest, thinner when energy is applied to it. But varnish applies most evenly when it's gently flowed onto a surface.

My flow-and-go method for brushing a clear finish on woodwork was taught to me by my grandfather who was a professional finisher. I've found his combination of finish preparation and brush handling to give my projects a final appearance that rivals the smoothness of spraying. The method works for most common wood finishes like oil-based varnish, brushing lacquer, water-based finish and shellac. But before dipping the brush in the can, we must choose and prepare the finishing material.

Picking and preparing the finish

Fast-drying finishes are harder to apply by brush than slower drying finishes. Oil-based varnishes dry slowly enough to allow ample time for leveling, allowing you to work at a leisurely pace. For that reason, oil-based polyurethane varnish is my favorite brush-on finish. At the other end of the spectrum, shellac is probably the most difficult common finish to apply, especially to large areas—it just dries too quickly. I limit my shellac brushing to small projects that I can completely coat in about 10 minutes. Likewise, most water-based finishes brush well but require a quick hand. Solvent-based lacquers are easier to brush, and retarders can be added to them to slow down drying.

Most finishes are too thick to brush right out of the can. Thinning with the appropriate solvent is usually necessary. Brushing a too-thick finish will show brush marks and streaks while an over-thinned finish tends to run, sag and drip. To get the ideal mix, start by transferring the finish to a clean coffee can, so you can thin only the amount you want to use. Now measure the finish's thick-

Checking the viscosity of a finish is the best way to know how much thinner you need to add to get the best finish flow. A stopwatch clocks the time it takes for a viscosity drip cup filled with finish to empty. Add more thinner until the time is optimal.

ness with a viscosity drip cup and a stopwatch. A viscosity drip cup holds a predetermined amount and has a precisely sized hole in the bottom; you fill it up with finish, then time how long it takes all the finish to drip out through the hole (see the photo above). Cups are available in paint stores and, unfortunately, come in many sizes (in other words, there's no simple standard). I usually work with about a pint of finish, thinning it a little at a time and checking its viscosity as I go. If I over thin it, I add a little finish from its original container. I find a reading of 13-14 seconds with a Zahn #3 cup, 48-50 seconds with a Zahn #2 cup or approximately 20-22 seconds with a Wagner cup seems about right.

Begin brushing

Before dipping into the finish, wet your brush with the thinning solvent to condition the bristles and to prevent the buildup of dried finish at the base of the brush. This minimizes the likelihood that any dried finish will flake off the brush and contaminate the freshly varnished surface, and it makes cleaning the brush easier. Strike off the

Remove the excess from a loaded brush by tapping the bristles lightly on the sides of the can, side to side. This prevents the brush from dripping and doesn't create air bubbles, which can end up on the finished surface.

excess solvent by dragging the bristles across the edge of the container.

Fill the brush with finish by dipping it so no more than half the bristle length is submerged. Capillary action will automatically fill the brush's reservoir (near the ferrule) with the proper amount of finish. Now tap the bristles on the inside of the can to

Choose the right brush for the job, and keep it clean

Woodworkers can choose from many brush types and styles including from left to right: nylon tapered bristle, nylon sash, ox hair, China bristle, nylon/polyester flagged bristle and nylon/polyester sash.

Practically any brush you can buy at a paint or hardware store is capable of applying a finish to woodwork. But if you want to brush on a smooth finish with an even, streakless appearance, you must choose the right brush for the job (see the photo above). The best brush has the correct type and style of bristles for applying the particular finish you choose. Generally, heavy-bodied finishes should be applied with a stiffer bristle brush while softer bristle brushes are better for applying thin finishes. Natural bristle brushes work best for applying solvent-based finishes.

A good-quality China bristle (hogs hair) brush has the proper stiffness and flexibility for applying oil-based varnishes, such as alkyd varnish and polyurethane. Ox-hair brushes, which are slightly stiffer than China bristle, hold their shape better when used for extended periods of time. Their stiffness also makes ox hair an excellent choice for smaller brushes of one inch or less. Softer fitch (skunk hair) brushes work best for applying thin finishes but camel-hair (actually, pony hair) brushes can be used.

Synthetic bristle brushes are best for waterborne finishes because natural bristles quickly splay in water and become unusable. The softness and flexibility of these brushes is determined by the polymers used for their bristles. Nylon bristles **are the softest and are good for general-purpose finishing. If you can afford only one brush, it should be nylon.** Nylon/polyester bristle blends **are slightly stiffer, and like ox hair, make excellent small-sized brushes. Pure** polyester bristles **are very stiff, generally too stiff for applying thin furniture finishes and should only be used for applying heavy-bodied paints.**

In addition to bristle material, brushes come with one of three tip styles: blunt cut, flagged **and** tapered. **Some tip styles are better for certain finishing jobs than others (see the drawings on the facing page).**

remove the excess finish and to prevent dripping. Don't drag the brush over the edge of the can—this might cause bubbles to form.

Using the basic brushstroke described in the sidebar on p. 188, I always finish the unseen areas of my project first. This gives me a chance to judge the flowing and leveling properties of the finish before I've committed myself to the show side of the piece. If the viscosity doesn't seem right, I add more finish to increase the thickness or more solvent to decrease it.

If you're brushing a complicated surface, such as a carving or a raised panel door, it's best to brush the areas farthest away first,

Choose the right synthetic bristle style

BLUNT CUT

Also called straight cut, these bristles are usually only found on cheap, low-quality brushes that are better used for dusting than varnishing furniture.

FLAGGED BRISTLES

With each filament broken into several small fiberals, flagged bristle tips have a fuzzy feel and appearance. Flagged nylon/polyester brushes are excellent varnish brushes.

TAPERED BRISTLES

These bristles taper from base to tip and end in a sharp point closely resembling natural bristles. Good for all varnishing, especially with water-based finishes.

Most finishing projects require using more than one brush. I use a 1-in. sash brush for coating small or intricate areas like moldings, spindles or tight inside corners. A 2-in. brush is my favorite for large flat areas. Brushes wider than 2 in. are inappropriate for furniture finishing. They're just too hard to control.

Cleaning brushes

Proper care and storage of any brush ensures optimum performance and longevity. Each brush needs to be thoroughly cleaned and wrapped for hanging storage between uses. First, remove excess finish by scraping the brush's bristles across the lip of the finish container followed by wiping off the residue with a paper towel. Wash the bristles in the same solvent used to thin the finish. Periodically, check your cleaning progress by bending the bristles with one hand and feeling along their base with the thumb of your other hand. A slimy feel indicates more cleaning is needed. Once all the finish has

Keep a brush clean and properly stored and it will last for years. After thorough solvent cleaning, bend the bristles and feel for remaining finish. Wrap the washed brush in brown paper and hang it up.

been removed, wash the brush in soap and water (I use dishwashing liquid, but any soap will do). After a clean water rinse to remove soap residue, wrap the brush tightly in brown paper to dry. Storing the wrapped brush by hanging it vertically on your shop wall prevents the bristles from taking a set and prolongs brush life. —*C.M.*

working outward from the center. I apply a coat to both sides of a door in one session by setting it on a nail board (a piece of thin plywood the size of the door with one nail in each corner).

Normally, I scuff-sand between each coat with 220-grit sandpaper to remove nibs or dust specks. Three or four coats is about right for most projects. After the final coat

has dried for a few days, I rub out the finish and apply a coat of paste furniture wax.

Dealing with defects

Drips, runs and sags are a normal part of any finishing operation. Fresh runs and sags can be removed from the surface by back brushing the affected area with an unloaded brush; capillary action draws off the excess

The basic brushstroke

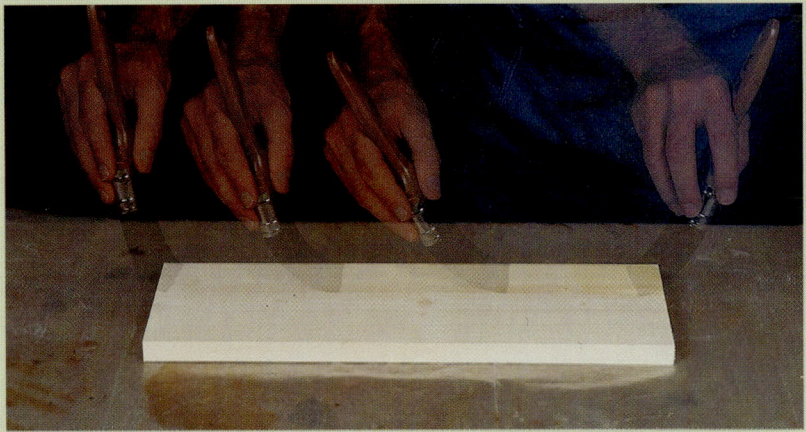

A smooth finish depends on smooth brush handling. My basic method begins with a back stroke 3 in. to 4 in. from the leading edge of the panel (right). Pull the brush smoothly, and lift it just before it goes over the edge. This back stroke virtually eliminates runs along the edge. I finish the stroke by starting just behind the back stroke's wet edge and pulling the brush in one slow and continuous motion across the panel (left). Pull the brush along slowly enough to allow an even sheet of finish to flow out of the brush, but fast enough to prevent pooling. My 2-in. brush holds enough finish for a single stroke about 20 in. long, which takes between five and seven seconds.

I hold the brush loosely by the ferrule with the handle cradled between thumb and index finger. I start with the brush at about a 45° angle and gradually increase the angle to almost 90° by the end of the stroke. As the bristle angle increases, more varnish flows out. When my brush approaches the trailing edge of the panel, I decrease the pressure slightly so the bristles don't run over the edge. Each successive stroke just barely overlaps the previous one. After the whole panel is coated, I tip off the finish by lightly dragging the bristle tips through the wet finish. Tipping off with an unloaded brush levels any uneven areas and removes bubbles. Any small bubbles left can usually be dispersed by lightly blowing on them from close range. —C.M.

Slicing off a dried drip with a sharp chisel is probably the cleanest way to remove the defect.

finish. Hairs, brush bristles or other goobers should be picked out immediately. A quick tipping off (see the sidebar above) blends and removes your fingerprints.

Sanding out a dried drip or run flush with the surrounding finish can create a halo around the defect. It's better to slice the drip off with a sharp chisel to remove the drip quickly and cleanly; only a little touch sanding is needed with 400-grit paper.

OIL-VARNISH MIXTURE IS DURABLE, EASY TO APPLY

by Garrett Hack

Finishing just isn't my cup of tea. Planning the design and construction details, picking the wood and carefully laying out the parts to match the wood's color and grain are all exciting. Cutting joints and planing by hand are pure pleasure. But putting on a finish is my least favorite part of building furniture. That may be one reason I've settled on a finish that gives me consistently satisfying results with a minimum of effort.

I first learned about this hybrid finish—a mixture of oil, varnish and turpentine—at the woodworking school I went to in Boston in the late 1970s. Since then, I've experimented with the ingredients, the proportions and the method of application. These days, I use this finish on everything from fine furniture and kitchen cabinets

Crowning touch—Author Garrett Hack tops his varnish-oil finish with wax.

Ingredients are simple; proportions are forgiving. Linseed or tung oil, varnish and turpentine make up the author's favorite finish. A pigmented oil stain can be added to give the mixture a little color.

to the handles on the tools I use around my farm.

The finish is mixed from either tung oil or boiled linseed oil and varnish, thinned with turpentine. It's easy to apply, doesn't require a special dust-free finish room and, like any oil finish, it won't obscure the texture and character of the wood. Yet because of the varnish, it offers more protection than oil alone.

The varnish also helps the finish build faster than a straight oil finish, eliminating much of the drudgery of application. Because the proportion of varnish is relatively low, this finish is as easy to repair or renew as an oil finish. And it can be tinted with artist's pigments or oil-based stains to match any wood. There's no need to fill pores on open-grained woods: Sanding the finish creates a slurry of wood dust, oil and varnish that fills the pores beautifully.

Don't sweat the finish proportions

When mixing this finish, I don't get overly scientific about measurements. The finish is very forgiving, and many proportions will work. Generally, I mix them in approximately equal measures. If I want more protection, I'll add up to 50% more varnish. If it's too thick (and always for the first coat), I'll add more turpentine to get better surface penetration. If I'm going to color the mixture, I add an oil stain or artist's colors, keeping it light initially and darkening it more if need be.

Spar varnish is a favorite

Varnishes have been around for a long time. Really old-fashioned varnishes are a mixture of plant resins (such as amber), oils and a solvent, which is heated and combined in formulations often kept secret by their makers. Even the techniques for applying these varnishes are carefully guarded by the few who still use them. Some of these varnishes take weeks to cure fully.

Modern varnishes are a combination of synthetic resins in an oil vehicle. Among the oils used by finishing manufacturers are soya, safflower, tung and linseed. The proportion of oil to resin in these varnishes ranges widely, and this affects how long they take to cure, as well as how tough and how elastic the cured finish film will be.

A spar varnish has a comparably high oil content, which takes longer to cure and leaves a fairly elastic surface that accommodates wood movement. Polyurethane varnishes dry quickly and form a tough, durable, but less elastic, coating. Also, after the finish has cured, repairs or additional coats don't bond well.

In terms of drying time, toughness and elasticity, alkyd-resin varnishes fall somewhere between spar varnish and polyurethane. They're not as tough as polyurethane, but they're more elastic, and any coats applied after the varnish has cured still bond well.

I have used all three of these varnishes in my finish with good results, but my favorite is spar. The main reason is color. Spar is the darkest. In combination with linseed oil, which also tends to darken wood, spar varnish significantly affects the color of some woods, like cherry. I happen to like the effect this mixture has.

Right away, cherry and bird's-eye and curly maple look older. But on darker woods like walnut, the color change is barely perceptible. If you want to preserve the light color of a wood like maple or ash, use a polyurethane varnish because it imparts the least color.

Most varnishes also have ultraviolet light (UV) inhibitors added to their formulations to keep the finish in the can from turning an unattractive yellow and to slow the natural aging effect of sunlight on wood.

All varnishes are naturally glossy. The softer luster of a satin or semigloss varnish results from the addition of a flattening agent, such as aluminum stearate or silica, which breaks up the reflection of light off the wood's surface. Stick with a gloss for the toughest finish, and use steel wool to get a satin finish, if that's what you're after.

Boiled linseed or tung oil and turpentine

For the oil component of my finish, I use either boiled linseed oil or tung oil (also known as China wood oil). Boiled linseed oil is made by steam-heating processed oil from raw flax and adding metallic drier compounds. The nondrying portion of the oil is removed, making what's left suitable as a finish.

Tung oil also is heat-treated, which speeds its curing time when exposed to oxygen. Tung oil is more expensive than linseed oil. However, it cures to a tougher, more water-resistant film, and it doesn't darken the wood as much. If you want maximum protection and a light color, use tung oil. Don't use raw linseed oil because it won't dry.

I thin my varnish and oil finish with turpentine. This increases surface penetration and speeds drying time. High-quality turpentine is getting harder and harder to find. It largely has been replaced by mineral spirits, which should work. I stick with turpentine because it's always worked well for me.

Brush it on; rub it off

The key to a really good finish with this mixture, or any finish for that matter, is to prepare the surface well. For me, this usually means a planed or scraped surface. I find this to be faster and more enjoyable than sanding. If you do sand, start with a fairly coarse grit, and work up to at least 220-grit. But it's less important which grit you end up with than how thoroughly you work through each grit to eliminate scratches from the previous grit.

For the first coat of finish, I brush on the mixture, flooding the surface and re-coating any dry areas that appear (see the photo at left below). After half an hour or less, any finish still on the surface will start to feel tacky. As soon as it does, I start rubbing with clean cotton rags to absorb it (see the photo at right below).

This initial coat is the easiest to apply because most of it soaks right in. Nevertheless, it's important to wipe off every bit of excess so that the surface doesn't turn into a sticky mess. When the surface is thoroughly rubbed dry, I'll set it aside for at least 24 hours before re-coating. Make sure you dispose of the rags properly. Either spread them flat outside until they've dried or put them in a metal bucket with a lid. Oily rags can combust spontaneously.

Subsequent coats of finish go on in the same way, except that they tack up more quickly and require more rubbing to remove

Flood the surface. The first coat will soak into the bare wood, so check the piece carefully for dry spots after it's been covered entirely. Re-coat areas that dry in the first 10 minutes or so.

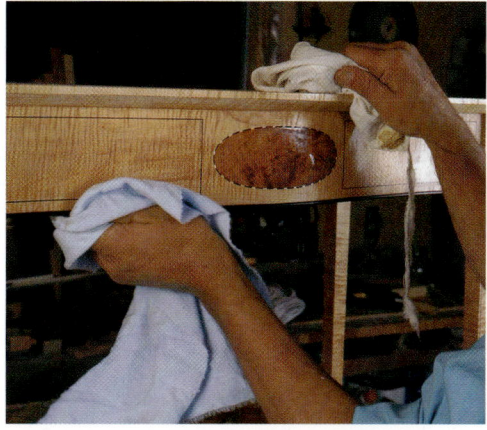

Rub off the excess. Pay close attention to the inside corners and the areas around details like cock beading, where the finish can collect. It's more difficult to remove excess finish after it has hardened.

Brush on subsequent coats, one area at a time. Keep checking areas you've already coated to see whether they've started to become tacky. After the first coat, the finish becomes sticky quickly.

Two rags are better than one. To remove excess finish after each coat, the author uses two rags. The first one picks up the majority of the residual finish; the second ensures the wood is really dry.

the excess. How fast these coats tack up depends on the temperature and humidity and on the type and amount of varnish in the mixture. Polyurethane varnishes cure within a few hours and can tack up very quickly; spar varnish can take twice as long.

When finishing a large piece of furniture, I work on one section at a time. I keep checking the areas I've already coated so that when the finish begins to tack up, I can start rubbing immediately (see the photo above). If I happen to get behind, brushing on a fresh coat of finish softens the tacky layer enough so that I can rub it down.

I like to use two rags, one for most of the excess finish and one for a final once-over polish (see the photo at left). Any places that aren't wiped clean will feel crusty. I don't worry about these too much because I can either rub them down with steel wool or rub especially vigorously when wiping off the next coat of finish.

How many coats to apply is a matter of choice and good judgment. Each layer adds a little more depth to the finish, some gloss and some additional protection. For a chest of drawers, three coats is fine. For a table that's going to see hard use, I would go with a minimum of four coats—five would be better. When I'm satisfied with the finish, I wait at least 24 hours, and then I top it off with a paste wax made from beeswax, boiled linseed oil and turpentine (see the sidebar on the facing page).

Using the finish to fill the grain

Another one of the beauties of this finish is that open-grained woods such as red oak or ash don't need to be filled before finishing. Lightly sanding the wet finish with 220-grit (or finer) sandpaper smooths the surface and creates a pore-filling slurry. I usually apply the first coat in the usual manner and sand the mixture after applying it for the second and third coats.

This method is easier than using a filler, and there are no problems with compatibility or bonding between the layers of finish. I avoid wet-or-dry, silicon-carbide sandpaper because the dark abrasive can color the pores. Instead, I use garnet or aluminum-oxide abrasives.

Rejuvenating the finish is easy

If the finish needs repair or if it just starts to look tired, it's easy to fix. First clean the surface well with 0000 steel wool, turpentine and a little boiled linseed oil, and then wipe the surface until the rags come clean. A light sanding with 320-grit sandpaper will take care of any stubborn areas the steel wool can't handle. Apply a fresh coat of finish, and rub it out with clean rags. After the finish has fully cured, reapply a wax topcoat.

Beeswax topcoat

My favorite topcoat is made of a combination of beeswax, boiled linseed oil and turpentine. This mixture is not as hard as a paste wax made with carnauba, but it's durable enough and it smells great.

In a double boiler on very low heat, I melt together a hunk of light-yellow beeswax (saved from comb honey I bought from a local beekeeper) and slightly less than equal amounts of oil and turpentine. I aim for a consistency similar to butter warmed to room temperature. It should be soft while maintaining its shape (see the inset photo below). If the wax mixture cools to something harder or softer than this, I add more oil or wax, whichever is appropriate, and rewarm. This recipe is very forgiving.

I apply the wax with 0000 steel wool, rubbing out the cured final coat of my oil-varnish mixture at the same time (see the photo at right). If the wax is the right consistency, it smooths out easily without feeling gummy. After a few minutes of

drying, I buff it with a clean rag to a satin sheen. To maintain the finish, just re-wax. —G.H.

ABOUT THE AUTHORS

Christian Becksvoort is a longtime cabinet-maker in the Shaker style and a contributing editor to *Fine Woodworking* magazine. He is the author of *The Shaker Legacy*.

William Duckworth was drawn to a career working wood after receiving an education in English literature and serving a brief stint in the publishing business. He spent almost two decades as a cabinetmaker and architectural woodworker before assuming his current duties as an associate editor at *Fine Woodworking*. He figures that he's ripped into several thousand sheets of plywood and other panel products.

Mark Duginske is a woodworker, author, and teacher who offers classes in his shop in Merrill, Wisconsin.

Curtis Erpelding is a furnituremaker living in Port Orchard, Washington. He has been affiliated with the Northwest Gallery of Fine Woodworking in Seattle for the past 21 years. In 1980, he received a grant from the National Endowment for the Arts. He has written several articles for *Fine Woodworking* magazine.

Maurice Fraser studied under designer Jere Osgood, and his work has appeared in the *Fine Woodworking Design Book* series. He is also a harpsichordist and part-time instrument maker and repairer. Currently, he is completing a woodworking book from his experience teaching at the Craft Students' League. He lives in New York City.

Tage Frid taught and inspired many woodworkers at the Rhode Island School of Design. He is now retired, although he is still a contributing editor at *Fine Woodworking* magazine. He lives in Rhode Island.

Zachary Gaulkin, a former editor at *Fine Homebuilding* magazine, learned to use hand tools while working for a Maine boatbuilder. He lives in Kennebunkport, Maine.

Tim Gilchrist works as a marketing consultant and builds furniture for fun in Simsbury, Connecticut.

Garrett Hack opened his own shop in 1973 and later studied furnituremaking at Boston University's Program in Artisanry. He designs and builds furniture in Vermont and is a regular contributor to *Fine Woodworking* magazine. He is the author of *The Handplane Book* and the upcoming *Classic Hand Tools*.

Sven Hanson designs and builds furniture and cabinets in Albuquerque, New Mexico, when he's not sailing and canoeing. However, he makes sure his work does not interfere with his family, which consists of his wife Margaret and Samoyed dog Tica.

Robert Hubert Jr. works for an architectural firm. He likes to build period and modern furniture for his Harvard, Massachusetts, home.

Frank Klausz is a native Hungarian and master cabinetmaker. He makes and restores furniture in Pluckemin, New Jersey.

Peter Korn works wood and teaches woodworking at his school, the Center for Furniture Craftsmanship, in Rockport, Maine. He is the author of *Working with Wood* and *The Woodworker's Guide to Hand Tools*.

Vincent Laurence is a former editor at *Fine Woodworking* and *Fine Gardening* magazines. Fences, gates, arbors, and outbuildings are now his primary woodworking metier. He lives in Newtown, Connecticut, with his girlfriend, two dogs and two teenagers.

Horst Meister is a toolmaker and woodworker who lives in Riverside, California.

Lars Mikkelsen is a self-taught professional woodworker who builds custom furniture and cabinets. Danish by birth, he has lived in the United States for 22 years, currently in Santa Margarita, California.

Chris Minick is a product development chemist at 3M Corporation and an amateur woodworker in Stillwater, Minnesota.

Sandor Nagyszalanczy, of Santa Cruz, California, is a professional furniture designer and craftsman with more than 20 years of experience. A former editor at *Fine Woodworking* magazine, he has written five books: *Woodshop Jigs and Fixtures, Fixing and Avoiding Woodworking Mistakes, Woodshop Dust Control, The Wood Sanding Book,* and *The Art of Fine Tools.*

Gerald Polmateer is a woodworker in Houston, Texas.

Strother Purdy used to edit articles at *Fine Woodworking* magazine. Now he edits books for The Taunton Press.

Mario Rodriguez is a contributing editor to *Fine Woodworking* magazine and woodworker living in Haddonfield, New Jersey. He also teaches woodworking at the Fashion Institute of Technology in New York City. He is the author of *Traditional Woodwork.*

Ken Textor's woodworking runs the gamut from delicate inlay work and furniture-making to timber-framed houses and boat-building. He lives on Arrowsic Island in Maine.

Jim Tolpin is a writer and woodworker in Port Townsend, Washington. He is the author of many books, including *Working at Woodworking, Building Traditional Kitchen Cabinets, The Toolbox Book,* and *The New Cottage Home.*

Peter Turner designs and builds furniture in a cooperative shop in Portland, Maine.

Pat Warner is a woodworker deep into routing and an instructor at Palomar College in San Marcos, California. He is the author of two books, *Getting the Very Best from Your Router* and *The Router Joinery Handbook.* A third is on its way. He lives in Escondido, California.

PHOTO CREDITS

INDEX

INDEX

EQUIVALENCE CHART

Inches	Centimeters	Millimeters		Inches	Centimeters	Millimeters
$^1/_8$	0.3	3		12	30.5	305
$^1/_4$	0.6	6		13	33.0	330
$^3/_8$	1.0	10		14	35.6	356
$^1/_2$	1.3	13		15	38.1	381
$^5/_8$	1.6	16		16	40.6	406
$^3/_4$	1.9	19		17	43.2	432
$^7/_8$	2.2	22		18	45.7	457
1	2.5	25		19	48.3	483
$1^1/_4$	3.2	32		20	50.8	508
$1^1/_2$	3.8	38		21	53.3	533
$1^3/_4$	4.4	44		22	55.9	559
2	5.1	51		23	58.4	584
$2^1/_2$	6.4	64		24	61.0	610
3	7.6	76		25	63.5	635
$3^1/_2$	8.9	89		26	66.0	660
4	10.2	102		27	68.6	686
$4^1/_2$	11.4	114		28	71.1	711
5	12.7	127		29	73.7	737
6	15.2	152		30	76.2	762
7	17.8	178		31	78.7	787
8	20.3	203		32	81.3	813
9	22.9	229		33	83.8	838
10	25.4	254		34	86.4	864
11	27.9	279		35	88.9	889
				36	91.4	914